JÜRGEN HABERMAS was born in 1929, and grew up in Gummersbach, Germany. He was educated at the Universities of Göttingen, Bonn, and Zurich, after which he worked for a while as a freelance journalist. In 1956 he became Adorno's assistant at the University of Frankfurt. From 1961 to 1964 he taught philosophy in Heidelberg, and from 1964 to 1971, philosophy and sociology in Frankfurt. From 1971 to 1983 he was Director of the Max Planck Institute for Research into the Life Conditions of the Scientific-Technical World, in Starnberg. Since 1983 he has once more been teaching at the Johann Wolfgang Goethe University in Frankfurt. Among his influential publications in English are: *Knowledge and Human Interests* (1971), *Theory and Practice* (1973), *The Theory of Communicative Action* (1984/1987), and *Moral Consciousness and Communicative Action* (1990).

Autonomy and Solidarity

Revised Edition

———————◆———————

Interviews with

JÜRGEN HABERMAS

Edited and Introduced by Peter Dews

VERSO

London · New York

First published by Verso 1986
This revised and enlarged edition published 1992
Interviews © Suhrkamp Verlag 1986, 1992 and *New Left Review* 1986
Introduction © Peter Dews 1986, 1992
All rights reserved

Verso
UK: 6 Meard Street, London W1V 3HR
USA: 29 West 35th Street, New York, NY 10001-2291

Verso is the imprint of New Left Books

ISBN 0-86091-367-8
ISBN 0-86091-379-4 (pbk)

British Library Cataloguing in Publication Data
A catalogue record for this book is available from the British Library

Library of Congress Cataloging-in-Publication Data
A catalogue record for this book is available from the Library of Congress

Typeset in Times by Leaper & Gard Ltd, Bristol
Printed in Great Britain by Biddles Ltd

Contents

Sources and Acknowledgements

'Ideologies and Society in the Post-war World': interview with Gad Freudenthal, Jerusalem 16 December 1977; first published in Hebrew in *Machschavot*, no. 48 (1979), pp. 68–79; republished in Habermas, *Kleine Politische Schriften I–IV* Frankfurt-a–M. 1981, pp. 467–90; translated by Rodney Livingstone.

'Conservatism and Capitalist Crisis': interview with Angelo Bolaffi, Starnberg 29 May 1978; first published in *Rinascita* 30–31, 28 July and 4 August 1978; English translation, *New Left Review* 115, May–June 1979, pp. 73–84; published in *Kleine Politische Schriften I–IV*, pp. 491–510.

'Political Experience and the Renewal of Marxist Theory': interview with Detlef Horster and Willem van Reijen, Starnberg 23 March 1979; first published in *Intermediair* (Amsterdam), 29 June 1979; English translation by Ron Smith, *New German Critique*, no. 18 (Fall 1979); published in *Kleine Politische Schriften I–IV*, pp. 511–32.

'The Dialectics of Rationalization': interview with Axel Honneth, Eberhard Knödler-Bunte and Arno Widmann, Berlin 22 May 1981, and Starnberg 10 July 1981; first published in *Ästhetik und Kommunikation* nos. 45–46 (1981), pp. 126–55; English translation by Leslie Adelson, Philip Boehm, Barton Byg, Karen Jankowski, and Istvan Varkonyi, *Telos* no. 49 (1981), pp. 5–31; republished in Habermas, *Die neue Unüber sichtlichkeit: Kleine Politische Schriften V*, Frankfurt-a–M. 1985, pp. 213–57.

'Conservative Politics, Work, Socialism and Utopia Today': interview with Hans–Ulrich Beck, 2 April 1983; first published in *Basler Zeitung*, 7 January 1984; republished in *Die neue Unübersichtlichkeit*, pp. 59–76; translated by Peter Dews.

'A Philosophico-Political Profile': written interview with Perry Anderson and Peter Dews, conducted November 1984; first published in *New Left Review* 151 (May–June 1985), pp. 75–105; republished in

Die neue Unübersichtlichkeit, pp. 213–57; translated by Peter Dews.

'Life-Forms, Morality and the Task of the Philosopher', interview with Perry Anderson and Peter Dews, Starnberg 6 December 1984; first published in this collection.

'Critical Theory and Frankfurt University': interview with Josef Früchtl; first part published in *links,* January 1985, pp. 29–31; republished in Habermas, *Eine Art Schadensabwicklung: Kleine Politische Schriften VI,* Frankfurt–a–M. 1987, pp. 57–63; second part published as 'Eine Generation von Adorno getrennt', in J. Frücktl and M. Calloni (eds), *Geistgegen den Zeitgeist. Erinnern an Adorno,* Frankfurt–a–M. 1991, pp. 47–53; translated by Martin Chalmers and Peter Dews.

'On Morality, Law, Civil Disobedience and Modernity': interview with Helmut Hein; first published in *Die Woche* (Regensburg), 15 May 1986; republished in *Eine Art Schadensabwicklung,* pp. 64–9; translated by Peter Dews.

'The Role of the Student Movement in Germany': interview with Angelo Bolaffi; first published in *L'espresso* (Rome), 25 January 1988; republished in Habermas, *Die nachholende Revolution: Kleine Politische Schriften VII,* Frankfurt–a–M. 1990, pp. 21–8; translated by Peter Dews.

'The Limits of Neo-Historicism': interview with J.M. Ferry; first published in *Die Neue Gesellschaft – Frankfurter Hefte,* vol. 36 (April 1989), pp. 370–4; republished in *Die nachholende Revolution,* pp. 149–56; published in an English translation by Stephen K. White in David Rasmussen (ed.) *Universalism vs. Communitarianism,* Cambridge Mass. and London 1990, pp. 207–13; translated here by Martin Chalmers.

'Discourse Ethics, Law and *Sittlichkeit*': interview with T. Hviid Nielsen, January 1990; first published under the title 'Morality, Sociality and Ethics', in *Acta Sociologica,* vol. 33, no. 2, 1990, pp. 93–114, and in German in *Die nachholende Revolution,* pp. 114–45; translated by Peter Dews.

All interviews except numbers 6 and 7 published here by kind permission of Suhrkamp Verlag. All translations from the German revised by Peter Dews.

Editor's Introduction

In an intellectual climate on the left strongly marked by a tendency to seek for truth in the fragmentary and the perspectival, to suspect comprehensive theoretical enterprises of authoritarian aspirations—even when such distrust is itself articulated on the grand scale—and in some cases even to reject the notion of theory itself as an imposture, the work of Jürgen Habermas stands out as a remarkable exception. For well over thirty years Habermas has pursued and developed a project which is rooted in the traditions of Critical Theory, the form of interdisciplinary Marxist social analysis initiated by members of the Frankfurt Institute for Social Research, under the aegis of Max Horkheimer, during the 1930s. As the inheritor of this tradition, Habermas accepts that philosophy can no longer sustain its claims to reveal the fundamental nature of reality; but he also denies that contemporary thought is obliged to choose between trivialized technicality or a grandiose arbitrariness. Philosophy *can* continue to deal with substantive questions, but only by acknowledging that it can no longer do so alone, through a collaboration with empirical disciplines. In Habermas's work philosophy functions as the problem-sensitive medium which integrates the results of the individual social and human sciences into a multifaceted, yet coherent, account of our history, our present dilemmas, and our prospects. In its most recent reformulation, the project which this conception informs has emerged as the attempt to produce a theory of modern society which will be neither complacent nor indiscriminately critical, which will be sensitive both to the failures of modernity and its achievements, to its distortions and its still-unrealized potential for a humane collective life.

But if Habermas's work is systematic, in a way which has no serious rival among contemporary philosophers and social theorists, it also confutes the facile equations which are often currently made between systematicity and dogmatism. Whereas his predecessors in the Frankfurt

1

School—as he remarks in these interviews—tended to restrict themselves to a comparatively narrow range of canonical texts, Habermas has opened out Critical Theory towards the most important currents of contemporary thought, while retaining its fundamental insights into the reified structures and menacing dynamic of capitalist society. This broadening of the frame of reference of Critical Theory has in large part taken place through a series of debates—some of which have become milestones in recent intellectual history—in which Habermas, while defending his basic convictions, has also learned something of enduring value from his opponents. Thus, in the early sixties, Habermas sided with Theodor Adorno in the well-known 'positivist dispute'—the debate with Karl Popper and his adherents over the philosophical foundations of the social sciences. Yet, while firmly defending the need for social science to be reflexively conscious of its own social function, against the technocratic thrust of Popperian 'critical rationalism', Habermas did acquire from Popper a sense of the fallibility of all knowledge-claims which was to become an important point of distinction between his own version of Critical Theory and that of his predecessors.[1] Similarly, Hans-Georg Gadamer's powerful restatement of the tradition of hermeneutic thought in *Truth and Method* aided Habermas to formulate his own critique of Wittgenstein, and to render more precise his objections to a positivist conception of the social sciences. Yet Habermas has also been a leading critic of the claims which Gadamer has made for the universal priority of understanding, arguing that a purely hermeneutic approach is not adequate to those phenomena of 'systematically distorted communication' which are the concern of ideology-critique.[2] In the 1970s Habermas's reading of systems theory, in particular the work of Talcott Parsons and Niklas Luhmann, enabled him to abandon the notion of a macro-subject of the historical process which he now believes to have encumbered much of the Western Marxist tradition. Nevertheless, he has continued to criticize systems theory for its reductionist account of social evolution as a process of increasing capacity for adaptation.[3] Finally, and most recently, Habermas has addressed himself to the antecedents and implications of post-structuralist thought in a book of lectures on the 'philosophical discourse of modernity'.[4]

---

1. Habermas's contributions to this debate are 'The Analytical Theory of Science and Dialectics' and 'A Positivistically Bisected Rationalism', in Theodor W. Adorno et al., *The Positivist Dispute in German Sociology*, London 1976, pp. 131–162, and pp. 198–225.
2. See 'A Review of Gadamer's *Truth and Method*', in F. Dallmayr and T. McCarthy, eds., *Understanding and Social Enquiry*, Notre Dame, 1977, pp. 335–363.
3. See, for example, 'Toward a Reconstruction of Historical Materialism', in *Communication and the Evolution of Society*, London 1979, pp. 174–5.
4. Jürgen Habermas, *The Philosophical Discourse of Modernity*, Cambridge, Mass. 1987.

In this last case, however, despite the genuine tributes which he has paid to Foucault,[5] Habermas leaves the impression of having far less to learn from his opponents—more than any other of his major writings, *Der Philosophische Diskurs der Moderne* is a combative work. The reasons for this difference of tone are readily apparent. For, whereas Habermas understands Critical Theory as the most self-reflexive outpost of the radical traditions of the Enlightenment, post-structuralist thought has launched an attack on the inheritance of the Enlightenment as a whole, severing the link between freedom and reason which has been central to modern political consciousness. Aware of the ambiguity of this move, Habermas, in a lecture first delivered in 1980, suggested that the radical credentials of post-structuralism should not be taken so readily for granted.[6] In doing so, he undoubtedly touched a raw point of contemporary intellectual life. For, since then, a widespread international debate has developed around these questions, including for example Habermas's own book on the discourse of modernity, an exchange between Richard Rorty and Jean-François Lyotard, and contributions by other defenders of the Critical Theory position.[7] This discussion, in which the influential arguments of recent French philosophy have been directly pitted for the first time against the major surviving current of the Western Marxist tradition, can be seen as revolving around a single central preoccupation: the question of whether we are currently experiencing the final exhaustion of the resources of modernity, and the transition to a much-prophesied 'post-modernity', or whether our present discontent and disillusionment stem from the fact that—in its capitalist and state-socialist forms—the possibilities of modernity have only been onesidedly and inadequately realized.

There are a number of reasons, however, why this debate between Habermas and his sympathizers, on the one hand, and thinkers influenced by post-structuralism, on the other, is unlikely to gain the balanced reception which it merits in the English-speaking world. Firstly, because of the esoterically technical or specialized character of

---

5. See Habermas's obituary article, 'Taking Aim at the Heart of the Present', in David Hoy, ed., *Foucault: A Critical Reader*, Oxford 1986, pp. 103–8.

6. Jürgen Habermas, 'Modernity versus Postmodernity', *New German Critique*, no. 22, Winter 1981. Reprinted in Hal Foster, ed., *Postmodern Culture*, London 1985, pp. 3–15.

7. See Jean-François Lyotard, 'Histoire Universelle et Différences Culturelles', and Richard Rorty, 'Le Cosmopolotisme sans Emancipation', followed by a discussion between Lyotard and Rorty, in *Critique*, no. 456, May 1985. For the Critical Theory position see Axel Honneth, 'An Aversion against the Universal: A Commentary on Lyotard's *Postmodern Condition*', *Theory, Culture and Society*, vol. 2, no. 3, 1985, pp. 147–56; and, most notably, Albrecht Wellmer, 'The Dialectic of Modernism and Postmodernism: The Critique of Reason since Adorno', in *The Persistence of Modernity*, Cambridge 1991, pp. 36–94.

much Anglo-Saxon philosophy in the twentieth century, broader questions of culture and society, which on the Continent would be the natural province of philosophy, have tended to be debated on the terrain of literary theory and literary criticism. Accordingly, post-structuralist thought, whose central concern with problems of discourse, textuality and interpretation reinforces this initial affinity, has far more readily been assimilated by art and literature departments than by philosophy departments in the English-speaking world. From here the characteristic themes and tropes of post-structuralism have permeated the more general texture of cultural theory and criticism, and have become familiar to a wider public of broadly left-wing sympathies. By contrast, Habermas's work is centred on problems in social rather than literary theory, and has been taken up to a much more limited extent—and with very little wider resonance—by sociologists, political scientists and philosophers. Secondly, not only does Habermas frequently write forbiddingly dense philosophical prose—in sharp contrast to the allusive, rhetorical, 'polyphonic' style of much post-structuralist work, which conceals its often considerable scholarship beneath an immediately enticing surface—but his references to a range of contemporary specialist literatures, and the rootedness of his thought in the problems of German philosophy from Kant, through Hegel to Marx and beyond, make the evaluation of the overall structure and intent of his corpus a formidable undertaking. Lastly, and most obviously, the French language, and consequently the French cultural tradition, are far more familiar to the average educated person in Britain or North America than are those of Germany. As a result of this constellation of factors there is a serious risk that the central assumptions and implications of the debate between post-structuralism and Critical Theory will be inadequately grasped by a broader public. In the worst cases, the conflict between the prophets of postmodernity and the defenders of modernity is liable to be trivialized into a choice between the playful style of post-structuralism and a somewhat oppressive Teutonic earnestness, with their presumed political extensions—a liberating pluralism on the one hand, a constraining systematicity on the other.

It is to be hoped that the present collection of interviews, which includes most of those which Habermas has reprinted in the four volumes of his shorter political writings, and a further interview with *New Left Review* not previously published, will help to broaden and redress the reception of Habermas's work in the English-speaking world. It is arguable that, despite their complexity, the structures of Habermas's theory have developed from a core of insights into our current historical situation, its dilemmas and possibilities, which are at least as intuitively plausible as those of the renouncers of modernity, even if they do not so directly express the contemporary mood of disenchantment. And, in the medium of the spoken word, these central convictions, the fundamental modes of response which inform Habermas's work, as well as many incidental sidelights and emphases not available in his more formal writings, emerge with especial vivacity. In the course of these discussions Habermas recounts his own political biography, explains his relation to his theoretical predecessors, analyses present-day cultural and social movements in the advanced capitalist world, and offers some pointers towards future possibilities, in a way which should make the essentials of his thought familiar even to a reader who has no prior knowledge of his work. In consequence, I do not intend, in the remainder of this introduction, to attempt an outline of Habermas's project as a whole, a task which has in any case already been ably accomplished.[8] It will perhaps be more useful to highlight a small number of areas in which Habermas's thought has most frequently been subject to attack, not to say misrepresentation, and to indicate how it might be defended against some recurrent objections, which have most recently been reformulated in post-structuralist guise. In doing so I shall employ the work of Jean-François Lyotard as my major point of reference. For Lyotard must be accounted not only the most politically alert of post-structuralist thinkers, but also the one who has spelled out most clearly the implications of recent French thought for our evaluation of modernity as a whole.

1. The Decline of 'Grand Narratives' and the Theory of History

In an influential book, Lyotard has defined postmodernity in terms of an increasing incredulity towards what he calls 'grand narratives', historical accounts of the past and correlative anticipations of the future of a people, nation, or other community, which perform functions of social integration and political legitimation. Members of contemporary societies, Lyotard argues, no longer find it possible to believe in their history as an epic of progress or emancipation. The promises of prosperity, freedom and justice associated with the Enlightenment project of scientific control over nature and a rational organization of society have signally failed to be realized, and we have no reason to suppose that they will be in the future, either in their bourgeois or their Marxist versions. Not only this, but even the regret for the absence of such metaphysical

---

8. For a fullscale account of Habermas's work, see Thomas McCarthy, *The Critical Theory of Jürgen Habermas*, London 1978. For a briefer survey, see Richard J. Bernstein's introduction to Bernstein, ed., *Habermas and Modernity*, Cambridge 1985, pp. 1–32.

guarantees of shared meaning has largely disappeared from 'post-modern' society. 'Most people,' Lyotard suggests, 'have lost the nostalgia for the lost narrative.'[9]

There are some striking parallels between this account of post-modernity and the 'end of ideology' debate which preoccupied English-speaking political scientists in the late fifties and early sixties. Indeed, it is curious to observe how the conception of ideology developed by American political science during the first Cold War is reduplicated in many of the themes of the 'left' Nietzscheanism of Paris during the 1970s. Daniel Bell's definition of a 'total ideology' as an 'all-inclusive' system of comprehensive reality', a 'set of beliefs infused with passion' which 'seeks to transform the whole of a way of life', captures the burden of this conception, which—independently of any direct Nietz-schean influence—is congruent with Nietzsche's fundamental convic-tions.[10] Nietzsche insists that any comprehensive theoretical or philosophical system must inevitably distort and simplify reality (for Bell, 'Ideology makes it unnecessary for people to confront individual issues on their individual merits'), that the energy which enters into the construction of such systems always derives from pre-rational needs and drives (for Bell, 'the most important latent function of ideology is to tap emotion'), and that concepts have an ineliminable pragmatic dimension (for Bell, 'not only does ideology transform ideas, it transforms people as well').[11] Furthermore, like Lyotard, the end-of-ideology theorists portrayed ideological thought as a compensation for the collapse of traditional religious worldviews, and attributed its decline to the political and social disasters of the twentieth century. Indeed, it is much the same litany of catastrophes, most notably facism and Stalinism, which is recited in both cases.[12] Here, however, the parallels between the two positions cease. For Bell, Shils, Lipset and company the post-war boom made possible the complacent assumption that Western societies had 'weathered the storm of ideologies', that a final dissolution of the principled opposition of left and right was taking place, in favour of a middle-ground consensus on the virtues of the mixed economy and the welfare state. Liberalism parted company with Nietzsche at the point at which a non-ideological standpoint was implicitly attributed to this

---

9. Jean-François Lyotard, *The Postmodern Condition*, Manchester 1984, p. 41.

10. Daniel Bell, 'The End of Ideology in the West: an Epilogue', in *The End of Ideology*, New York 1962, p. 400.

11. Ibid., pp. 405, 400, 401.

12. Bell mentions 'such calamities as the Moscow Trials, the Nazi-Soviet pact, the concentration camps, the suppression of the Hungarian workers': ibid., p. 402. Lyotard cites 'Auschwitz and Stalinism' as the liquidators of the hopes of modernity. See 'Sprache, Zeit, Arbeit', in Jean-François Lyotard et al., *Immaterialität und Postmoderne*, Berlin 1985, p. 37.

consensus. For the theorists of postmodernity, however, the informing political experience is precisely the collapse of the welfarist consensus, with the consequent proliferation of new forms of political opposition, themselves the inheritors of an earlier upsurge of lifestyle experimentation. Accordingly, Lyotard follows Nietzsche through to a drastic pluralism, suggesting that the 'grand narratives' have been irreparably fragmented into a multiplicity of 'language-games' whose truth-claims are localized, and which are played with an ironic consciousness of their own relativity.

Against this background, it is important to note that Habermas has never denied the metaphysical core of the classic philosophies of history—indeed, he would concur with Lyotard that what he terms the 'objectivistic philosophy of history' must be considered as the last embodiment of an 'illusion of order' which was first generated by myth, and later preserved by philosophical systems. What Habermas refuses to accept, however, is that—from Vico onwards—the philosophy of history has *simply* been a means of satisfying a craving for coherence and order. Rather, he suggests, the philosophy of history emerged in response to novel historical experiences associated with the rise of capitalism. In an essay dating from 1972 Habermas lists four fundamental experiences which played a role in this process: an awareness of accelerated and directed social change, resulting from the growth of forces of production, and from attempts to control the effects of this growth; a consciousness of the gap between the need for regulation of increasingly complex social processes, and a lagging capacity for control which generates unpredictable side-effects of its own as it advances; a sensitivity to the unresolved conflict between the universal scope of bourgeois moral principles and the continuing 'state of nature' which exists between national communities; and, lastly, the disintegration of traditional world-views as securers of social identity.[13] In Habermas's account, the historico-philosophical sketches of the eighteenth century, and the theories of social evolution of the nineteenth, were attempts to comprehend and propose solutions to these problems, through a construal of universal history with scientific intentions. Such theories address the contradictory fact that human beings continue to suffer the consequences of a historical process which is in some sense the outcome of their own actions. Habermas views Marx's critique of capitalist society as a materialistic transformation of this tradition, like its predecessors connecting an awareness of the crisis of contemporary

---

13. See Jürgen Habermas, 'Über das Subject der Geschichte: Diskussionsbemerkungen zu falsch gestellten Alternativen', in *Kultur und Kritik: Verstreute Aufsätze*, Frankfurt 1973, pp. 390–393.

society with an interpretation of the pattern of human history as a whole.

Insofar as experiences of uncontrolled contingency and of the ambivalence of progress—rather than its absence—remain central to contemporary consciousness, Habermas appears justified in arguing that 'all counter-ideologies, which claim to have overcome the problems of the philosophy of history, come under suspicion of escapism.'[14] To suggest—as Lyotard does—that theories of history are necessarily metaphysical, either because of their narrative forms or because of their scale, is simply to reproduce the fundamental prejudices of positivism. Such a position excludes the course, which Habermas advocates, of radicalizing the philosophy of history by eliminating its dogmatic residues. In this respect there are two fundamental difficulties to be resolved. The first concerns 'objectivism'—the belief in a 'meaning' of history which is logically independent of any practical orientation towards the transformation of society. In his early writings, Habermas contends that Marx had already overcome this problem, having understood that 'the meaning of history can be theoretically recognized to the extent that human beings set about making it practically true.'[15] The second difficulty concerns the empirical controls on such a philosophy of history, or—more broadly conceived—the problem of the relation between philosophy and science.

Habermas's early conception of such an 'empirically falsifiable philosophy of history with practical intent' emerges with particular clarity in a discussion of Merleau-Ponty which he wrote in 1957, as part of a report on recent philosophical debates around Marxism.[16] Habermas argues that—among Western Marxists—it is Merleau-Ponty who has come closest to grasping the distinctive epistemological status of Marx's theory, insofar as he seeks to undermine the notion of history as governed by an inexorable logic, without lapsing into Sartre's equation of revolutionary practice with an abrupt, meaning-bestowing act of transcendence. Merleau-Ponty's position is summarized in a manner which reveals more than a hint of Adorno's influence: 'Where the logic of history, the condition of any possible philosophy of history,

---

14. Jürgen Habermas, 'Between Philosophy and Science: Marxism as Critique', in *Theory and Practice*, London 1973, p. 251 (trs. altered).

15. Ibid., p. 248 (trs. altered). More recently, Habermas has suggested that both Hegel and Marx, in the course of their careers, make the transition from a practically-oriented to an 'objectivist' interpretation of history: *The Philosophical Discourse of Modernity*, pp. 60–63.

16. Jürgen Habermas, 'Literaturbericht zur Philosophischen Diskussion um Marx und den Marxismus', in *Theorie und Praxis*, 2nd edn., Frankfurt 1971, pp. 387–456. The discussion of Merleau-Ponty appears on pp. 425–428.

remains without any metaphysical guarantee, the philosophy of history is itself no longer philosophical; it rather becomes the critical prologue to a practice, to which it delivers up its own logos along with the logic of history as a whole ... The experimental philosophy of history no longer searches for a hidden meaning; it saves such a meaning by producing it. Strictly speaking there "is" no meaning, only a progressive elimination of unmeaning.'[17] However, although Habermas praises Merleau-Ponty for this elucidation, there is one crucial respect in which he disagrees with the French phenomenologist's position. Merleau-Ponty's acceptance of the contingency of political practice, of the fact that 'the revolutionary event is not inscribed anywhere, in any metaphysical heaven', does not lead to an appreciation of the need for an empirical investigation of the preconditions of social transformation. The qualification of the proletariat as the bearer of revolution, for example, is not seen as something to be empirically demonstrated. Ultimately, Habermas suggests, Merleau-Ponty cannot attribute any independent role to social-scientific analysis within his conception of philosophical critique because he is unable to break with the traditional assumption that philosophical insight must be self-validating, and consequently fails to appreciate that 'an analysis of the question of meaning will only enter the dimension of the meaning of history when it comprehends this question from the determinate, historically-constituted situation in which it appears or disappears.'[18] Thus, for Habermas, the metaphysical features of the philosophy of history can only be eliminated through a relation of philosophy *both* to practice and to the empirical social sciences. A practical theory, he suggests, must be 'dependent on the social sciences, so long as it does not believe that it can get by with a dialectic which—prior to and at the basis of all history—unfolds in accordance with the hourstrokes of metaphysical necessity. So long as it rather considers dialectic to be as contingent as history itself, it must allow everything which it wishes to know to be empirically given, and this means with the procedures of the objectifying sciences; of course, the results of these are treated by philosophy as the material for its interpretations.'[19]

This conception of a close collaboration, and reciprocal dependence, of philosophy and the social sciences is central to Habermas's work as it develops through the 1960s. By the early 1970s, however, Habermas will be forced to recognize that even such a collaboration is not sufficient to strip the philosophy of history of certain dogmatic residues, of a kind which we shall be considering in more detail in a moment. As a result,

17. Ibid., pp. 425–426.
18. Ibid., p. 427.
19. Ibid., p. 443.

Habermas eventually drops the ambiguous notion of a 'philosophy of history' altogether, and, during the 1970s, embarks on the collaborative project of a reconstruction of historical materialism as a theory of social evolution. The most distinctive feature of this reconstruction is Habermas's argument that what Marxists have traditionally referred to as the 'forces of production' and the 'relations of production'—labour-power, technical knowledge transformable into instruments of production, and organizational skills on the one hand, and the manner in which labour-power is combined with the means of production and the social product distributed, on the other—must be considered as two separate dimensions in which progress can take place. Marxists have usually placed most emphasis on the forces of production in their explanations of historical development, arguing that it is the relations of production which must eventually come into line with an expansion of the productive forces. Habermas, however, developing a distinction between 'work' and 'interaction' which has been central to his thought ever since the beginning, discerns an autonomous logic in the moral-practical sphere of the relations of production. Furthermore, since it is ultimately only socialized *individuals* who can learn, even if their attainments may eventually become part of a culturally-transmitted collective fund of knowledge, psychological theories of cognitive and moral development—here Habermas takes Piaget and Kohlberg as his guides—can provide the basis for a theory of evolutionary stages in the domain of law and morality, of ego-demarcations and worldviews, and of individual and collective identity formations. Habermas is anxious to stress that such a 'twin-track' theory of social evolution neither abandons materialism nor revives a teleological conception of history as inevitable progress towards a pre-ordained goal. To identify a series of stages in the development of normative structures is not to reduce the dynamics of history to an internal history of mind, nor is it to deny the possibility of stagnation or regression by asserting the inevitability of the transition from one stage to another. The materialism of Habermas's theory consists in the view that such transitions only take place as a means of resolving crises in the domain of social production and reproduction, while the rejection of any 'logification' of history results from the fact that both such crises and their successful resolution are regarded as contingent events—there is no guarantee that learning-processes will be institutionalized.[20] By drawing a sharp line in this way between the

---

20. Jürgen Habermas, 'Historical Materialism and the Development of Normative Structures', in *Communication and the Evolution of Society*, pp. 120–122. A helpful brief account of the development of Habermas's views on history is provided by Axel Honneth, 'Vorbemerkungen', in Urs Jaeggi and Axel Honneth, eds., *Theorien des historischen Materialismus*, Frankfurt 1977, pp. 453–464.

'logical space' of possibilities of development and the contingency of the historical process, Habermas is able finally to overcome the ambiguities of the philosophy of history. A general theory of social evolution, he suggests, can provide a promise of 'meaning'—in the sense of an overcoming of contingency—no longer available from collapsed metaphysical worldviews. But it does so not through the rationalization of hazard, but rather by making possible an analysis of the present on which a practical overcoming of uncontrolled contingencies can be based.

2. Subjectivity and Emancipation

Even if it is admitted that a general theory of history is not intrinsically 'metaphysical', and may even be indispensable for the analysis of contemporary social developments, there remains a further reason, which demands to be taken seriously, for the current distrust of notions of 'revolution' and 'emancipation'. To a certain extent in Marx himself, and in the Hegelian Marxist tradition—beginning with Lukács' *History and Class Consciousness*—the notion of a subject of the historical process, which is eventually able to comprehend itself as such, plays a major role. Even in the work of Adorno, who, in *Negative Dialectics*, develops a radical critique of many aspects of the Hegelian Marxist tradition, the view that society is a 'potentially self-determining subject' remains central. Thus, in his 'Introduction' to *The Positivist Dispute in German Sociology*, Adorno exposes the reification of social reality through the argument that 'society is objective because, on account of its underlying structure, it cannot perceive its own subjectivity, because it does not possess a total subject and through its own organization it thwarts the installation of such a subject.'[21]

The validity of this conception, however, according to which the impersonal objectivity of social structures can be theorized in terms of alienation, has long been open to question. As Habermas points out in *Der Philosophische Diskurs der Moderne*, the viability of the corresponding conception of revolution as a reappropriation of alienated powers was already one of the central issues between the first generation of Left and Right Hegelians. In opposition to the notion that political power could be dissolved into the self-organization of society, the Right Hegelians argued that the individualism and competitiveness of bourgeois society

---

21. Theodor Adorno, 'Introduction', in *The Positivist Dispute in German Sociology*, p. 33.

must rather be held in check by the state, and that any attempt to abolish this counterweight could lead only to chaos. 'How can one collectively administer', one liberal follower of Hegel enquires, echoing many more recent arguments, 'that which does not constitute a closed whole, and which is daily generated and formed anew through the infinite and infinitely manifold production of individuals?'[22] This critique was radicalized by Max Weber, who predicted—before the Russian Revolution—that abolition of private ownership of the means of production would not lead to a self-managed society, but only to an intensification of bureaucracy, and has also been a feature of post-structuralist thought. It is implicit in Foucault's insistence on the ineliminability of relations of power, and becomes more explicit and topical in Lyotard's recent discussions of 'immateriality'—a term which he associates with the erosion of identity, the breaking-down of stable barriers between the self and a manipulable world produced by our implication in opaquely labyrinthine technological and social systems.[23] A similar account of late capitalism has been developed by Fredric Jameson, who is, however, markedly more ambivalent about its implications.[24] In general, the phenomenology of 'postmodernity' gives the lie to the notion that society could ever become 'transparent' to itself, through a process which could be conceptualized as the self-reflection of a collective social subject.

In much of his earlier work, Habermas had relied on the concept of a subject of the historical process, although he considered this subject to be the human species, rather than a social class such as the proletariat, and although he argued that the subject of history—in the form of global humanity unified by modern networks of commerce and communication—was not to be hypostatized, but was itself a product of the historical process. However, Habermas has become increasingly aware of the basic problems generated by the conceptual framework of the philosophy of consciousness. One major turning point can be located in his debate with the systems theorist Niklas Luhmann, which was published in 1971. Here, for the first time, Habermas stresses the inappropriateness of theorizing social collectivities in terms of a constitutive subject. He suggests that even in Hegel—despite a shift towards intersubjectivity—a monological absolute subject is ultimately restored, with significant consequences for the Marxist tradition, including his own position in *Theory and Practice* and *Knowledge and Human*

---

22. Oppenheim, cited in *The Philosophical Discourse of Modernity*, p. 395.

23. See Jean-François Lyotard, 'Immaterialien', and 'Philosophie in der Diaspora', in *Immaterialität und Postmoderne*, pp. 9–26.

24. See Fredric Jameson, 'Postmodernism, or the Cultural Logic of Late Capitalism', in *New Left Review*, no. 146, pp. 53–92.

Interests.[25] In this context even French structuralism—an intellectual movement from which Habermas is in most respects distant—is sympathetically referred to as resulting from a justified dissatisfaction, with the application of concepts derived from the philosophy of reflexion to social processes. Habermas himself, however, prefers to turn towards systems theory for the conceptual tools with which to overcome this weakness in the tradition of Western Marxism. Thus, in his 1976 essay on the reconstruction of historical materialism, Habermas argues that 'Historical materialism does not need to assume a *species*-subject that undergoes evolution. The bearers of evolution are rather societies and the acting subjects integrated into them; social evolution can be discerned in those structures that are replaced by more comprehensive structures in accordance with a pattern that is to be rationally reconstructed.'[26]

However, just as with other major conceptual borrowings, Habermas's assimilation of systems theory takes place through the medium of critique. Habermas rejects attempts to make systems theory alone the basis of a theory of social evolution, arguing that a self-sufficient functionalism cannot appreciate the fact that increases in complexity are in each case only possible at the learning level attained in the organizational principle of the society in question. In other words, in terms of the distinction between functional and normative structures which we have already noted, the modes of action embodied in social systems first have to be made possible through evolutionary learning processes in the moral-practical dimension. In his more recent work Habermas has explored the implications of this conception of evolutionary processes in terms of the relation between systems and the 'life-world'. In the domain of everyday life concerned with the transmission of culture, social integration, and the socialization of individuals, what Habermas terms 'communicative action', the co-ordination of action through implicit or argumentatively attained agreement, is indispensable. By contrast, the achievement of systems such as the capitalist economy and bureaucratic administrations is to operate via 'steering media'—money and power—which enable us to dispense with the common orientation of actors. In one respect this dualism of system and life-world, which Habermas has placed at the centre of the most ambitious formulation of his social theory to date, *The Theory of Communicative Action*, is simply an attempt to solve one of the oldest conundrums of

---

25. Jürgen Habermas, 'Theorie der Gesellschaft oder Sozialtechnologie?', in Habermas and Niklas Luhmann, *Theorie der Gesellschaft oder Sozialtechnologie—Was Leistet der Systemforschung?*, Frankfurt 1971, pp. 176–181.
26. 'Towards a Reconstruction of Historical Materialism', p. 140.

sociology—the problem of reconciling the apparently autonomous logic of social processes with the equally inescapable fact that society is the outcome of human interactions. However, this distinction also enables Habermas to develop a new account of the contradictions and characteristic forms of political struggle of advanced capitalism. In line with his general conception, Habermas argues that it is only on the basis of a 'modernization' of the life-world (the process whereby the concepts of truth, moral rightness, and truthfulness or authenticity, which are inseparably interwoven in traditional forms of life, become differentiated into three distinct spheres of value) that systems can separate out from the life-world—as they did fully for the first time under capitalism. For much of its historical existence capitalism has survived and expanded by consuming the substance of traditional forms of life. However, we have now reached a stage, Habermas contends, when the uncontrolled growth of autonomous systems has begun to undermine its own foundations, as it were, by commodifying and bureaucratizing life-world activities which are intrinsically bound to communicative action. The result is the generation of social pathologies, of the kind which have called forth the defensive and communitarian impulses manifest in the New Social Movements.

On the basis of this conception, in which it is not systems as such, but their 'colonization' of the life-world, which generates phenomena structurally analogous to those which Marx designated with the term 'alienation', Habermas is able to pinpoint the ambiguity in Marx's work which has led to the current distrust of traditional conceptions of revolution and social emancipation. 'Marx's error', Habermas suggests, 'can be traced back to that dialectical clamping together of system analysis and life-world analysis, which does not permit a sufficiently sharp separation between the level of system-differentiation achieved by modernity and the class-specific forms of its institutionalization ... Otherwise he would not have been able to overlook the fact that any modern society, no matter what the nature of its class-structure, must demonstrate a high level of structural differentiation.'[27] Echoing a critique which has been developed from different angles, and in widely differing theoretical contexts, by authors such as André Gorz and Alec Nove,[28] Habermas argues that because Marx borrows a conceptual

---

27. Jürgen Habermas, *The Theory of Communicative Action*, vol. 2, trans. Thomas McCarthy, Boston 1987, p. 340 (trs. altered).

28. See André Gorz, *Farewell to the Working Class*, London 1982, especially chapters 2–5; and Alec Nove, *The Economics of Feasible Socialism*, London 1983, especially chapters 1–2. Although formulated more intuitively than in Habermas, the suggestion that Marxism has traditionally underestimated the autonomy of systems is central to both these works.

apparatus from Hegel which is neutral in relation to the distinction of system and life-world, he is misled into viewing the capitalist system as 'nothing more than the ghostly form of class-relations which have been inverted and fetishized into anonymity'.[29] This has the unfortunate consequence that Marx's theory of revolution awakens the illusory expectation that 'in principle all social relations which have been objectified, rendered systematically autonomous, can be brought back within the horizons of the life-world.'[30] It is then a comparatively easy matter, as we have already seen, for opponents to unmask the 'unifying power of reason' as an illusion in the face of such 'stubborn complexities'.

The critique of Marx's social theory and of his theory of revolution clearly has important consequences for our conception of the goals and procedures of a contemporary socialist politics. Because Marx's explanatory model for the pathologies of capitalism remains Hegel's *entzweite Sittlichkeit*—a torn-apart traditional life-world—which he theorizes in terms of a self-divided macro-subject, he is able to group these disturbances around a single, central class antagonism. Once we abandon this model, however, by distinguishing between the modernization of the life-world, and the reification of an already modernized life-world, we must admit the more diverse and contingent character of the pathological traits of advanced capitalism, and reject the notion that the knowledge and organization of the social totality can be conceptualized as the self-reflection and self-transformation of a social subject. A no less important consequence is that the prospect of a thoroughgoing internal reorganization of administration and economy on the basis of workers' control is no longer plausible. For the efficiency of these subsystems, which is in fact their *raison d'être*, derives from their use of 'steering media' which can be considered as impoverished and standardized languages, abstracted from the more context-specific forms of agreement which are required for the co-ordination of action in the life-world. Habermas denies, however, that the recognition of these constraints must lead us to abandon the very ideal of a democratization of society. Rather, such democratization must take the form of a fostering of 'counter public-spheres', 'centres of concentrated communication which naturally arise out of the micro-domains of everyday practice',[31] and which can focus the impulses of the life-world. In this way state and economy could be sensitized to the goals established by participatory decision-making processes. These counter public-spheres must, of course, maintain themselves below the level of complexity

---

29. *The Theory of Communicative Action*, vol. 2, p. 339 (trs. altered).
30. *The Philosophical Discourse of Modernity*, p. 67 (trs. altered).
31. Ibid., p. 422.

which would carry them over the threshold of the life-world, operating instead at the interface of a life-world and system. Only in this way, Habermas suggests, can the ideals of solidarity and self-determination built into modernity be reconciled with the level of system-complexity on which modern societies rely for their material well-being.

3. Morality and Ethical Life

The criticisms of the Marxist tradition which we have considered in the previous section are based on the argument that the complexity and objectivity of social systems are not simply abstract, dependent moments of the self-relation and self-movement of a potentially revolutionary subject of society. As we have seen, Habermas both accommodates and counters this objection by suggesting that it is the immanent rationality of linguistic *inter*-subjectivity which resists submission to the functional imperatives of economy and administration. However, Habermas has also had to respond to objections from another, very different quarter— here the contention is not that subjectivity is impotent in the face of objective social processes, but rather that the notion of a 'rational' consensus, based purely on argumentation, which Habermas employs as the normative foundation of his critical social theory, is chimerical. Objections of this kind have frequently been brought by thinkers in the hermeneutic tradition, most notably Hans-Georg Gadamer, who, in his important debate with Habermas in the late sixties, accused Habermas of being unconsciously guided by the image of an 'anarchistic utopia', in so far as he believed it possible to submit all inherited authority to a demand for rational justification.[32] For Gadamer, 'It is not so much our judgments as it is our prejudices that constitute our being'[33]—'tradition' reaches deeper than any possible explicitly attained consensus. More surprisingly, given the iconoclastic posture of much post-structuralist thought, a similar lesson can and has been drawn from Jacques Derrida's portrayal of subjectivity as always caught up in the play of a 'general text' whose meaning it can never make fully perspicuous to itself. It has also informed Jean-François Lyotard's attempts to develop a 'post-modern' conception of justice. Unlike some of his contemporaries, Lyotard fully acknowledges the central role which the ideal of autonomy has played in modern politics, the principle that 'only that totality of

---

32. See Hans-Georg Gadamer, 'On the Scope and Function of Hermeneutical Reflection', in David E. Linge, ed., *Philosophical Hermeneutics*, London 1976, p. 42.
33. Hans-Georg Gadamer, 'The Universality of the Hermeneutic Problem', in ibid., p. 9.

prescriptions will be considered just which is produced by the social body to which these prescriptions apply.'[34] However, Lyotard also dismisses such self-determination as an impossible ideal, since, as participants in a life-world, our selves are shaped by forms of 'narrative knowledge', networks of belief and evaluation which are the implicit basis from which all argument begins. 'People begin by listening to a language', Lyotard affirms, 'not by speaking it, and what they hear as children are stories ... That implies the contrary of autonomy, heteronomy. It also implies that, fundamentally, it is not true that a people can ever give itself its own institutions.'[35]

In this area, too, Habermas has modified his position, introducing further discriminations, over the last ten years or so. In some of his earlier statements Habermas had given the impression that the concept of what he terms an 'ideal speech situation'—a situation of dialogue characterized by full reciprocity, and by an absence of external coercions and internal distortions—could provide the lineaments of a possible future form of life. Now, however, Habermas acknowledges that the content of particular life-forms depends on traditions, no matter how reflexively appropriated, and that 'socialized individuals cannot relate hypothetically to the form of life or to the life-history through which their own identity has been formed.'[36] Recently Habermas has summarized, in terms of a series of arguments developed by Albrecht Wellmer, the limitations which such considerations place on a 'discourse ethics'— an ethics based on the principle that a norm can be considered objectively right if it would be consented to in free discussion by all concerned as consonant with their interests.[37] Firstly, practical discourse cannot generate the content of norms, but can only serve as a means of resolving disputes concerning norms and practices which have already become problematic: 'Without the horizon of the life-world of a specific social group, and without conflicts of action in a specific situation ... it would be senseless to want to conduct a practical discourse.'[38] Secondly, a discourse ethics cannot resolve questions of the 'good life', since 'ideas of the good life are not representations, which hover before us as an abstract ought; they stamp the identity of groups and individuals in such a way that they form an integrated component of the

---

34. Jean-François Lyotard and Jean-Loup Thébaud, *Just Gaming*, Manchester 1985, p. 25 (trs. altered).

35. Ibid., pp. 68–9.

36. Jürgen Habermas, 'Discourse Ethics: Notes on a Program of Philosophical Justification', in *Moral Consciousness and Communicative Action*, Cambridge 1990, p. 104 (trs. altered).

37. See ibid., pp. 103–6.

38. Ibid., p. 103.

particular culture or personality.'[39] Thirdly, because of their degree of universality, moral insights acquired under conditions of practical discourse must be complemented by a non-formalizable hermeneutic sensitivity, in order to be applied to concrete situations. Lastly, moral discourses themselves stand under a number of restrictions: since they are concerned with the interpretation of needs they are necessarily permeated by motifs of aesthetic and therapeutic critique which cannot themselves be conclusively validated; since the problems with which they deal result from a disturbance of intersubjective relations, an element of the 'struggle for recognition' is built into them; finally, the achievement of consensus is by no means the socially predominant form of conflict resolution, so that ethical principles are confronted with the difficulties of instatement through strategic political action. All these factors, Habermas suggests, bring into play the 'power of history over against the transcending claims and interests of reason.'[40]

Recently, Habermas has argued that these conflicts between history and reason can be summarized under the heading of the relation between morality and 'ethical life', in the Hegelian sense of *Sittlichkeit*— the concrete customs of a community.[41] For it was Hegel who first definitively exposed the formalism of Kantian ethics, showing that the mere principle of universalizability cannot generate determinate moral norms, and is dependent for its content on the actual practices of a society. In this respect Habermas admits that his discourse ethics, which radicalizes Kant by proposing that universal norms should be the outcome of a discussion in which individual needs and interests are expressed, pays for its enhancement of the rationality or moral norms with a number of drawbacks—most importantly, an abstraction from concrete situations of application, and a loss of the force of empirically effective motives.[42] On the other hand, Habermas also contends that it is no longer possible for the critics of formalism—without the guarantee of Hegel's absolute spirit—simply to appeal to *Sittlichkeit*, to what happens

---

39. Ibid., p. 108.
40. Ibid., p. 106.
41. See Jürgen Habermas, 'Über Moralität und Sittlichkeit—Was macht ein Lebensform "Rational"?', in Herbert Schnädelbach, ed., *Rationalität*, Frankfurt 1984, pp. 218–235.
42. See ibid., p. 228. Kant, of course, was well aware of both the problem of application and the problem of motivation posed by his moral philosophy. In *Groundwork of the Metaphysic of Morals* he admits that the a priori laws of morality 'require in addition a power of judgement sharpened by experience, partly in order to distinguish the cases to which they apply, partly in order to secure for them admittance to the will of man and influence over practice; for man, affected as he is by so many inclinations, is capable of the Idea of pure practical reason, but he has not so easily the power to realise the Idea *in concreto* in his conduct of life.' *The Moral Law* (Kant's Groundwork of the Metaphysic of Morals), translated and analysed by H. J. Paton, London 1948, p. 55.

to be done, unless they are willing to countenance an unqualified moral relativism. Habermas's current solution to these difficulties is to suggest that questions of justice in the narrow sense, normative questions, must first be separated from evaluative questions of the good life—the former being amenable to procedures of rational argumentation, while the latter are not—and then reintegrated at a later stage. The resulting problem of the historical mediation of morality and ethical life is made considerably easier for us, Habermas contends, by the fact that modern life-worlds 'come to meet us halfway'. This is true both in relation to the problem of application and of motivation. Firstly, hermeneutic tact does not entirely dissolve the transcending force of principles into the relativity of particular situations. In some cases we can interpret the history of the application of a principle as a learning-process, in which partial and interest-distorted attempts at installation retrospectively appear as such in the light of the universal content of the principle in question. Habermas gives the example of the establishment of fundamental norms such as freedom of speech and the adult franchise in modern parliamentary democracies to illustrate such a learning-process. He points out, in addition, that the more the institutions of a society are organized in accordance with such principles, the more their further extension is facilitated. Secondly, while it must be admitted that a universalistic morality which is not 'to hang in the thin air of good intentions' must be anchored in personality structures, it can be argued that modernized life-worlds, which push processes of individuation beyond the limits of an identity tied to specific social roles, towards the flexibility of what Habermas terms 'ego-identity', tend to provide such an anchorage. In this respect too, modern societies can be said to compensate for the abstraction of modern morality.

One further problem which arises in this context, and to which Habermas has devoted considerable attention in recent years, is how to accommodate the concept of 'progress' within an approach which accepts the duality of morality and ethical life. For, if we admit that conflicting ideas of the good life cannot be arbitrated through discourse in the same way as questions of justice, we must also admit that there can be no formal criterion which would allow us to pronounce one form of life superior to another. Here again Habermas has considerably modified traditional Marxist conceptions of historical progress. Marx himself, as the *Communist Manifesto* shows, often downplayed the costs of the shattering of traditional ways of life, in favour of what he considered to be the emancipatory dynamic of the capitalist mode of production. Although he is not entirely immune to the poignancy of the destruction of ancient cultures—particularly in a colonial context— Marx's historical optimism leads him to assume that rationalization and happiness, secured through the full realization of human capacities, must eventually coincide.[43] In Habermas's view, however, we can no longer claim Marx's confidence. While firmly opposing any politically-motivated romanticization of the past, which conveniently neglects the levels of material misery prevalent in pre-modern societies, Habermas nevertheless insists that our assessment of a form of life as successful or unsuccessful, good or bad, ultimately depends on unformalizable 'clinical' intuitions: a mediaeval society—even with higher levels of oppression—might be considered less alienated than a modern capitalist metropolis. The abandonment of the philosophy of history, which we have already examined, in favour of a theory of social evolution, which filters out universal structures from concrete forms of life, and strictly separates the logic from the dynamics of development, requires us to 'give up critically judging and normatively classifying totalities, worldviews, epochs, forms of life and cultures, complexes of life as a whole.'[44] It is important to add, however, that this line of argument does *not* plunge us into relativism as far as our own society is concerned. For if it is true that the substance of a way of life cannot be justified from a universalist standpoint, it is equally true that moral demands which run counter to the degree of rationalization which a society has already achieved will generate social pathologies—as the extreme case of fascism in the twentieth century graphically shows. To this extent we can say that, for us, as members of a modern society, there is no turning back—if we are to move towards a less commodified and bureaucratized form of life, it cannot be through a return to an undifferentiated life-world, but only on the basis of the forms of communicative action which modernity has already released.

4. Truth, Consensus and Conformity

There remains one final charge against Habermas which merits discussion in this context, and which—again—has been perhaps most clearly and forcefully stated in *The Postmodern Condition*. In the work of influential contemporary thinkers such as Lyotard and Feyerabend—behind whom, of course, stands the figure of Nietzsche—the very notions of 'truth', 'objectivity', 'consensus', are seen as possessing a

43. A fine illustration of the balance of Marx's sensibilities on this subject is provided by his article on 'The British Rule in India', in *Surveys from Exile*, Penguin/NLR edn., Harmondsworth 1973, pp. 301–307.

44. Jürgen Habermas, 'A Reply to my Critics', in John B. Thompson and David Held, eds., *Habermas: Critical Debates*, London 1982, p. 254.

coercive moment, as implying the enforced unification of plurality. In his more recent writings Lyotard has sought to break out of this coercion by adopting the Wittgensteinian notion of language-games, which are inherently multiple and irreducible to any universal model of language. Habermas's error can then be portrayed as the belief that 'humanity as a collective (universal) subject seeks its common emancipation through the regularization of the "moves" permitted in all the language-games'. The Critical Theorist's 'narrative of emancipation' unfortunately relies on a *telos* of collective agreement which 'does violence to the heterogeneity of language-games'.[45]

There are three distinct levels at which this critique of Habermas must be criticized in its turn. Firstly, at the philosophical level, Lyotard's arguments depend on a chronic confusion between *language-games* and *validity-claims*. He fails to distinguish between the differentiation of the life-world into three distinct spheres of value, concerned respectively with cognitive, moral and aesthetic questions, and what Habermas terms a 'pluralization of diverging universes of discourse [which] belongs to specifically modern experience'.[46] This confusion is particularly apparent in Lyotard's repeated twinning of Kant and Wittgenstein, exemplified by his recent statement that 'it is basically through Kant and Wittgenstein that I understood that there is no metalanguage in general'.[47] For to say that there is no metalanguage in general is ambiguous, interpretable either in a 'horizontal' or a 'vertical' sense. On the former—more Wittgensteinian—construal, what is meant is that there are no specifiable universal features of language at all: universality is fragmented into a variety of linguistic practices. On a Kantian interpretation, however, what is meant is that there are *several* metalanguages, governing different spheres of value. Far from defending a cognitive or moral pluralism, Kant's concern is precisely to uphold the possibility of claims to universality in different spheres, by clarifying the distinct epistemological statuses of different kinds of judgement. Thus, while admitting the plurality of language-games in contemporary culture, it is possible to argue that validity-claims (which are not themselves a specific kind of linguistic activity, but arise within different

---

45. *The Postmodern Condition*, pp. 66, xxv. For a useful commentary on this argument, which fails, however, to question its basic assumption, see Manfred Frank, *Was ist Neostrukturalismus?*, Frankfurt 1983, pp. 102–115.

46. Jürgen Habermas, 'Questions and Counterquestions', in *Habermas and Modernity*, p. 192.

47. 'Sprache, Zeit, Arbeit', p. 41. This confusion appears particularly clearly when Lyotard almost inadvertently lists Habermas's three aspects of validity, but describes them rather as 'régimes de phrases' ('regimes of sentences'): 'Appendice Svelte à la Question Postmoderne', in *Tombeau de l'Intellectuel et Autres Papiers*, Paris 1984, p. 84.

linguistic activities) *cut across* this multiplicity. In other words, there will be clashes of viewpoint concerning cognitive, moral and aesthetic questions, but we cannot claim that these conflicts are *in principle* unamenable to discussion, and to possible resolution. Habermas makes a similar point in the course his critique of Max Weber, who, like Lyotard, tends to run together value-contents and aspects of validity. 'Weber goes too far', Habermas suggests, 'when he infers from the loss of substantial unity of reason a polytheism of gods and demons struggling with one another, with their irreducibility rooted in a pluralism of incompatible validity-claims. The unity of rationality, in the multiplicity of value-spheres, rationalized according to their inner logics, is secured precisely at the formal level of the argumentative redemption of validity claims.'[48]

Secondly, on the political level, Lyotard's position is unsatisfactory insofar as it does not even address the issue of social conflict. One of the principal reasons for this is the anodyne connotations of the term 'language-game', which Lyotard employs with excessive laxity. Had he employed an alternative term such as 'social practices', and had he considered that this category would include activities such as pumping pollutants into the environment, closing down industries in depressed areas, and driving under the influence of alcohol, he would have found it less plausible to portray conflict merely as a kind of verbal jousting ('agonistics') internal to each language-game. A further important reason is that, as soon as Lyotard attempts to address the problem of the reciprocal relations of 'language-games' he is confronted with the nemesis of all relativism. For to argue that 'the recognition of the heteromorphous nature of language-games' implies 'the renunciation of terror, which assumes that they are isomorphic and tries to make them so',[49] is again to rely on an equivocation, between 'recognition' as the registering of a state of affairs, or as an acknowledgement of validity. Unless such a recognition, in the second sense, is more than simply one language-game among others, it is difficult to comprehend how Lyotard can claim priority for it. Had Lyotard reflected a little further on this, he would have appreciated that Habermas's theory of consensus has nothing to do with the homogenization of language-games, or with the establishment of the supremacy of one language-game, but rather with the condition of possibility of plurality: the regulation of the effects of social practices on each other in the light of the freely expressed interests of all those concerned.

But not only is Lyotard's position philosophically and politically

---

48. *The Theory of Communicative Action*, vol. I, trans. Thomas McCarthy, Boston 1984, p. 249.
49. *The Postmodern Condition*, p. 66.

dubious, it is also historically inaccurate, in so far as it fails to perceive that the universalization of principles and the individualization of lifestyles are two sides of the same process. In modern societies, Habermas suggests, the co-ordination of action becomes increasingly dependent on explicit, argumentatively attained agreement, rather than on the background consensus of the life-world. But, to the extent that this is the case, concrete life-forms and general life-world structures increasingly separate out from each other. It is possible for a proliferation of subcultures to take place precisely because the need for agreement on basic rules of social interaction is satisfied at ever higher levels of abstraction. Because he entirely neglects this universalistic component of modern consciousness, Lyotard equates an emancipatory pluralism with a retreat into fragmented and particularistic forms of consciousness, which has to some extent replaced the function of ideologies, with their 'dangerously' promissory and utopian content.[50] The basic philosophical confusion behind this position emerges clearly in Lyotard's recent suggestion that 'the decline, perhaps the ruin of the universal idea can liberate thought and life from totalizing obessions.'[51] Strangely enough, for a thinker who has recently made so much of Kantian motifs, Lyotard assumes that the universalism of Enlightenment moral consciousness must collapse along with the ambitions of traditional metaphysics. In consequence, he misinterprets Habermas as believing that 'the aim of the project of modernity [is] the constitution of sociocultural unity within which all the elements of daily life and of thought would take their places as in an organic whole.'[52] Lyotard is unable to distinguish between a concern with the re-establishing of connections between split-off specialist cultures and an irreversibly modernized life-world, and a longing for the lost totality of pre-modern culture.

In fact, one of the major distinctions between Habermas's work and the traditions of Hegelian Marxism from which it emerged is Habermas's Kantian insistence on the irreducible distinctions between value-spheres. Thus, at the risk of attack from more ecologically-minded radicals, Habermas has argued that the differentiation of modern life-forms must be preserved, 'in order that the reflexivity of traditions, the individuation of the social subject, and the universalistic foundations of justice and morality do not all go to hell.'[53] Far from advocating an organically integrated society, his vision is rather of a transformation

---

50. Ibid., p. 72.

51. Jean-François Lyotard, 'Tombeau de l'Intellectuel', in *Tombeau de l'Intellectuel et Autres Papiers*, p. 21.

52. Jean-François Lyotard, 'Answering the Question: What is Postmodernism?', in *The Postmodern Condition*, p. 72.

53. 'The Dialectics of Rationalization', p. 108 below.

from a society dominated by instrumental rationality to one in which the currently isolated spheres of the cognitive, the moral and the aesthetic can be brought into a new equilibrium and interaction, a task which he compares not to a melt-down into a new totality, but rather to the setting-in-motion of a mobile which has become obstinately entangled. This vision is encapsulated in Habermas's statement, from one of these interviews, that the 'motivating thought' which lies at the heart of his work concerns 'the reconciliation of a modernity which has fallen apart, the idea that without surrendering the differentiation which modernity has made possible in the cultural, the social and economic spheres, one can find forms of living together in which autonomy and dependency can truly enter into a non-antagonistic relation, that one can walk tall in a collectivity that does not have the dubious quality of backward-looking substantial forms of community.'[54]

Conclusion

The incoherence and omissions of Lyotard's thought, considered as the paradigm for a self-proclaimed postmodern philosophy, point towards some of the general, underlying problems with post-structuralist-inspired accounts of postmodernity. As we have already noted, in considering Lyotard's attitude to the philosophy of history, the Nietzschean influence on post-structuralism ensures that the metaphysical character of theories is equated with their systematicity. For Habermas, however, it is not systematicity as such which poses the problem, but the fact that philosophical systems—interpretations of the world as a whole—were based upon a fundamental principal immunized against critical probing, that philosophy traditionally conceived itself as a discourse operating at a level entirely distinct from that of empirical confirmation or disconfirmation. Habermas shares with the post-structuralists a sense of the crisis of philosophy after Hegel, of its struggle to step over into another medium. But he continues the materialist argument of the original Frankfurt School in suggesting that this medium must consist of a practically-oriented collaboration between philosophy and empirical social science. Through such a co-operation philosophy preserves the social and human sciences from empiricist and elementarist myopia, while the sciences lend philosophy a substantive, but non-dogmatic, content. For Habermas, in other words, it is not the *universality* of philosophical truth-claims which is to be abandoned, but rather their non-fallibilist aspect. Post-structuralism, however, through

54. Ibid., p. 125 below.

its critique of the universal, is driven into an abandonment of systematic cognitive claims, indeed frequently into a quasi-aesthetic suspension of truth-claims as such. The result of this manoeuvre, however, is that genuine attempts at social and cultural analysis become vulnerable to anecdotal and inadequately theorized evidence, a fact which explains the constitutive vagueness and portentousness of general accounts of postmodernity. Indeed, this vulnerability can be seen in the diffusion of the term postmodernism itself. In the domains of architecture and the visual arts, the word possesses a determinate meaning, referring to a renunciation and critique of distinct traditions, of a levelling techno-cratic functionalism in architecture, and of a programme of negation in modern art which leads from abstract expressionism, through mini-malism, to conceptual art (the last modernist movement which could be meaningfully described as avant-garde). It is certainly the case that these localized crises are symptomatic of more fundamental problems of modernity, problems of technology, of aesthetic experience and commodification, of environmentalism and democratic control. But this in itself does not justify the inflation of the term 'postmodernity' into a term of epochal diagnosis, an announcement of the collapse of the 'Enlightenment project' as a whole.

One cannot, in other words, provide a coherent account of post-modernity without a determinate concept of modernity; and such a concept cannot be developed a priori, but is necessarily dependent on the theorization of long-term historical processes, of the kind which Habermas attempts in his reconstruction of historical materialism. Lyotard and other contemporary thinkers often seem to ignore this basic requirement, assuming that it is sufficient to recite the disasters of the twentieth century in order to blacken the entire Enlightenment heritage. At the crudest level this position appears to imply a denial of the meaningfulness of any counterfactual history, the belief that no epoch can contain possibilities other than those which have been actually realized. Thus Lyotard affirms—in explicit opposition to Habermas—'Modernity is not "incomplete", rather it has been liquidated. After Auschwitz and Stalinism it is certain that no-one can maintain that the hopes, which were bound up with modernity, have been fulfilled. To be sure, they have not been forgotten, but rather destroyed.'[55] The implausibility of this argument is intensified by the fact that it is only in the light of the democratic and humanitarian aspirations of the Enligh-tenment that fascism and Stalinism appear in their full horror. In general, the discourse of postmodernity, in its constant oscillations between depression and exhilaration, its bitter-sweet ambivalence,

---

55. 'Sprache, Zeit, Arbeit', pp. 37–38.

provides evidence in favour of Habermas's contention that modern consciousness is essentially constituted by an intersection of historical and utopian perspectives, the one—for example, in the form of the memory of the political disasters which Lyotard evokes—providing a necessary ballast for the other. For Habermas, what has been exhausted is not utopian energies as such, but a particular model of utopia based on the notion of self-realization through labour, which is dubious both in its philosophico-anthropological origins, and in its lack of purchase on modern industrial processes. Whether the decline of this particular model of self-realizing subjectivity signals a collapse of belief in the possibility of progress as such depends upon one's theoretical conception of the potentials of modernity.

In the case of post-structuralist thought, the rational principle of modernity is equated—although more often implicitly than explicitly—with cognitive-instrumental thought. This then permits post-structuralist theories to invoke the characteristic experiences of aesthetic modernism—of a subjectivity freed from the demands of utility and morality—as the radical other of Enlightenment reason and societal modernization. In viewing cultural modernity as a disruptive intruder, post-structuralism and neo-conservatism coincide, although the polarity of values is reversed from one position to the other. For the neo-conservatives, the spread of life-styles and attitudes inspired by aesthetic modernism poses a threat to the ideology of achievement and obedience which is essential to the continuing process of capitalist modernization. For post-structuralism, by contrast, the celebration of the untamed energies of mind and body—of madness, intensity, desire—is the only means of opposing a modernity conceptualized exclusively in terms of economic and administrative rationalization. It is important to note that Habermas by no means underestimates the emancipatory potential of modern culture, although he would argue—against the onesidedness of post-structuralism—that a concern for human and civil rights, and for democratic self-determination, is no less central to cultural modernity than the values of expressive subjectivity. He even accepts the contemporary 'cult of immediacy, the deflation of noble forms, anarchism of the soul, the celebration of the concrete all along the line, relativism even in the theory of science'—developments which go against the grain of many of Habermas's basic convictions—as expressions of 'the need for concretion, the wish for engagement, the attempt to test the critical content of ideas here and now, to take ideas seriously in the way one live's one's life.'[56] In their post-structuralist form, however, these

---

56. Jürgen Habermas, 'Introduction', in Habermas, ed., *Observations on the Spiritual Situation of the Age*, Boston 1984, pp. 21–22 (trs. altered).

attitudes have implications which cannot be exempted from criticism. Perhaps the most significant of these concern the rejection of an anticipatory relation to practice in philosophical thought, and a reliance on the normative content of aesthetic experience itself.

In one sense, Lyotard is perfectly correct in suggesting that Adorno's thought can be seen as teetering on the brink of post-modernity, if we understand by this the collapse of any rationally-justified belief in the possibility of a better future. Indeed, the classical Frankfurt School as a whole, once it had come to doubt the revolutionary role of the proletariat, emphasized the fragility of its own critical perspective—and devoted a great deal of energy to the problem which this fragility posed. In his 1937 essay on 'Traditional and Critical Theory', Horkheimer remarks that—from the conventional standpoint—a critical theory of society could only appear as 'an aimless intellectual game, half conceptual poetry, half impotent expression of states of mind'.[57] And in his complementary essay of the same year, Marcuse, too, admits that 'strong emphasis on the role of phantasy seems to contradict the rigorously scientific character that critical theory has always made a criterion of its concepts', but nevertheless insists—more defiantly than Horkheimer—that 'without phantasy, all philosophical knowledge remains in the grip of the present or the past and severed from the future, which is the only link between philosophy and the real history of mankind.'[58] It is in the work of Adorno, however, that the shift of emphasis from historical process to the subjective resources of the individual, the view that 'reason has retreated behind a windowless wall of idiosyncrasies, which the holders of power arbitrarily reproach with arbitrariness',[59] takes its most extreme form. While it is true that in Adorno the possibility of reconciliation is not arbitrarily posited, but is rather the logical outcome of an immanent critique of identity-thinking, nevertheless, in Adorno's later works—particularly *Negative Dialectics*—an almost unbearable tension is generated, an absurd disproportion, between the utopian glimmerings, on the one hand, and the total system of delusion, on the other. It is revealing that, in the early seventies, Lyotard finds his own experience as a former militant of the far Left reflected in this tension; and that it is precisely by means of a contrast with Adorno—who was, at that time, little known to France—that Lyotard articulates the break from the tormented negativity of a

---

57. Max Horkheimer, 'Traditional and Critical Theory', in *Critical Theory*, New York 1972, p. 209.

58. Herbert Marcuse, 'Philosophy and Critical Theory', in *Negations*, Harmondsworth 1968, p. 155.

59. Theodor Adorno, *Minima Moralia*, London 1974, p. 70.

prospectless critique, to an affirmative Nietzschean stance, a break which he describes in *Économie Libidinale* as 'la résolution d'une longue douleur'.

From one point of view, this shift can be seen as motivated by sound political intuition, which is also embodied in the Hegelian inheritance of Marxism—an awareness that, as Albrecht Wellmer has recently recalled—'theory must have an appropriate concept of the already *existing* forms of freedom, if it is to anticipate emancipation not as the mere negation, but as the *"Aufhebung"* of this freedom'.[60] In the philosophy of postmodernity, however, the conservation and super-session of existing freedoms no longer comes into question at all, any more than it does in the facade of playfulness and individuality which postmodern architecture superimposes on anonymous concentrations of wealth and power, or in the reconciliation with the art market of neo-expressionist painting. Rather than abandoning the utopian perspective and retreating into stoicism, Lyotard tends to consider it as already realized in the present, thereby collapsing the relation of philosophy to a transformative practice no longer considered necessary. The problem with this position, however, is that it is no less based on wish-fulfilment than the position which it replaces: Lyotard's suggestion, for example, that 'the extension of the technical criterion, even in its capitalist usage, to the majority of activities does not only have the effect of subjugating them to the interests of the system', but also 'favours the discovery that every activity is also an art (*technè*)',[61] is far from convincing. The perpetuation of illusion implicit in this attempt to escape the tension between the real and the ideal was well perceived by Adorno in his critique of Nietzschean *amor fati* in *Minima Moralia*: 'Love of stone walls and barred windows is the last resort of someone who sees and has nothing else to love. Both are cases of the same ignominious adaptation which, in order to endure the world's horror, attributes reality to wishes and meaning to senseless compulsion.'[62] Furthermore, the accusation which Lyotard levels against Habermas, of a refusal to draw the necessary distinctions between language-games, of a longing for the 'unity of experience', appears bizarre in the light of what can be seen as the fundamental project of *The Postmodern Condition*: an attempt to portray the cognitive and the aesthetic as *already* reconciled, under the headings of 'paralogism' and 'experimentation', and then to employ this

---

60. Albrecht Wellmer, 'Terrorism and the Critique of Society', in *Observations on the Spiritual Situation of the Age*, p. 304 (trs. altered).
61. Jean-François Lyotard, 'Introduction' to *Des Dispositifs Pulsionnels*, 2nd edn., Paris 1980, p. 11.
62. *Minima Moralia*, p. 98.

conflation as basis for an account of justice. In general, post-structuralist thought, with its strong resistance to categorial distinctions, and its inflation of concepts such as 'desire', 'power', or even 'language-game', seems in a poor position to accuse other theoretical traditions of totalizing aspirations.

The second enduring difficulty of post-structuralist thought concerns the discrepancy between a philosophical anti-humanism and a continued commitment to political principles whose content cannot be derived from aesthetic experience alone. Habermas pays tribute to the sensitivity of post-structuralism to the 'complex injuries and subliminal violences' of contemporary societies, but goes on to suggest that this sensitivity is implicitly dependent on 'the image of an undamaged intersubjectivity which first appeared to Hegel in the form of an ethical totality'.[63] The values of grace and illumination, ecstatic delight, corporeal integrity, wish-fulfillment and protective intimacy, which post-structuralist thinkers espouse, do not cover the moral bill which they implicitly draw on an intact everyday life-practice. There is a disparity between declared and disguised normative foundations which can only be explained in terms of an undialectical rejection of subjectivity: the failure to recognize that the concept of the subject in modern thought does not merely imply a damagingly objectified relation to self, but also contains the promise of a self-conscious practice in which solidarity and autonomy can be reconciled. Habermas's argument appears confirmed by the fact that hints of this unacknowledged foundation occasionally intrude—almost like a lapsus—into the texts of post-structuralism. In *Discipline and Punish*, for example, Foucault remarks that the prisoner caught within the Panoptic system 'is seen, but he does not see; he is the object of information, never a subject in communication.'[64] More generally, the development of French thought in the 1970s reveals—and Lyotard's well-meaning, but theoretically incoherent, interdictions of coercion and 'terror' clearly illustrate this point—that a liberal-universalist safety net was always tacitly spread beneath the highwire of the new Nietzscheanism. Nietzsche well appreciated, and accepted, the consequences of a full-blown perspectivism. He understood that, if claims to universality can never be more than the mask of particular forces and interests, then 'life' cannot take the form of harmonious plurality of standpoints, but is '*essentially* appropriation, injury, overpowering of the strange and weaker, suppression, severity, imposition of one's own forms, incorporation and, at the least and mildest, exploitation.'[65] It is

63. *The Philosophical Discourse of Modernity*, p. 337 (trs. altered).
64. Michel Foucault, *Discipline and Punish*, Harmondsworth, 1979, p. 200.
65. Friedrich Nietzsche, *Beyond Good and Evil*, para. 259.

from this implication of 'left' Nietzscheanism, almost as much as from Marxism, that the 'New Philosophers' recoiled in horror in the later 1970s, ushering in the current French preoccupation with pheno-menological ethics, liberal political theory, and the philosophy of human rights.

These theoretical gyrations, in their contrast with the steady develop-ment of Habermas's project, must ultimately be understood against the background of national history and politics. In a country where a revolu-tionary tradition—reinforced by the experience of the Resistance—spans the distinction between Left and Right, outright attacks on the 'totalitar-ianism' of Enlightenment inevitably take on something of the appear-ance of self-indulgent play: the political reaction to Marxism in France has taken the form of an oversimplified espousal of democratic and human rights. In Germany, however, the country which, in Marx's phrase, has shared in the restorations of modern peoples, without sharing in their revolutions, the heritage of the bourgeois emancipation movements cannot be taken so readily for granted. The general contours of Habermas's work spring far more sharply into relief if one bears in mind the fragility of progressive bourgeois traditions in Germany, and indeed the origins of the Federal Republic itself: not the achievement of a capitalist class in pursuit of its own freedoms, or of a popular upheaval, but an imposition of victorious foreign armies. Habermas's critique of capitalism has never relied on an undervaluation of the historical achievement of the constitutional state: rather it is based on the inability of bourgeois society to fulfil its own initial democratic promise. In view of Habermas's repeated engagement, over the last ten years or more, in a defence of liberties, of the rights of dissent and civil dis-obedience, against an encroaching neo-conservatism, Lyotard's hints that the stress on 'communicational consensus' implies a 'call for order, a desire for unity, for identity, for security, or popularity', sound rather hollow.[66] It is tempting to reply that such consequences are far more likely to flow from a badly-thought-through assault on Enlightenment universalism.

Particularities of historical location and political culture need not simply result in a distortion or biasing of thought. Anomalous situations may also make possible a more acute insight into what is in fact a more general problem or condition. Habermas's shift from a production to a communications paradigm within Marxism can be seen in this light. By theorizing the moral-practical as an autonomous dimension of historical development, Habermas is able to resolve the problem to which

---

66. 'Answering the Question: What is Postmodernism', p. 73.

accounts of postmodernity also propose a solution—the problem of linking up with existing forms of freedom and overcoming the sterility of total critique—without lapsing into a self-deluding transfiguration of the status quo. Participatory democracy, implying the restraint of the currently uncontrolled imperatives of economy and bureaucracy, is not simply a groundless utopian ideal, but an impulse and an aspiration which is actively embedded in modern societies. Furthermore, once the blinkers of an analysis based exclusively on the dialectic of instrumental reason—and which is shared by earlier Critical Theory and poststructuralism—are shed, this aspiration appears unmistakably as central to the Enlightenment project. It is true that Habermas's work does not hold up a mirror to contemporary experiences of fragmentation, loss of identity, and libidinal release, in the manner which has enabled post-structuralist writing to provide the 'natural' descriptive vocabulary for the culture of advanced consumer capitalism. But neither does it pay for its expressive adequacy and immediacy with a lack of theoretical and historical perspective.

The importance of such perspective is, of course, most clearly underlined by the contrast between postmodern theory's melodramatic portrayal of the grand finale of modernity, and Habermas's contention that modernity is necessarily subject to recurrent crisis, insofar as it is the first form of society which cannot draw uncritically on the resources of tradition, but is obliged to unfold its fundamental norms from within itself. From this standpoint, the post-structuralist thinkers appear simply as the most recent of a long line of critics who—under the pressure of social crisis—have doubted the capacity of modernity to generate such norms. Admittedly, there are difficulties and ambiguities in Habermas's present position, as there would be in any project of comparable scope. For some, the stress on the irreducibility of system to life-world sets up too sharp a distinction between domains of action, and represents an unjustified a priori containment of democratic aspirations. For others, Habermas's account of the rational structures of communication fails to link up adequately with the necessarily concrete forms of political association and struggle. Furthermore, it could be contended that Habermas's central concern with the reification of the life-world tends to obscure the continued importance of traditional forms of gender- and class-based domination—although, in the latter case, Habermas appears to believe that the future quiescence of major class conflict will depend on the retention of at least the basic fabric of the welfare state.[67] However, the most cogent objections to Habermas have usually come

---

67. For critical essays raising some of these issues, see the special number of *New German Critique* on Habermas, no. 35, Spring/Summer 1985.

from within the Left, and this means from amongst those committed to the achievements of modernity, and aware of the difficulties and dangers of their casual dismissal. No postmodern thinker has yet succeeded in demonstrating that the vision of an 'undamaged intersubjectivity' has lost its hold over the modern political imagination; or that the autonomous logic of communicative action which modernity has laid bare is *inherently* incapable of sustaining a social order beyond the constraints and oppressions of both authoritarian socialism, and an increasingly troubled late capitalism.

Postscript to the Introduction[*]

Since the publication of this collection of interviews in 1986, Habermas has increasingly had recourse to the interview format, as means both of presenting the latest developments in his theoretical work and of responding to current political and cultural events. This tendency has cuminated in the publication of a book-length interview, *Vergangenheit als Zukunft*, which explores in depth Habermas's responses to the second Gulf War, the reunification of Germany, and the recent momentous transformations in European and world politics in general.[1] Given the bulk of this new material, it would have been impossible to incorporate it all into a 'collected interviews' of manageable size. I have therefore chosen from among the more recent interviews those which seemed to share the closest thematic focus. It will be found that the most prominent issues highlighted in the additional texts are the history and significance of the Frankfurt School, the development of post-war Germany and the question of German national identity, and Habermas's latest philosophical work on the relations between morality, ethics and law.

Although none of the further material included here touches directly on the recent revolutionary changes in Europe, Habermas has of course been much concerned with both the theoretical and political problems they have raised.[2] It may therefore be appropriate to say something briefly here about the repercussions of these changes for the contemporary status and project of Critical Theory.

---

[*] This postscript was completed during a stay at the University of Tübingen, as a Fellow of the Alexander von Humboldt Foundation. I would like to thank the Foundation for their support.

1. Jürgen Habermas, *Vergangenheit als Zukunft*, Zurich 1991.
2. See Jürgen Habermas, 'The Rectifying Revolution', *New Left Review* 183, September–October 1990.

Habermas's central concern has always been the theory of contemporary capitalist society, with the consequence that discussion of the now defunct state socialist societies of Eastern Europe has only ever occupied a marginal place in his work. In *Legitimation Crisis*, Habermas referred to these societies as 'post-capitalist class societies', thereby retaining a trace of the standard Marxist notion that such societies might represent, in however distorted a form, a certain advance over capitalism, although at the same time arguing that a new principle of social organization would supersede both capitalism and state socialism.[3] However, in *The Theory of Communicative Action*, which represents the mature statement of Habermas's social theory, advanced capitalist and bureaucratic socialist societies are described as two forms of 'post-liberal society', which—in certain respects—can be seen as mirror images of each other. In advanced capitalist societies, the autonomous dynamic of the economic system becomes the determining factor in a developmental process which, in the case of the welfare-state democracies, is restrained and counterbalanced—although within definite limits—by administrative measures. By contrast, in bureaucratic socialist societies, it is the functional rationality of the state apparatus which acquires evolutionary primacy.[4]

Despite the difference in the predominant system—the economy in the first case, the state administration in the second—both types of society suffer, according to Habermas's account, from parallel difficulties. The crises arising from the uncontrolled dynamic of capital accumulation, in the one instance, are mirrored by the internal limits of the rationality of planning in the other. Thus

> in bureaucratic socialism crisis tendencies are generated by the mechanisms of a self-blocking administrative planning in the same way as they are, on the other hand, by the endogenous interruptions of the accumulation process. The paradoxes of the rationality of planning can be explained in a similar manner to those of exchange rationality, by the fact that action-orientations come into contradiction with themselves through unintended systemic effects. The crisis tendencies are worked through not only in the partial system in which they arise, but in the complementary system of action, onto which they can be displaced. Just as the capitalist economy is dependent on organizational

---

3. See Jürgen Habermas, *Legitimation Crisis*, Boston and Cambridge 1976, p. 17. For a discussion of this passage and of Habermas's other references to state socialist societies, cf. Andrew Arato, 'Critical Sociology and Authoritarian State Socialism', in John B. Thompson and David Held (eds) *Habermas: Critical Debates*, London and Basingstoke, 1982.

4. See Jürgen Habermas, *The Theory of Communicative Action*, Vol. 2, Boston and Cambridge 1987, pp. 383–6.

activities of the state, so the socialist planning bureaucracy is dependent on the self-steering mechanisms of the economy.[5]

In Habermas's analysis, a pathology-inducing colonization of the life-world by systems occurs in both cases, although the form which it takes in each is very different:

> The overextension of the medium of legal-administrative power results in a similar intrusion of systemic mechanisms into the life-world. The points of incursion are not private households, but politically relevant memberships. Here, too, a sphere relying on social integration, namely the political public sphere, is transferred over to mechanisms of system-integration. But the effects are different; in place of the reification of communicative relations, we have the *shamming* of communicative relations in bureaucratically dessicated, coercively harmonized domains of pseudo-democratic will-formation. This *politicization* stands in a certain symmetrical relation to a reifying privatization.[6]

Given the parallel features of this comparative analysis of the crisis tendencies of capitalist and state socialist societies, it is not surprising that, until comparatively recently, Habermas entertained the possibility of a development within East European societies which would mirror the welfare-state 'taming' of capitalism. In *Vergangenheit als Zukunft* Habermas admits:

> Naturally I hoped—more at the time of the Prague Spring, less during the Brezhnev era—that bureaucratic socialism would one day liberalize and take a learning step, introducing a functional equivalent for the advance of the welfare-state compromise in the West. In that case, although on a lower level of development, the system-specific advantages and disadvantages would have confronted each other in a complementary way: to simplify somewhat, development of the productive forces and capacity for innovation over here, greater social security and possibly a qualitatively controlled growth over there. This hope is now buried.[7]

If one considers this hope as the expression of adherence to a form of 'convergence theory', then, as Claus Offe has recently pointed out, the historical record itself might have suggested some time ago the un-reliability of such a standpoint:

---

5. *Ibid.*, p. 385 (trs. altered).
6. *Ibid.*, p. 386 (trs. altered).
7. *Vergangenheit als Zukunft*, p. 101.

The 'oil-slick' theory, which predicted an automatic, surface-smothering disruption in the steering logic if the economic system were to be impeded at a single *point* (for example, through the state regulation of the price of a single commodity in a market economy), proved to be inappropriate for those systems for which it was originally invented, namely the capitalist democracies of the West. However, it proved to be entirely accurate for the state socialist regimes. As the results of the economic reform debate of the sixties and seventies in the Eastern Bloc show, these societies were simply unable to incorporate a sufficient, and yet not harmful, dose of the opposing principle.[8]

However, if one examines more closely Habermas's own theory of steering media, presented in *The Theory of Communicative Action*, an adumbration of the deep structural reasons why expectations of a possible complementary development were destined to be disappointed can already be discerned. Crucial here are the differences between money and power which Habermas explores. Some commentators have assumed that Habermas views the functioning of these media as more or less analogous, but in fact Habermas lists a series of major distinctions. Power, he stresses, first cannot be precisely quantified in the same way as money, second tends to become bound to specific individuals and therefore cannot circulate so freely, and third cannot be 'deposited' without erosion unless it is constantly actualized.[9] Most important in the present context, however, is the fact that 'In contrast to money, power can only be established through organizations and applied for the goals of a collective.'[10] Thus, in addition to a 'backing' (gold, or means of coercion) and legal regulation, power also requires a further basis of trust, namely *legitimation*, for which there is no equivalent in the case of money. Furthermore, whereas money makes possible a self-interested exchange between equals, the person who receives an order is structurally disadvantaged in relation to the holder of power. This disadvantage, Habermas claims, can only be compensated for 'with reference to collectively desired goals'.[11]

On the basis of this comparison, it is possible to see why the state socialist societies were bound to suffer from an irremediable structural disadvantage. For the introduction of market mechanisms, as a way of relieving the overloaded rationality of planning, could only lead to a covert pluralization of interest groups, and thereby subvert the ideological pretence of collective social goals which was essential to the

---

8. Claus Offe, '*Das Dilemma der Gleichzeitigkeit*', *Merkur*, vol. 45, no. 4 (April 1991), p. 279.
9. See *The Theory of Communicative Action*, Vol. 2, pp. 267–9.
10. *Ibid.*, p. 270 (trs. altered).
11. *Ibid.*, p. 271 (trs. altered).

legitimation of the administrative system, and more especially to its social primacy.[12] The greater flexibility of market-dominated societies in this respect is unmistakable—precisely because of the comparative insulation of the market from the pressure of legitimation, a space can be left open for the interplay between administrative power and the communicatively-generated power of public opinion within the broad political domain. By contrast, a society organized through the primacy of administrative power must exhaust itself in a self-defeating effort to control the discursive sources of legitimation. As Habermas states, 'If we put aside normative assessments, then state socialism can be seen as an inflationary overloading of administrative power. In societies of this type, the mechanisms of bureaucratic regulation not only destroyed the autonomy of economic processes controlled in a decentralized way by the market, but also the *communicative rationality of the life-world.*'[13] Nevertheless, the bonds of life-world communication could not be definitively torn asunder, as the collective powers of resistance manifested in the events of 1989 made clear.

Individuation and Singularization

In his brief, evocative essay 'Über das mimetische Vermögen' ('On the Mimetic Faculty'), Walter Benjamin posed the question whether the human ability to generate 'non-sensuous similarities' (*unsinnliche Ähnlichkeiten*) across a whole field of activities has decayed in the course of historical development, or whether it has merely undergone a transformation. In the case of language, Benjamin presents the semiotic dimension—the combination of sound and sense—as merely the bearer of this mimetic capacity, which was once revealed in the play of correspondences between macro- and microcosm which dominated the human life-cycle. Contemporary language may appear to be stripped of this mimetic power, but in fact—Benjamin suggests—such power may have entirely migrated into language, to the extent of liquidating its original magical forms of expression. Even without these forms, with their esoteric and hierarchical features, the patterns of purely linguistic

---

12. In the article cited above, published in 1982, Andrew Arato suggested that it might be possible for the state socialist societies to promote market reforms while avoiding 'spill-over' and the reconstitution of civil society, by retaining control of politics and culture and drawing on pre-democratic sources of legitimation. ('Critical Sociology and Authoritarian State Socialism', pp. 208–10.) Although not an implausible speculation at the time, the historical evidence has now reinforced theoretical considerations implying the structural impossibility of such a course.

13. *Vergangenheit als Zukunft*, p. 116.

meaning may continue to allow similarities and correspondences to appear, with the abruptness and illumination of a lightning flash.[14]

If we understand the notion of mimesis as evoking the human ability to reach out across the non-identity between persons and things, without crushing this non-identity, then Benjamin's philosophical fable expresses a hope which is equally implicit in Habermas's theory of communicative action. Habermas does not view the rationalization of the life-world one-sidedly in terms of an ineluctable and identity-threatening dilution of the substantial resonances of tradition. Rather, the web of communicative relations in modernity becomes simultaneously finer and more complex:

> As individuation advances ever further, the individual subject becomes more and more caught up in a network of reciprocal vulnerabilities and of openly revealed needs for protection. A person can constitute an inner centre only to the extent that he or she can find self-expression in communicatively generated interpersonal relations.[15]

Similarly, Habermas argues in *The Philosophical Discourse of Modernity* that

> Rationalization of the life-world means both differentiation and condensation—the condensation of the floating texture of a web of intersubjective threads which holds together those components of society, culture and the person which become ever more sharply distinguished.[16]

More recently, however, Habermas has found it necessary to add further qualifications to this account. Around the time of *The Theory of Communicative Action*, the concept of the life-world was presented in a predominantly defensive mode. Habermas suggested that 'It is no accident that social movements today have taken on cultural-revolutionary traits.... Social movements derive their driving force from the threatening of well-defined collective identities.'[17] But now Habermas stresses the need not just for repair and restoration, but also for the building of new forms of *Sittlichkeit*. Perhaps the major reason for this is an ambiguity in the notion of individualization, which has been

---

14. Walter Benjamin, 'On the Mimetic Faculty', in *One-Way Street*, London 1979, pp. 160–63.

15. Jürgen Habermas, 'Morality and Ethical Life: Does Hegel's Critique of Kant Apply to Discourse Ethics', in *Moral Consciousness and Communicative Action*, p. 199 (trs. altered).

16. Jürgen Habermas, *The Philosophical Discourse of Modernity*, Cambridge 1987, p. 346 (trs. altered).

17. *Ibid.*, p. 365 (trs. altered).

forcefully highlighted by Ulrich Beck, in his influential book *Risiko-gesellschaft*. Beck argues that, with the disintegration of the nuclear family as the last form of cross-generational and cross-gender social synthesis, the individual is becoming burdened with the entire responsibility for his or her own fate. Yet at the same time, the individual is more than ever radically dependent on the vagaries of the labour market, and the accompanying systems of culture and consumption. The result is that

> In the individualized society each person, in order to avoid the punishment of permanent disadvantage, must learn to understand him or herself as a centre of action, a planning bureau, in relation to his or her career, capacities, orientation, partnerships, and so on.[18]

Building on this analysis as a means of interpreting the aestheticized concept of freedom promoted by many forms of post-modern social theory, Axel Honneth has argued that what such theories implicitly celebrate is the liberation of the individual from the disintegrating pre-modern *Sittlichkeit* which held together modern industrial society. Emerging into the semantic vacuum of a life-world which has been culturally and communicatively hollowed out by the mass media, the individual tends to structure his or her biography on the basis of the prefabricated lifestyles propagated by these very same media.[19] Autonomy-confirming structures of recognition are lacking.

Habermas himself now stresses the teetering of contemporary social development between individuation and what he terms 'singularization'. 'The social individualization brought about by system differentiation', he admits, 'is objectively an ambiguous phenomenon.'[20] True individuation is only possible if the members of a modern society can themselves learn to create 'socially integrated forms of life'. This in turn cannot be achieved

> by way of purposive-rational decisions, which are directed towards one's own preferences, but only if those concerned recognize each other as autonomous subjects capable of action, and confirm each other as individuals who can take responsibility for their own life history.[21]

---

18. Ulrich Beck, *Risikogesellschaft*, Frankfurt 1986, p. 217.
19. See Axel Honneth, 'Pluralisierung und Anerkennung: Zum Selbstmissverständnis postmoderner Sozialtheorien', *Merkur*, vol. 45, no. 7 (July 1991).
20. Jürgen Habermas, 'Edmund Husserl über Lebenswelt, Philosphie und Wissenschaft', in *Texte und Kontexte*, Frankfurt 1991, p. 48. Habermas refers to 'singularization' in 'Individuierung durch Vergesellschaftung: Zu George Herbert Meads Theorie der Subjektivität', in *Nachmetaphysisches Denken*, Frankfurt 1988, p. 238.
21. 'Edmund Husserl über Lebenswelt, Philosophie und Wissenschaft', p. 48.

Given the current pressures in the former Communist world to dismantle recently forged solidarities, by handing over the direction of social development to parliamentary elites and the forces of the market (pressures starkly illustrated by the bewilderment of the East German public as the West German electoral machines invaded the field), it can be plausibly claimed that this is the task which now faces the members of societies both East and West.[22] As the Hungarian writer György Dalos stated in May 1990, shortly after the first free elections:

> With the necessary establishment of these institutions there comes the danger that something will get lost in the process: namely the ability to think otherwise.... Intellectual impulses which do not fit in with the dominant stream of a culture can disappear, even given the widest possible public sphere. The whole previous activity of the East European opposition originally consisted in the production of ideas which were not destined for daily political use. I am in favour of the preservation of this tradition, in other words the continuation of dissidence by other means.[23]

However, with regard to the development of such an intermediate, morally-charged political sphere, distinct from the 'daily use' of systematized politics, a further difficulty arises. In a powerful essay, 'Bindung, Fessel, Bremse' ('Binding, Fettering, Braking'), Claus Offe has explored the sociological implications of the fact that Habermas, in his most recent work, has become increasingly sensitive to the need for concrete life-forms which can meet the 'post-conventional' identity of individuals half way, and thus make possible the effectuation of universalistic moral principles. For Habermas,

> Moral insights would remain without consequences for practice, if they could not rely on the driving force of motives and the recognized social validity of institutions. They must, as Hegel affirms, be transformed into the concrete duties of everyday life ... every universalistic morality is dependent on *corresponding* forms of life.[24]

Offe himself agrees with this conception, arguing emphatically that the bare commonality of language, combined with a public sphere filtered through the mass media, and the modernized structures of the life-

---

22. On these pressures see Andrew Arato, 'Revolution, Civil Society and Democracy', in *Praxis International*, vol. 10, nos. 1–2 (April and July 1990).
23. György Dalos, 'Über die Verwirklichung der Träume', in Rainer Deppe, Helmut Dubiel and Ulrich Rödel (eds) *Demokratischer Umbruch in Osteuropa*, Frankfurt 1991, p. 188.
24. 'Moralität und Sittlichkeit', p. 28.

world, are in themselves not sufficient to sustain a universalistic moral point of view: between the level of socialization and the level of the state encouraging and sustaining institutions are required.[25] Habermas himself has in the past expressed confidence that such fostering life-forms and practices are in fact emerging in modern societies.[26] Yet, if in fact social development is, rather, taking the path which Beck describes, then a vicious circle is generated. Supportive institutions and life-forms are required in order to enable subjects to transform moral insight into practice. Yet at the same time, as Habermas himself now admits, subjects must be able to *generate* new life-forms on the basis of moral recognition, in order to evade the fate of singularization.

The answer to this dilemma lies in the fact that social theory is itself a practical factor in the situation which it describes. Despite the pessimistic cast of his account of individualization, Beck too perceives new opportunities for freedom and equality in the current breakdown of the traditions of industrial society. As long as there is an *orientation* to solidarity, expressed in Beck's concluding appeals for an intensification of 'sub-politics' and 'counter-politics', then solidarity itself cannot have been entirely eroded.[27] A positive cycle may also be set in motion between morality and *Sittlichkeit*, but this is not something which can occur automatically, or indeed according to an institutional programme. As Habermas states:

> The step-by-step incorporation of moral principles into concrete forms of life is not something which one can entrust—as Hegel did—to the progress of absolute spirit. It can only be achieved in the first instance through the collective struggles and sacrifices of social and political movements.[28]

After 1989, however, two models which coexisted uneasily within the Marxist tradition must be finally set aside in discussing such possibilities of social transformation: first, the model of revolution as the expansive, totalized self-realization of a social subject; and second, the model of revolution as an instrumental restructuring of social forms and processes. Given the necessary systemic independence of the economy in modern societies, which the failure of state socialism definitively demonstrated, a new critical politics—as Offe argues—will increasingly

---

25. See Claus Offe, 'Bindung, Fessel, Bremse', in Axel Honneth et al. (eds) *Zwischenbetrachtungen: Im Prozess der Aufklärung. Jürgen Habermas zum 60 Geburtstag*, Frankfurt 1989.

26. See Jürgen Habermas, 'Über Moralität und Sittlichkeit: Was macht ein Lebensform "Rational"?', in Herbert Schnadelbach (ed.) *Rationalität*, Frankfurt 1984, p. 231.

27. See *Risikogesellschaft*, pp. 368–74.

28. 'Moralität und Sittlichkeit', p. 29.

be a politics of self-control and self-limitation, and not of unfettered emancipation.[29] The dynamic public spheres which a democratic socialist politics should aim to develop can only retain their effectivity if they constitute a force external to central processes of political decision-taking, exerting pressure for a just and responsible shaping of the evolution of economy and society. (Such a politics, of course, would also promote the internal democratization of specific institutions, including those involved in production, but without any dogmatic preconceptions concerning the possible extent of such a process.) Furthermore, solidaristic life-forms cannot be brought into being through calculation or administrative fiat, but only through the reflective practical transformation of the inherited patterns of relations and commitments which constitute our present identities. In this sense the demanding negotiation of boundaries and continuities implied by the politics of self-limitation—although remote from Marx's vision of revolution—may offer us a salutary opportunity to rediscover the dialectical complexity of Marx's original concept of 'praxis'.

Peter Dews
1991

---

29. See 'Bindung, Fessel, Bremse', *passim.* Also, Jean Cohen and Andrew Arato, 'Politics and the Reconstruction of the Concept of Civil Society', in *Zwischenbetrachtungen: Im Prozess der Aufklärung*, pp. 482–503.

1

Ideologies and Society in the Post-war World

I should like to begin with the general theme of our Special Issue, 'Thirty Years After'. For us these thirty years refer to the founding of the State of Israel. What does this date mean to you? What hopes did you have in 1948, what expectations have been fulfilled after thirty years and what disappointments have there been?

If any expectations have been fulfilled, they are not the ones we had as schoolboys at the time. Following a brief interregnum lasting a few years, the Currency Reform ushered in the reconstruction of the capitalist economy and a social restoration whose dynamism exceeded my wildest imaginings at the end of the war. My expectations and those of my friends were in fact somewhat idealistic. We were living in a state of shock at the Nazi atrocities, which were first revealed at the Nuremberg Tribunal, and a little later in a series of documentary films. We believed that a spiritual and moral renewal was indispensable and inevitable. Nothing much came of it. And it did not take thirty years to perceive this. I remember an election-campaign meeting of the chairman of the national-conservative German Party in 1949, all decorated with the black-white-and-red flag. I ran out on the spur of the moment when they sang the first stanza of *Deutschland über Alles.*[1] Some months later the same man, Herr Seebohm, became a minister in the first Federal Government under Adenauer. In short, the hopes I had at that time were so unrealistic that I cannot begin to relate them to the present day.

Then let me give the question a personal slant. How did the world appear to you as a 15/16 year old who had experienced five years of war and

---

1. Since 1945 only the third stanza is officially acknowledged. Black, white and red were the colours of Prussia and the Reich.

43

spent his entire youth under the Hitler regime? What influence did this have on your intellectual development? And did these factors have a general significance?

Although the town in which I returned to school in the autumn of 1945 was not very badly damaged, we experienced our world as it was reflected in the spare prose of Andersch, Richter and, later, Böll, in the so-called *Trümmerliteratur* [literature of the rubble] and in anti-fascist memoirs. Books that come to mind are Ernst Kogon's *SS State*, Günter Weisenborn's *Memorial*, and then Sartre's *The Flies* and *In Camera*. Material deprivation (hunger and cold to begin with), the reduction of the economy to basics, the purely local nature of the authorities, the duplication of the administration into civil and military spheres, then the predominance of small groups and primary relations after the collapse of the central institutions and organizations—at the time all this constituted the horizon which delimited our unsociological view of the world. Our problems were moral and existential in the first instance. The grand anthropological concepts we brought to bear were grotesquely irrelevant to the social and economic problems of a reconstruction which, as soon became apparent, had been set up irreversibly along capitalist lines. And for me personally all this took place against the background of a mood of War Socialism and a programme of the 'Third Way' which would cut across all party differences.

We younger people were mainly absorbed in a step-by-step recuperation of the modern movement which had been suppressed in Germany. This meant in the first instance the years following the First World War: the Haubrich Collection opened our eyes to expressionist painting; we read expressionist poems from Trakl to Benn, and were introduced to functionalism and the Bauhaus. Sartre's novels and O. F. Bollnow's account of existentialism led us back to Kafka and Rilke. The contemporary cultural scene was dominated by novels like Thomas Mann's *Dr Faustus* and Hesse's *The Glass Bead Game*. Films like *The Third Man* stamped the experience of an entire generation.

Looking back now I realize with some astonishment just how German and how provincial these perspectives were, even though for us they opened up a whole new world. While I was still studying in Bonn, that is to say up to 1954, I found myself in a university environment where, in the arts and social sciences, the thirties and forties had not implied any break, and the traditions of the 1920s were simply resumed without debate. Admittedly, in philosophical anthropology we now read Plessner as well as Gehlen, and in phenomenology we learned about Eugen Fink and Ludwig Landgrebe as well as Oskar Becker. We also made use of the books Löwith had written in emigration. But we were told nothing about Marx, any more than about analytical philosophy, Freud, sociology or social theory. While I was still at school I had read the pamphlets of Marx and Engels, which were published in East Berlin and distributed by the Communist bookshop in Gummersbach, at a time when there was not much else to read apart from Rowohlt magazines.[2] By chance I also came across Lukács's early writings while I was still a student. Of course the scene changed dramatically during the fifties. With the return of René König to Cologne, Plessner to Göttingen, Francis to Munich and Horkheimer to Frankfurt, sociology was re-established as an academic discipline. Sociological ideas even entered public consciousness. Thanks to the writings of Bloch and Adorno we discovered, to our astonishment, that Marx was not over and done with, that the Marxist tradition was of more than historical and philological interest, and could be of relevance to systematic inquiry. The same was true of psychoanalysis. I had, in fact, studied psychology and had even heard of 'depth psychology'. But it was not until 1956, when I heard the Freud lectures which were organized on the initiative of Max Horkheimer and Alexander Mitscherlich, that I grasped the fact that Freud had created a scientific theory which had to be taken seriously, and a school of psychoanalysis of far-reaching importance. Finally, we became familiar with the dominant philosophical school in the Anglo-Saxon countries through the writings of Carnap, Wittgenstein and Popper. We realized that the theory of science and linguistic analysis had set standards of rigour which continental philosophy could no longer satisfy. In literature, music and art, in art-criticism and art-theory too, the reception of that genuine modernism which is sustained by a radical avant-garde consciousness became more widespread, but not, if I remember rightly, until the second half of the fifties. As the chief interpreters of this modernism, Adorno, and through him Benjamin, played a vital role.

You ask about the influence of Hitlerism on my intellectual development and also what possible general significance it had. Well, all biographical facts have an idiosyncratic element. Perhaps I could say in general that the intellectual and cultural provincialism we were plunged into by the Nazis was not overcome at a stroke, but relatively slowly. The traditions of the Enlightenment and of radical modernism did not become generally accepted before the end of the fifties. However, when they did achieve a breakthrough, it was with fewer reservations than at any previous time in German history. Incidentally, this breakthrough

---

2. Before Rowohlt started to print their paperback books, following the occupation of Germany, they published books in newspaper format.

would have been scarcely conceivable without the outstanding intellectual impact of the last generation of German-Jewish scholars, philosophers and artists who returned to Germany after everything was over, either in person or through their works and writings. Their productivity had been dammed up during the emigration, but it now flowed all the more vigorously. I myself did not become aware of the part played by intellectuals of Jewish origin in the cultural development of the Federal Republic until 1959, when I prepared a study of the role of Jewish philosophers in German Idealism as part of a series of broadcasts portraying aspects of German-Jewish intellectual history.

Why do you emphasize that? In what sense did Jews have an influence as Jews in German intellectual life, particularly after 1945?

Gershom Scholem has said what there is to say about the price the Jews had to pay for their assimilation into German culture throughout the nineteenth and twentieth centuries. On the other hand, not even Scholem denies that German culture enjoyed one of its happiest moments at the very period when the ghettos opened and the assimilation of the Jews began. This explains the enthusiasm of Jewish intellectuals for the epoch of German Classicism, and it provides one reason for the incomparable creative benefits brought to German culture by the Jews from that time on. Despite the rich fruits that fell to German culture as a result of this process, not even the Jewish intellectuals, the 'cultured Jews' [*Bildungsjuden*] as the contemptuous phrase went, were permitted to achieve a complete assimilation. And of course this applied with even greater force to other Jews. Hence the condition of exile persisted in the midst of the most creative assimilation. The Zionists then drew their own consequences from this situation.

When we contemplate the ambivalence of German-Jewish intellectual history, we can perceive the unique opportunity which a crass irony of history had given to the last generation of Jewish intellectuals, once the Nazis and their intellectual retinue had succeeded in poisoning or obscuring even our best traditions. We young people, who were privileged not by our merit, but simply by our age, were able to acquire a distinctive perspective from the teachers who now returned from emigration. H. Plessner once defined this perspective in the words: without estrangement, no understanding. What it amounts to is that those who had long been part of German culture, without every really belonging to it, taught us how to identify with our own, with German traditions, and yet while standing within them, to keep a certain distance from them, which enabled us to continue them in a self-critical spirit, with the scepticism and the clairvoyance of the man who has already once been fooled.

I would like to go back to my initial question. You described the hopes you had immediately after the war as unrealistic, and ruled them out as a standard by which to judge the present. What about the hopes and disappointments of the last thirty years? Which events had the most powerful influence on you?

Whatever view is taken today of the political significance of Stalin's Note of March 1952,[3] this was a date that played a major role in my own life because, in rejecting this offer, the Federal Government ensured the military integration of the Federal Republic into the Western hemisphere. This meant that we had to abandon all hope of a neutralist solution which might have prevented the two social systems on German soil from becoming sealed off from each other. The change in *Ostpolitik* introduced a decade and a half later by Willy Brandt was no more than the logical extension of this first (and only) basic *foreign policy* decision taken by the Federal Republic.

As far as international relations in general are concerned, I am not unaware of the significance of the strategic balance between the superpowers. But I cannot claim to have ever been passionately interested in East–West relations. The conflicts with an inbuilt development dynamic are to be found on the North–South axis. That could be seen very early on, at least as far back as the Bandung Conference. But it was not until later that the problematic nature of this relationship became dramatically clear, and was first taken seriously, on the domestic front. In this context the American intervention in the civil war in Vietnam, the Chinese Cultural Revolution and the oil crisis have highlighted the underlying tensions more effectively than the national liberation movements themselves.

In Germany the Adenauer-Erhard regime established itself for the long term, following its return to power with an absolute majority in 1953, even though there was to be sharp conflict on the question of equipping the *Bundeswehr* with nuclear weapons. Against this backcloth of a long period of political stagnation, the election of Heinemann as Federal President and the formation of the first Brandt government in 1969 were events that made a deep impression on me.

I was also relieved to see that the student movement did not

---

3. Stalin's Note of March 1952 to the three Western powers proposed a peace treaty with Germany and the creation of a united, neutral Germany on the basis of the frontiers agreed at Potsdam in 1945. The Allies, with Adenauer's approval, refused to discuss a peace treaty until after general elections had taken place throughout the whole of Germany. It is widely believed in Germany, particularly on the Left, that the last opportunity for a real settlement was thus missed.

immediately trigger off the much-feared backlash but led instead to a loosening of the political fronts, a liberalization of the intellectual climate and even to the spread of radical democratic ideas. But the profound shifts of attitude that marked this phase did not last long. From around 1972 the reactions set in. In addition economic crises made their appearance. They are still with us today and are cleverly manipulated by a crisis management that uses them as a means of maintaining a feeling of anxiety and inducing a sense of 'realism', behind which are hidden the economistic values of the postwar reconstruction generation (as embodied in Helmut Schmidt). Today, stimulated by these newly aroused economic fears, neo-conservative attitudes are gaining ground. They involve the abandonment of the abstract universalism of the Enlightenment, the discrediting of notions of progress, the revaluation of traditional ways of life, historicist modes of thought, the development of subcultures based on oriental traditions, and so on.

In this context I find the vulnerability of our political culture disturbing. This vulnerability becomes more apparent the more tightly acts of terrorism—themselves hard to explain—intermesh with a bureaucratic control of ideas which flourishes in the shadow of terrorism. I mention terrorist outrages in the same breath as the practice of vetting applicants for the public service (and recently this has included their relatives as well) because both the terrorists and those who derive advantage from terrorism promote a form of consciousness that is very typical of the way in which Germans tend to fetishize security under the rule of law. This fetishizing of the rule of law did not succeed in defending us against Hitler's legalistic rise to power, but time and again it has dulled our capacity to distinguish between an authoritarian and a democratic form of state.

If you were to compare the social systems in East and West—what you would call 'late-capitalist' and 'state-socialist' societies—how would you judge the achievements of the past thirty years? Which hopes have been fulfilled and which haven't?

A large and rather difficult question. Anyone who grew up as I did in West Germany after the war, in other words, face to face with the DDR, had no chance of being under any illusions about the repressive conditions prevailing in the Soviet sphere of influence. Those of us who became socialists under the intellectual influence of an unorthodox Western Marxism did so despite, and not because of, conditions in the Eastern bloc. I am unable to persuade myself that, from the standpoint of social evolution, state socialism is any more 'mature' or 'progressive' than late capitalism. It is probable that both forms of society represent variants of the same stage of development in which, as we can see from the growing dependence of the countries with state-controlled trade on the capitalist world market, the USA, the EEC and Japan are still the pacesetters. If you really want to analyse trends in social development you probably have to look at the internal conflicts in the advanced capitalist societies, and at the conflicts generated by the international division of labour, in other words the North–South antagonisms.

I can understand neither those students in our universities who, after the collapse of the protest movement, went over to a party on the Soviet model, nor the so-called 'New Philosophers' in Paris who remained unaware of the true nature of bureaucratic socialism until they had read Solzhenitsyn—and who now throw out the baby with the bathwater. These things are two sides of the same coin. I welcome the move towards Eurocommunism in the Western parties—although it has been far too long in coming. But I only say this by way of explaining why for me Soviet Marxism could never be the privileged object of vast hopes or profound disappointments, and why I was never able to get excited about it.

How would you characterize the two social systems today? How far do they share common problems, similar crises? What direction are they moving in? What analogies or distinctions would you draw?

If one has to address such huge issues in the framework of an interview, in other words, casually, I suppose one has to be willing to simplify. In both East and West we have modern class societies, that is to say societies in which the state and the economy assume distinct forms. I am using the word 'class' in its Marxist sense. Class structures persist as long as the means of production and socially useful labour-power are deployed according to preferences which reflect sectional interests in society. At any rate they do not express the universal interests of the population as a whole, or the compromises the population might be prepared to make. In state-socialist societies the bureaucratic elites which control the means of production form an opaque, complex system. This system is essentially authoritarian and has shown itself to be impervious to democratic decision-making processes with regard to the priorities of society as a whole. In late capitalist societies the power structures are even less transparent. To the extent to which the priorities of society take shape in an unplanned way, as the secondary conse-quences of the strategies of private enterprise, class structures survive here too. Control over the means of production by political elites, on the one hand, and by private privilege, on the other, are variant forms of class relations at the stage of development reached by modern societies.

It is noteworthy that Western societies are the more successful in *both* dimensions, in the development of the forces of production and in what Max Weber called 'legal domination'. Carter's 'human rights' policy has obvious ideological components, but it can base itself on the fact that it is only in Western nations that the precarious and continually threatened achievements of bourgeois emancipation and the workers' movement are guaranteed to any extent worth mentioning. This applies, incidentally, to the Federal Republic too, despite the disturbing weaknesses and the shallow historical roots of our political culture. And we know just how important bourgeois freedoms are. For when things go wrong it is those on the Left who become the first victims.

Where do you see the main crisis tendencies on both sides?

That can't be answered in a few words. Both systems find themselves confronting similar problems in their own way. Putting on one side the question of the strategic relations of the super-powers, the first set of problems arises in the wake of bureaucratization, of the development of overcomplex forms of organization, in relation to the running of the state administration and the economy. These developments ensure that crisis-management becomes a permanent problem on every level, a problem of which the public becomes increasingly conscious and one which, as I have already suggested, gives rise to diffuse anxieties and possibilities of intimidation. The fear of crisis favours forces that can present themselves as the guardians of order. On occasion it can be a party like the PCI which assumes this role; but the Bonapartist, or perhaps rather Francoist danger stems from the fact that such power vacuums can arise in the first place.

I have already discussed the second set of problems, those arising from the power relations which structure the world economy, and from the international division of labour. Thirdly, ecological problems will intensify but probably on a longer time-scale than suggested by the dramatic prognoses of the early seventies. But I do not feel especially competent to judge these matters.

As to the specific trends in Western societies, I must admit that I do not have much confidence in the predictive power of the various economic crisis theories. But I do believe that the continuing vitality of the capitalist global economy is giving rise to a succession of problems which could impede the further advance of the accumulation process. And in that event I do not see how capitalist societies could adjust, if not to zero growth, then at least to a greatly reduced and qualitatively regulated process of growth, without its affecting the very foundations of capitalism.

It may be an idiosyncracy of mine, or perhaps rather a legacy of the Frankfurt School, that, of all these side-effects, I find myself most fascinated by those which jeopardize social and cultural integration— that is to say, the potential crises that initially assume socio-psychological form. Referring to these new problems of motivation and legitimation Dan Bell talks of 'the cultural contradictions of capitalism'. Such matters may not be of burning importance in Israel, given present circumstances. But this situation could easily change. If the present genuine prospects for peace were realized, and a settlement reached with her Arab neighbours, an economic development could result in which Israel would emerge as a sort of German Federal Republic of the Middle East.

Let us stay with a comparison of the two systems, for a moment. Which strata are responsible for changes in each case? What is the role played in this context by movements such as the student movement on the one side, and the dissidents on the other?

You cannot draw a direct parallel between the two movements; they are not functional equivalents. In countries where social integration has to be secured by means of a state-licensed world view, any criticism emanating from the intellectuals represents a direct political threat. Dissidents who are willing to put themselves at risk can put the state's power of veto to good use. Furthermore they can lay claim to rights that are in part guaranteed by existing law, in part integral components of the official ideology. In either case they can appeal to the humanist content of socialism. The more they take their stand on socialist principles and develop a radical, yet fundamentally immanent critique, the greater the threat they pose to the party bureaucracy. By the same token, the more they tend to criticize socialism from outside and forge alliances with conservative forces in the West, the weaker their influence is likely to be. Of course their chances of success are also related to the speed with which structural pressures of modernization are making the outmoded ideological mechanisms of integration ineffective. They depend too on an effective feedback between the internal socialist opposition and the Eurocommunist parties in the West. I can see trends here that justify a cautious optimism. However that may be, these opposition movements are in the tradition of the European Enlightenment, the bourgeois liberation movements and the classical workers' movement.

The youth rebellion of the sixties is a complex phenomenon with a *different* historical significance. Here I can only venture hypotheses. Regarded as a social movement, the students had at best a nuisance value which, under certain circumstances, sufficed to achieve a malfunctioning of various aspects of society, but not to bring about a rational transformation of fundamental social structures—something which the dissident movement might conceivably achieve in the future. Looking back now on the protest movement that sprang up in the universities in the West, I see it as arising from certain favoured social strata, and as marked by the circumstances of the economic boom. As such I regard it as a special case of those neo-populist currents which cannot be properly absorbed by the political parties. Such movements react to the forms of economic and administrative rationality which permeate every aspect of life in the wake of the process of capitalist growth. Such forms penetrate deeper and deeper into the self-regenerating processes of nature, and consume the historical substance of traditional, pre-bourgeois ways of life, but without creating any new forms of solidarity or any new possibilities of a non-instrumental relation with nature, whether with outer nature or with the human body. The student movement was a transitory phenomenon, but it resembles other grassroots movements of a similarly ambivalent character, partly progressive, partly backward-looking. Comparable needs are articulated in the women's movement, in the ecological protest groups, in citizen's initiatives, in the resistance of the anti-nuclear lobby, in regionalist movements, unofficial strikes and factory occupations. The student movement directed people's attention in a spectacular way to these new areas of potential conflict.

Could you say something more about these movements from the standpoint of alienation? To what extent can people become conscious of an objectively existing alienation? Are the anarchist Left, the ecological movement, the anti-psychiatry movement also the expression of what we might call a falsely objectified alienation? Do these movements tend to miss the point because they only address the symptoms, since their members have in fact internalized the normative structures of capitalism all too thoroughly? Is there such a thing as an unconscious class struggle? And are there ways of raising it to consciousness?

I don't much care for the term 'alienation'; it is too woolly. In bourgeois cultural criticism it signifies a sort of anthropological or even metaphysical disaster. In American social psychology 'alienation' covers almost every form of deviant, or even simply non-conformist behaviour. In the young Marx the concept was clearly linked to the structure of alienated labour, of the labour process under conditions of commodity production. It is precisely when one wishes to retain such a concept of alienation in social theory that one is forced to concede that a definition based exclusively on the production process has become too narrow. We have to take the arguments of the systems theorists seriously. All modern economies are so complex that a complete shift to participatory decision-making processes, that is to say, a democratic restructuring at *every* level, would inevitably do damage to some of the sensitive require-ments of contemporary organizations. If we wish to maintain such organizations at their present level of complexity, then it is probable that the idea of socialism can no longer (and need no longer) be realized by means of the emancipation from alienated labour. It may be that initiatives to democratize global economic priorities and to create humane working conditions can only come from outside in future, by which I mean that a *thoroughgoing internal* reorganization of the economy in accordance with the principles of self-administration is neither possible nor necessary. Such an *external* linking of the economy—to overstate the case a little—to democratic decision-making processes is a necessary condition, though not a sufficient one, for communal forms of collective life, for forms of life which are no longer regulated by the uncontrolled process of accumulation, or moulded by forms of economic and administrative rationality. Conversely, without a reorganization of living conditions, the basis for an effective democratic will-formation will be missing. I have put this very crudely and mis-leadingly in order to establish a particular, not undangerous thesis: a concept of alienation in contemporary social theory would have to be reformulated in a more abstract way. It would lead away from the analysis of the commodity form towards a critique of instrumental and functional rationality.

What would that mean when applied to the movements we were speaking of?

You mentioned the revival of anarchist thinking on the Left. You might also have included the rediscovery of Surrealism in the sixties, or the intellectual spin-offs of the student movement—for example, Foucault's critique of the forms and norms of bourgeois rationality in medicine, law and sexuality (already anticipated in the *Dialectic of Enlightenment*), or such practical consequences of the protest movement as anti-psychiatry, the critical law movement, criticism of the media (along the lines of Enzensberger's theory of the media), as well as the experiments in anti-authoritarian education, the 'democratization of art', and the emergence of a professional radicalism among doctors, architects, lawyers, scien-tists, the clergy, and so forth. These are all phenomena which resist decoding in terms of the classical concept of alienated labour because, without exception, they are the outcome of experiences outside the sphere of production. You are absolutely right that they contain a potential whose ambivalent nature needs much closer scrutiny before we can arrive at a theoretical explanation. It seems that we are faced neither with organized resistance of a clearly political nature, nor, as your question would seem to suggest, with a new kind of false consciousness. What we have is rather a highly selective set of sensitivities and rebellions, confined to certain strata, directed against reifying tendencies in predominantly cultural sectors which have suffered the encroachment of economic and administrative rationality. They are also in my view reactions against the displacement of social conflicts into realms which hitherto have come into the category of the private sphere, the merely psychological. That is to say they are reactions against the off-loading of social costs onto the isolated individual. Such mechanisms for resolving conflict are gaining in importance in countries like the Federal Republic where social integration still functions smoothly at the level of institutions, the trade unions, political parties, law courts, the mass media, and so on. We will discover in the coming decades whether the potential for deviant behaviour, the substance of conflict, which today is being transferred to the private and cultural spheres, will be absorbed by rapidly growing social bureaucracies. We will see whether this substance, which is currently revealed in criminal activities, schooling problems, psychosomatic illness, alcoholism, the proliferation of group therapies, the retreat to rural communes, the fascination with gurus, the revival of meditational techniques (even in the Churches) and also in a new religiosity, and is fragmented into various sub-cultural domains, can be processed administratively, that is within the permitted forms of rationality. If so, this would give rise to a huge administrative apparatus dedicated to the control of motivation and, basically, to social therapy. This apparatus would stretch from the security services and the authorities concerned with controlling opinion, through a psychologized penal system, socio-psychiatric institutions, psychotherapeutic guidance systems for parents, young people and the old, and through to the public education system. In my view one of the great achievements of the student movement and its offshoots is that a start has been made on deprivatizing such sources of conflict and on opening them up to forms of practical rationality. I would not speak in terms of an unconscious class struggle. But a theory which could analyse these new areas of conflict would have to start from the premise that structurally-based class conflict is in a state of suspension in politically sensitive key areas and has instead been shifted into the margins of society.

Could you say something more specifically about the role of the intellectual in contemporary society? To start with: what were the most important ideologies in Europe between 1948 and 1978? What is your view of existentialism in particular?

If by 'ideology' you mean the most important intellectual movements, the most influential, philosophically-inspired styles of thought, I would in fact nominate existentialism for the post-war period, particularly in its Sartrean variant; after that I would mention positivism, which brought technocratic conceptions in its wake; and lastly, Western Marxism, which assumed phenomenological and later structuralist features in France, while in Germany it developed along Hegelian lines, in a tradition leading from Lukács and Korsch to Critical Theory. Like my friend K. O. Apel, I have always regarded existentialism and positivism in the wider sense as complementary phenomena. Between them they implement a division of labour. Positivism, and in this context I would include Popper's philosophy under this heading, sees its task as being to establish the objective status of the sciences, to privilege them as the sole legitimate form of knowledge and the only way to achieve systematic cognitive progress. The theoretico-political impulse underlying the Vienna Circle was to draw a demarcation line between science and 'metaphysics', in other words, all other kinds of knowledge, which were thereby downgraded to mere forms of expression. The aim was to expel the charlatans once and for all from the temple of an Enlightenment which was now to be made watertight at the cost of a general levelling down. The search for demarcation criteria has long since been abandoned, but this impulse continued for a long time to animate the main currents of analytical philosophy. For its part, existentialism engaged in a complementary politics of demarcation. From the early Jaspers right through to the late Kolakowski the protagonists of this tendency have been agreed that an objectivist concept of science guarantees an autonomous sphere *beyond the reach of binding argument* to philosophical faith, intuitive thought, myth and, in general, all the non-objectifiable experiences of historical existence. Both schools reject as 'gnostic' everything which resists the dichotomy between an empiricist interpretation of science and an appeal to the powers of faith. Most characteristically, they reject the Marxist theory of society and psychoanalysis, since both attempt to introduce the element of self-reflexion into the construction of scientific theories. Critical Theory, for example, retains a concept of reason which asserts itself simultaneously against both scientific mutilation and existentialist downgrading, and which is furthermore also critically applied to itself. In consequence a complacent faith in rationalism is ruled out, and neither does the philosophy of history degenerate into mystification. The *Dialectic of Enlightenment* attempts to salvage the normative substance of concepts such as ego-autonomy and the emancipation of society, by criticizing the ideological misuse of such concepts just as relentlessly as it does the positivist campaign to cleanse our consciousness of transcendental perspectives entirely.

You refer to the Dialectic of Enlightenment. *It is a book that appeared thirty years ago. Is it still representative of the Critical Theory you defend today?*

It was not until the late sixties that the Frankfurt thinkers began to be considered as a school in the eyes of the politicized students and the general public. The fact is that a coherence of views powerful enough to form a school only existed in emigration in New York, when the old members of the Institute for Social Research, Pollock, Marcuse, Löwenthal, Adorno, Kirchheimer and Neumann, were working together closely and productively, with Horkheimer as the moving spirit. This phase lasted until 1940. After the War, Horkheimer and Adorno were influential in the Federal Republic, as was Marcuse somewhat later. It was only at this stage that Critical Theory gained a wide audience; and this was not primarily through philosophical works such as Adorno's *Negative Dialectics* or *Aesthetic Theory,* but rather as a sort of pessimistically tinted cultural criticism. This fact actually exposes some real weaknesses. Adorno took the aphoristic mode of philosophizing to extremes. He made the idea of thinking in fragments into a programme, keeping his distance, an excessive distance in my view, from the general scientific enterprise. This led to three principal weaknesses. In the first place, Critical Theory never really took the theoretical contributions of the social sciences and analytical philosophy seriously. It never engaged with them systematically, as it should have done, given its own intentions. Hence, secondly, it took refuge in an abstract critique of instrumental reason and made only a limited contribution to the empirical analysis of the over-complex reality of our society. And finally, it failed to give an unambiguous account of its own normative foundations, its own status. Adorno denied that it was possible to provide a systematic grounding of the concept of reason to which he always implicitly appealed. This aporia, incidentally, is one reason why I have attempted to elaborate a theory of communicative action, of action orientated towards validity claims.

The demise of the Frankfurt School has often been announced.

I mention these three defects because they are a negative pointer to the direction in which my colleagues and I are trying to advance our theoretical work today. But there is no longer any question of a school, and that is undoubtedly a good thing. Furthermore, there have been trends in the Federal Republic during the seventies which react pretty sharply to what many people consider to be the 'cultural hegemony' of the Left. The forms taken by this change in climate [*Tendenzwende*] differ from country to country. To the critique of the 'New Philosophers' in Paris, and of the conservative sociological theorists grouped around East Coast journals like *Commentary* and *Social Policy* in the USA, there corresponds in the Federal Republic only a motley coalition which revives anti-Enlightenment ideological positions, and endows them with an emphasis which manages to be both liberal-conservative and scientistic at the same time. It draws on a broad heritage stretching from Carl Schmitt to certain variants of neo-Aristotelianism, taking up Gehlen and Heidegger *en route*. These diffuse trends only acquire a certain political and ideological coherence by virtue of their resolute assault on the common enemy.

And what role do intellectuals play in society? I am less interested in the sociological aspects of this question than in those concerning the philosophy of science. In this context how would you define the difference between your conception of science and that of Karl Popper? Could you say something about the accusation of decisionism that you levelled against Popper?

Popper's model of empirical-analytical science fails to do justice to the most fruitful theoretical developments in the social sciences, from Durkheim, Freud, Mead and Piaget down to Chomsky, Luhmann, Kohlberg and others. I do not need to emphasize that I have learned an enormous amount from Popper. He is one of the great figures in that admirable process of self-criticism through which the analytical theory of science has matured and cast off its dogmatism, culminating in the insight, which emerged from the controversy with Kuhn, that the rational reconstruction of the history of science is itself a hermeneutical enterprise *par excellence*. Of course, my view is that, in his legitimate criticism of the practice of reducing the theory of science to the investigation of the syntax and semantics of scientific language, Popper—to put it crudely—has not gone far enough. Even C. S. Peirce took a more radical view than Popper of the pragmatic dimension of scientific logic and of the systematic importance of the 'context of discovery' (and the 'context of application'). To my way of thinking Popper draws far too rigid a distinction between the logic of scientific discovery on the one hand, and its psychology and sociology on the other. The difference of opinion you have in mind is connected with this.

In his reconstructive analyses Popper does away with both the context of discovery and the context of application, from which the theories of the social sciences emerge and in which they become effective. Hence in his view only those sociological approaches have a legitimate status which yield information usable in social technologies, and which find their practical point of reference in piecemeal social engineering. As opposed to this, I would defend the traditions of research in social theory and psychoanalysis, as well as in cognitive developmental psychology, which have a different practical point of reference; they aim to enlighten people and groups who are in need of orientation about themselves and about their social situation, the network of interests and the formative processes which make their activities possible, control them, and—in certain cases—subject them to pathological constraints.

The reproach of decisionism is connected with something else, namely the problem of rational foundations. Popper over-extends the methodological power of the negative with his theory of falsification, and makes the critical method of refutation autonomous. In this he is not unlike Adorno (and for that matter he finds himself in agreement with the radical Jewish traditions whose roots have been uncovered by Scholem). In consequence he denies himself the possibility of validating criticism itself as a rational activity. For Popper criticism is ultimately just *one* option among others. He is forced to rely on a *decision* for rationality, on a critical attitude, a readiness to engage in criticism, and on the traditions that produce such a disposition. I believe I can show that a species that depends for its survival on the structures of linguistic communication and cooperative, purposive-rational action must *of necessity* rely on reason. In the validity claims, however implicit, by means of which we are obliged to orientate ourselves in our communicative actions, a persistent, albeit repeatedly suppressed, claim of reason lies concealed.

Of course there are no metaphysical guarantees of any sort that this claim of reason will prove historically efficacious or assume an institutional form. But I believe that a partiality for reason has a different status from any other commitment.

How do you interpret the fact that in the Anglo-Saxon world the roles of the sociologist and the philosopher are rigorously separated, whereas your work is sociological and philosophical at the same time?

There is a trivial answer to that question. In the German educational system subjects like psychology and sociology only became distinct disciplines relatively late on. The process of professionalization started later in Germany than in the USA. Right up to the fifties we had philosophers who could still be taken seriously as psychologists (Rothacker), anthropologists (Gehlen) or sociologists (Plessner), maintaining combinations of a kind which Max Scheler represented in the 1920s. In the case of the old Frankfurt Institute members there is the additional factor that, in the Marxist tradition, a division of labour between philosophy on the one hand, and economics, psychology and the social sciences in general on the other, was only held to be meaningful if they were integrated within the context of a general programme of theoretical enquiry. The programmatic statements of the old Institute for Social Research, Horkheimer's Inaugural Lecture as Director in particular, all give expression to the conviction that only if philosophy establishes links with the social sciences can it survive as a significant discipline concerned with substantial questions, and thus escape the fate of withering away into a merely formalistic discipline. And by the same token, the social sciences can only be preserved from declining into a sterile positivism by functioning within the framework of a philosophically-based theory of society. Furthermore, Horkheimer—and this relates directly to your question—had actually distinguished Critical Theory from 'traditional' theory by the claim that Critical Theory remains conscious of its connection with practical life. How can the philosopher hope, if not to eliminate, then at least to undermine reflexively the role divisions of academic enquiry, if he allows himself to be cut off from all substantive questions and hence from a theoretically-informed stance toward contemporary political issues? As for myself, I am like one of the Last of the Mohicans. I studied mainly philosophy and psychology with Rothacker, learned sociology as Adorno's assistant, took my second doctorate in political science under Abendroth, and subsequently occupied Horkheimer's chair in Philosophy and Sociology. In 1971, after I had left Frankfurt, the chair ceased to cover the two disciplines. At the institutional level, then, the neat division of labour I referred to earlier was established in the Federal Republic—doubtless to the great satisfaction of our strictly sociological sociologists.

But your original question was less concerned with the institutional side. Can there and should there be philosophers who, without lowering their theoretical standards, and indeed by virtue of their theoretical expertise, can conceive of their profession as entailing a public, politically effective role? I think the answer is yes; and as the example of Charles Taylor proves, such people can also exist in the Anglo-Saxon world, and even in Oxford.

Furthermore, can and should a philosophy exist which communicates with the individual sciences, not just on a metatheoretical level, but in terms of substantive issues? If you defend the concept of distinct unitary sciences, however you interpret the term, both questions have to be answered in the negative. By contrast, I believe that to the extent that the human sciences convert philosophical questions into problems capable of scientific analysis, they will diverge increasingly from this empiricist model, and that in this context philosophy has a duty to promote strong theoretical strategies which are opposed to inductionism and elementarism. I regard philosophy as the hitherto irreplaceable representative of a claim to unity and universality, which of course can be satisfied seriously either in the human sciences or not at all.

One last question: to whom is your philosophy addressed— to the person who wishes to learn about an object by approaching it from the outside, or to the individual who desires to find his bearings in his own lived world, the individual caught up in the problems of life?

If we set aside the problems of life for the moment, I do not think we have to choose between a sociological knowledge which lays claim to objectivity, and a practical knowledge-interest that aims at the transformation of information into what we may call understandings of particular situations, and life-orientations. But that is only true where sociological theory is not objectivist to start with, where, unlike behaviourist learning theory, it does not by its choice of basic concepts rule out every reference to, and every possibility of translation into, the traditional concepts which structure our daily lives.

But what relevance has a social theory to the life of the individual?

Do you mean to imply that theories in the tradition of Marx and Hegel are unable to fill the gap left by existentialism? A theory of society can perhaps provide a perspective, can offer—to put it cautiously—hopes and starting-points for the conquest of unhappiness and misery which are generated by the structure of social life. But it can do nothing to overcome the fundamental perils of human existence—such as guilt, loneliness, sickness and death. You could say that social theory offers no consolation, has no bearing on the individual's need for salvation. Marxist hopes are of course directed towards a collective project, and hold out to the individual only the vague prospect that forms of life with greater solidarity will be able to eradicate, or at least diminish, that element of guilt, loneliness, fear of sickness and death, for which social repressions bear the responsibility. But that is a poor substitute for consolation. It could even be said that a consciousness of the radical absence of consolation is fostered in the first place by theories which inform us about the stages of social development, more mature forms of organization, and the practice through which new social formations can be brought into existence, and in so doing repudiate religious notions of salvation. How can there be universal solidarity with the victims of merciless historical progress, when past crimes, when the sufferings, the humiliations and the misery of past generations, appear irreversible to the secular gaze, and beyond redress? Benjamin, groping for response to the horror of all this, developed the idea of an anamnetic solidarity, which could bring about atonement solely through the power of remembrance. Perhaps we can discern in Benjamin's sometimes crypto-theological reflections the outlines of a way of thinking which would attempt a serious answer to your question. I believe you will be more likely to find it there than in the early existentialist philosophy of Sartre. The problem is one which faces all modern societies once the religious traditions that point beyond the purely human realm have largely lost their former authority. I observe palpable regressions into new forms of paganism which undercut the ego-identity that was achieved by means of the major religions. If that is the case, then how can, if not the substance, then at any rate the humanizing power of traditions that protect us against such regressions, how can the legacy of religion be salvaged for the secular world? For the moment we can only say: not *as* a religious legacy.

Very well then, we should not ask too much of social theory. But how far can it exert a practical influence on the individual? And if you do aim at such an influence, what sort of commitment would you envisage?

Any practical, action-orientated influence on individuals and groups cannot be any better than the interpretations and explanations which the theoretical premises make possible in their application to specific situations. Beyond that, I can only give a strictly procedural reply: if a commitment is to be voluntarily entered into, then there must be sound reasons for it. Theories too can provide solid grounds. But reasons mediated by theory can only acquire will-forming force in political and moral-practical discourse. And since every commitment is concrete and specific, you cannot have any standard form of discourse, any discourse once and for all. In other words, not even a theory with practical intent can provide any more or anything other than, in the optimum case, a set of plausible hypotheses. It will depend on *continuities*, not only in the system of knowledge itself, but also in the discursive will-formation and in the self-reflexion of those who orientate themselves in action. For that there can be no substitute.

2

Conservatism and Capitalist Crisis

There is much discussion today of the nature and causes of the crisis racking the advanced capitalist countries. How should we define its structural characteristics and draw up an initial balance sheet?

In general we can say that the economic crisis has got steadily worse. By now everyone knows that we are not dealing with a short recession, and that unemployment will be a problem well into the 1980s. This is an obvious fact. What we should explore is the impact of the slump on the consciousness of the working class. In Germany the crisis is having a disciplinary effect. That is, within the framework—or more accurately on the basis—of legally guaranteed social security, it has proved possible to nip protest movements in the bud. Although not entirely unexpected, this process demands some explanation. The constraining pressure of the crisis has not only prevented any electoral turbulence, it has evoked deep conservative sentiments amongst the population, which have found a cultural echo amongst intellectuals and in the rhetoric of political parties. This neo-conservative current, which first emerged in the early 1970s, has been enormously strengthened in the new economic environment.

In 1973 you gave a talk at the Goethe Institute in Rome whose title was Was Heisst Heute Krise? *Five years later, how would you reply to the same question: what is the meaning of 'crisis' today?*

I would say that in the last few years it has become clear that the origins of the crisis still lie in the economic system of capitalism, but that the Welfare State no longer allows the crisis to explode in an *immediately* economic form. Instead, when there is a recession and large-scale unemployment, the symptoms of the crisis are displaced into strains within the cultural and social order. Recent years have rather confirmed me in the conviction that today the onset of an economic crisis does not generally lead to a political response, either by organized workers or trade unions—or in our own case in Germany, by the Social Democratic Party—of a rationally calibrated type. Instead, reactions to the crisis take the very mediated form of an overloading of the mechanisms of social and cultural integration. The result is a much bigger 'ideological discharge' than in periods of capitalist development characterized by high employment. The direction of this discharge is two-fold. On one hand the work ethic is incredibly re-inforced: there is a rehabilitation of competitive behaviour, pursuit of gain, and exaltation of virtues conducive to a high mobility of labour. For it is necessary to induce people to accept work they would not otherwise perform of their own free will, or for which they have not had the necessary preparation. The accent is thus placed on an acquisitive ethic and instrumental virtues. This orientation penetrates deeply into the first years of schooling, to the point of dominating the whole educational system.

The other direction taken by this 'ideological discharge' is a revitalization of traditional virtues and values: in the first instance those of an anti- or a-political private life, whose literary reflection is a new subjectivism, and a revival (in its own way a pleasing one) of poems and novels in lieu of critical or analytic works on the present historical epoch, or sociological and political treatises. The result is an essentially rhetorical response to the bureaucratization and other negative consequences of capitalist growth. But I think that we have to take seriously that aspect of the propaganda of the Right which deals with real needs and offers a conservative solution to real problems. For in the criticisms of bureaucratism, as in the revaluation of traditional ways of life, in the spontaneous reactions not only against the destruction of the environment but against the dangers of atomic energy, and even in the resistance to administratively imposed educational reforms, there is a basic problem at stake which was a very important one for both Marx and Weber. In the course of capitalist development and of a politically uncontrolled process of accumulation, the partial administrative and economic rationality that is functional to such an economic system gradually penetrates and restructures ever broader spheres of life, which should on their own be evolving completely different forms of rationality—that is, practical and moral agencies, democratic and participatory processes of forming a collective will. In other words, there is thus actually a greater need today for types of relations within which more subjectivity and more sentiment can find expression, in which affective conduct is taken more into account.

To conclude, one could say that the increased 'ideological discharge' that I have been discussing operates to diffuse conservative interpretations of problems which are properly speaking secondary dysfunctional effects of politically uncontrolled capitalist growth.

Should one include under this heading the outbreaks of apparently non-political protest, which seem typical of many Western countries today?

These represent the new element in what I call the 'potentials for protest'. The novelty of the situation in West Germany—it is probably different in Italy—is that the type of protest which dominated the national scene at the end of the sixties and the beginning of the seventies, emerging from the universities and spreading to strata of young workers and apprentices, has died down. This must also be numbered amongst the disciplinary effects of the crisis. In its place we have on the one hand the emergence of forms of revolt taking the direction of terrorism, and on the other hand less dramatic but emotionally powerful currents of neo-populist protest. The latter are a reflection of the inability of the traditional parties and trade union bureaucracies to canalize or specify key themes and conflicts adequately. I see in these protests the sign of a dissatisfaction which leads to an estrangement from parties as such. We have other indications of this: for example, public opinion polls now show that at any rate a significant percentage of the population is discontented, not merely with this or that party, this or that policy, but with the party system as such. This is the first time that this has happened in the Bundesrepublik since the war. Of course in other countries, this potential for protest has been canalized in petty-bourgeois directions: we need only think of Poujadism in France or the emergence of parties against taxes in Denmark. But in West Germany no canalization of this kind has so far occurred; we are still at the first stage of attempts to form parties on such economic issues. However, I am convinced that as soon as these currents organize themselves into parties, it will become clear that their real potential for protest cannot be encapsulated in this form. By nature they cannot let themselves be institutionally interpreted by parties and routed through parliaments, without the base of these movements feeling itself cheated.

You think that it is impossible or impracticable to organize or 'parliam-entarize' these protests?

The present potentials for protest are heterogeneous and hard to analyse: anti-nuclear movements, civic initiatives which develop in response to very diverse circumstances—for instance, at the neighbour-hood level, to stop a motorway destroying or dividing a residential area. If we ask ourselves what are the causes behind such protests, I would say that in the first instance they represent a reaction against administrative procedures and methods. Let us take, for example, the resistance to educational reforms in Germany: in this case parents react against their loss of a field which they have always considered *naturally belongs to them*, and which they now see stolen from them by an extension of the sphere of competence of the public authorities. For this reason I am sure that they would resist 'right wing' reforms no less: for what provokes their protests is not so much the educational content as the administrative form of the intervention concerned.

If we ask ourselves what these various movements of protest have in common, I would say that they reveal an increasing sensitivity towards, and readiness to rebel against, secondary dysfunctions of capitalist growth. There is a rising awareness of the 'infiltration' of capital into areas of life which until now were shielded from it by tradition, and within which the values of capitalist society (competition for status, pursuit of gain, instrumentalization of existence) were not hitherto dominant. Such currents do not represent the classical potential for protest delineated by Marxism, although workers are naturally also involved in them. Their social composition is heterogeneous. For example, the mobilization against nuclear plants in West Germany swept up conservative peasants as well as parts of the rural establishment like apothecaries, teachers, doctors or lawyers. Alongside them were detachments of students and young workers on the left, the heirs of 1968.

But surely such campaigns are of less importance than the emergence of the women's movement, which is by now a world phenomenon?

The women's movement is in many respects structurally distinct from this process. In the first place, of course, it represents a much greater potential. It does not spring from transient causes, but from a fundamental problem: unequal rights. In the second place, it is as much a part of the traditional bourgeois as the socialist movement for emancipation. From the ideological point of view it must be counted amongst those great mass movements which take up universal principles of equality. This does not apply to other contemporary movements of protest.

But women have gone beyond the demand for equality, converging with critics of Marxism as a mere theory of social equality to call for liberation?

Very true. But here there are some striking similarities with the processes I have just described. The social conflict which lies behind the women's movement is linked to the fact that capitalist economic development is now violating the hitherto relatively protected preserve of the bourgeois family in Western society, in particular among the middle classes. Women are beginning to form part of the reserve army of labour; moreover this change, until recently largely confined to the working class, is now affecting more and more bourgeois strata. The result is a conflict in parallel with the other protest movements, but which unlike them cannot be canalized in a traditionalist direction. In this lies the radical difference of the women's movement. Other protests can be keyed to attempts to conserve or recapture what has already been. For women there is no such possibility. There is no viable return, there is no *status quo ante* which is desirable or is worth restoring. For this reason there exists *a priori* a critical potential in the women's movement.

But if it is true that these conflicts do not immediately reproduce the classical Marxist picture of class conflict, they are nevertheless still structurally determined by the process of capitalist development. Is not the political need to reconnect cause and effect, in a conscious practice, all the greater?

As Marxists, our task is to interpret the experiences that find expression in these movements in such a way that our reading of them is ratified by the strata so mobilized: that is, we must be able to render our hypothesis that these phenomena are caused by the politically uncontrolled development of capitalism credible to them. If we fail, then this potential for protest can very easily be captured by parties of a conservative type. In West Germany, for example, the CDU and even the Bavarian CSU have adopted the catchword 'human administration' to confiscate the critical potential of anti-bureaucratic reactions for their own ends. For the moment such a prospect is not imminent, but it could happen—all the more so because by their very nature these potentials for protest cannot generate their own organizational forms, capable of action appropriate to their aims. The most they can do on their own is to precipitate a *rupture*—that is, depending on the circumstances, a rupture in the system of organized parties. If such tendencies were to prevail, their outcome would be decided by the responses to the rupture when it occurred. In principle there could be two possible reactions. One would be a move towards a major decentralization of the process of formation of the collective will, with the involvement in it of spheres of life which until now have been deemed private and non-political. The other would prepare the way for a conservative party of order bent on resolving all these problems by administrative means, using the potential for protest they arouse simply as legitimation for a suspension of democratic rights, or in certain conditions even of the constitutional norms of a legal state.

Is there not a further possibility: the emergence of a new 'extremism' oscillating between autonomy and corporativism—in other words between a defence of its own radical alterity as itself the form and content of a political strategy, and a utilization and manipulation of welfare provisions; between a rejection of politics as a mere form of mediation and integration, and a corporatist use of certain political conquests and rights?

The unravelling of the controls of central leaderships and central bureaucracies in the party system is a very ambivalent process. It can develop towards a neo-fascist corporatism, or it can reinforce anarchic tendencies to a point where they provoke reactions which no one could seek or want. It is necessary to insist that this is not a process without dangers, that can be supported blindly. But there can be no doubt that there is a real problem here, to which the parties of the Left must address themselves rationally. *How* they should do so is not a simple thing to say. To start with, they must elucidate and explain these processes, so that the potential for protest does not move in a corporatist direction. Secondly, to the extent that competition with other parties and an ever more centralized state apparatus allows, they will have to decentralize their own forms of organization, rendering them more supple and capable of absorbing and capturing the autonomous critical potentials within society, which if left to their own devices risk becoming destructive. This is only a hypothesis of mine: I have no ready-made answer. If I can speak of the matters that I know only from a distance, I think that even the PCI could find itself in a dangerous situation where it could become the functional equivalent of an authoritarian party of order. Such historical-political constellations can take shape rapidly and unexpectedly. They will be the less likely, the more the PCI can decentralize the intimate structure of its organization, even if it is clear that in the first instance such a change would limit its freedom of decision and movement. I am well aware, in effect, that every bureaucracy has its rational attributes. There are no easy solutions: I can only hope that the PCI will be capable of giving a positive example of how to react to the new potentials for protest. Of course, we have not yet spoken of terrorism, which unfortunately makes all these questions much more difficult.

But are we not also witnessing today the emergence of a neo-liberal ideology which formally proposes to put back the clock of history before Keynes, but factually seeks to exploit the crisis of the Welfare State to impose a certain brand of economic policy?

On the Right, the real lines of battle are moving away from Keynesianism and towards the new monetarism of Friedmanesque orientation. Naturally, this trend has its political counterpart in demands for the destruction of the Welfare State and the limitation of bureaucracy. If there is a real attempt to impose these policies, the trade unions will have no alternative but to develop an offensive strategy, in West Germany as well. We would see the reappearance of the classical type of struggle which has long lain hidden behind the veil of neo-Keynesianism. It is really impossible to imagine the Welfare State being dismantled without a massive reaction from the traditional workers' organizations. For that very reason I do not regard such an attempt as either probable or imminent. It is more likely that efforts will be made to muddle through, for worse rather than better, with forms of modified Keynesianism. A government that sought to proceed otherwise would have to be able to mobilize very powerful conservative reserves, and we would then find ourselves in a situation very different from the present one— much nearer to a mobilization of the fascistoid potential in contemporary society.

Finally I would venture the opinion that in the medium term the economic system can succeed in living with these difficulties very well. The truth is that it should be able to 'normalize' what seemed explosive only a few years ago. But on one condition: that the social security system continues to hold good. This system is now under stress and it is certainly not easy to maintain it at its present level. Yet it is precisely its deficits that allow it to maintain social peace, by displacing social conflict forward in time. Capitalism's capacity to adapt is very great: it is an incredibly flexible order, which still possesses significant cultural and motivational reserves. It is suprising how it has been able to combine different forms of social integration. This is an old idea of the Frankfurt School in the 1930s: when its theorists arrived in America they realized that what needed explanation was not so much the phenomena of capitalist economic crisis as the mechanisms of capitalist cultural integration. Today I would still say that this set of problems is of the greatest importance. Conflicts are provoked by economic mechanisms which are in themselves well known and sufficiently analysed. The real question is: how are they subdued and controlled, or displaced into marginal sectors of the system? What price must be paid for these outcomes? What other conflicts are brought into play in lieu of this central one? Finally, and most crucially, will contemporary economic difficulties increase to such a magnitude that the present model, which lives on 'small crises', will be unable to function any longer, and will usher in a crisis of classical dimensions? It would then remain to be seen how such a crisis would end. I think, given the strong possibility of a fatal outcome, that we could not invoke or await such a 'grand crisis' with a light heart.

We probably need to develop another sort of analysis for Italy and perhaps for other Mediterranean countries, where on the one hand the role, weight and strategy of the labour movement, and on the other hand the economic room for manoeuvre of capital, differ from those in Germany. However, your arguments essentially confirm the view, adumbrated by Gramsci, that there has been an enormous expansion of the sphere of politics since the 1920s and with it the capacity of the bourgeoisie to utilize economic crises politically—to the discomfort of economistic readings of Marx's works, which seem to be re-emerging in 'orthodox' positions against which you have explicitly polemicized.

The real position which differentiates me from traditional Marxist analyses is my conviction that even with the methods of the classical critique of political economy, we cannot make precise economic predictions today: for these presuppose an autonomous, self-repro-ducing economic system. This I do not believe in. In fact, the laws governing the contemporary economy are no longer identical with those analysed by Marx. This does not mean that his analysis of its mechan-isms is inaccurate, but rather that this analysis only remains valid so long as the intervention of the political system is ignored, and in turn the guiding of the political system itself by economic mechanisms. For this reason I cannot agree with Altvater's analyses, for example. In contrast to him, I consider the problem of economic prediction to be an empirical question to which answers can in principle be given, but for which in practice we do not yet possess sufficiently developed explanations. We are dealing with a very complex system which operates an interaction of economy and *Kulturstaat*: it must be analysed in detail. A purely economic analysis is not a basis for accurate prognoses. It could be argued that what we need is a functional equivalent to the theory of Marx. But we do not possess one: each of us works and labours to understand systems which have become much more complex than in his time. So far as the mechanisms of the economic system proper are concerned, on the other hand, one might even say that they are relatively transparent today, to a point where there is little need for an extensive political economy, or critique of ideology, to understand how they work. Anyone who watches the television news in West Germany, for example, can see that an economic policy is being pursued which flouts any overall planning in favour of attempts to stimulate investment by indirect inducements alone. To ignite the 'motor of accumulation', options are being imposed which are manifestly unfavourable to working people. By now it is patent to everyone that business is trying to exploit the present economic difficulties for its own advantage.

Is it really so patent? Even in Italy, where the consciousness and combativity of the working class is certainly higher than in West Germany, there is no self-evident untruth—at least in a narrowly economic sense—in the claim of certain industrialists that if only workers would accept lower wages, there would be higher investments and therewith more jobs.

Of course, there is a whole series of economic mystifications and slogans which do need criticism. I only wanted to say that it is obvious to everyone that you cannot influence the behaviour of investors by indirect methods. In this respect the system is now more transparent. On the other hand, if we are speaking of the interaction of economic mechanisms with political-cultural institutions, we would have to insist that they have actually become more complex and impenetrable, to specialists as well.

There is a parallel between the economic crisis and the symptoms of a crisis of rational investigation. But the real problem is surely why these processes have not yet given rise to a true crisis of legitimation?

I would rather speak of *tendencies* towards such a crisis. We can all see the difficulties of attempts to solve the tendencies to economic crisis by administrative means. But these have not in practice had major delegitimizing effects so far. At least in West Germany, the management of economic policy has been staged for the public in a very effective way. The immediate results of this staging have been on the one hand the processes of intimidation and discipline that I have mentioned and on the other hand a possibly reinforced cynicism towards the way the system redistributes its costs. Hence the incipient estrangement from the political system, whose indicators I have already touched on. However, we certainly cannot speak of a real crisis of legitimation: people continue to vote, and in their vast majority vote for the traditional parties. Whereas, setting aside the phenomenon of terrorism and its stabilizing effect on conservative reaction, a real crisis of legitimation would signify a collapse of the traditional party system and the formation of a new party whose aims would at least transcend the existent economic system. This will not happen so long as the neo-populist currents do not grow to a point where they acquire a much greater strength and pose a real challenge to the established order; or— alternatively—so long as the government parties do not introduce economic policies that are an outright challenge to the trade unions.

Speaking of the 'crisis of legitimation', you have argued that the extension of citizens' possibilities for democratic action would help to prevent a putative disintegration of contemporary society. But is a democratic response to the crisis of a complex society really possible? Might not this complexity impose a society dominated by specialists, in which decisions are made apart from its citizens? Can the 'ungovernability' of Western democracies today favour a real democratization—let us call it a socialization of politics—or is a victory of technocrats and experts inevitable, a victory of complexity over democracy?

I am of the opinion that a greater democratization of our societies, in the sense of a decentralization of current decision making, and joint involvement in decisions previously taken either privately or administratively, through more discursive processes of formation of the collective will, would have two consequences. On one side, it could certainly lead to a loss of efficiency. It would not *have* to be so, but it *might* be. This is the objection advanced today by the theoreticians of the existing system. They hold that complex systems can only change their modes of operation and base themselves on participatory decision making at the cost of their functionality and rationality. There is enough truth in these objections for Marxists to have to ask themselves whether socialism today, under present conditions, can still really mean a *total* democratic restructuration from top to bottom, and vice versa, of the economic system: that is, a transformation of the capitalist economy according to models of self-management and council-based administration. I myself do not believe so. I think it would be sufficient to introduce *above* the decisions of the base into the productive structures of the economy, as their political premises; and *below* to democratize the decision making within production as such to a point where all those imperatives which even under capitalism are expressed in such notions as the humanization of the world of work are satisfied. In other words, I wonder—this is an empirical question which cannot be answered abstractly, but only through experimental practice—if we should not preserve part of today's complexity within the economic system, limiting the discursive formation of the collective will precisely to the decisive and central structures of political power: that is, apart from the labour process as such, to the few but continuously made fundamental decisions which will determine the overall structure of social production and, naturally, of distribution.

On the other hand I am convinced that we want democratization not so much in order to improve the efficiency of the economy as to change the *structures* of power: and in the second place to set in motion ways of defining collective goals that merely administrative or power-oriented decisions would lead astray or cripple. It can be shown that there are collective needs which cannot be satisfied so long as the decision-making process remains administrative or power-oriented. This is the real reason for demanding their democratization; it is also the reason why those needs which are today expressed in the form of autonomous movements are articulated in an unorganized way, for until now the traditional mechanisms for taking decisions have excluded them. Thus, leaving aside the fact that a way of life that is in general worthy of men and women can only be realized if fundamental decisions are taken by the people who are affected by them—in other words the intrinsic value of democracy as such—the present system generates ample evidence that democratization, greater popular participation and decentralization of the processes of formation of the collective will are essential because the *market + administration* cannot satisfy a whole series of collective needs.

The crisis of the 1930s was overcome by the emergence of governments and administrations with greatly increased powers over democratic political bodies of opinion formation. This happened both in the East and the West—in the latter in many different forms, ranging from the New Deal to Nazism and Fascism. Can we emerge from the present crisis in the opposite direction, by a growth of democracy? Eurocommunism represents at once a critical reflection on the historical errors of the workers' movement which produced Stalinism, and a search for a democratic road to socialism—that is, for the form of a transition understood not as a sudden and absolute rupture but as a gradual process which will guarantee greater popular participation and a more democratic structure of power.

We must start from the fact that social systems as complex as highly developed capitalist societies would founder in chaos under any attempt to transform their fundamental structures overnight. In this respect you are absolutely right. I can only imagine a revolution as a long-term process which makes possible: (a) an experimental transformation, guided at every step by its successes and failures, of central decision-making structures; (b) simultaneously, if not indeed as an actual premise of this change, an 'acclimatization' to new democratic forms of life, through a gradual enlargement of democratic, participatory and discursive action. Such a path would, above all, prevent that mobilization of affective forces in a crisis which has always been a weapon of fascism. In fact, it is precisely in the throes of a transformation of complex societies that there is a particular danger of the emergence of parties appealing to fear, insecurity, and the latent disposition to prejudice hidden in all of us. In such circumstances the slogans of a fascist, or at any rate authoritarian-administrative, alternative gain assent and support. Hence the need to respect these two minimum conditions if we are to accomplish a prudent and long-term process of transformation. The task is a very difficult one, for which an extraordinarily intelligent party is necessary.

A flexible and non-bureaucratic one too.

Such a party must expose itself to the process of democratization, accepting all the possible consequences: in other words the risk of harming and even losing its capacity for bureaucratic action. These are, of course, empirical processes, in which the role of theory can at most be to set out the alternatives before us.

Can it not also indicate possible solutions, by studying the relations between knowledge and power? This would seem to be the explanation for the interest in Foucault's 'micro-physics of power' in Italy and elsewhere today.

Foucault imagines that a bourgeois rationality was somehow imposed on all spheres of life in the eighteenth century, which must now be generically done away with. I am not convinced by his undialectical negation. It is rather necessary to show that what Weber called 'rationalization' and which Foucault has well explored in a very different way—in the field of culture, sexual relations, criminality and insanity—is dangerous because it is partial. For it is characterized by its universalization of a single fundamental form of rationality—instrumental, economic and administrative reason. But we must be careful not to throw the baby out with the bath water and take flight in a new irrationalism. Foucault visibly falls into that danger.

But has he not also developed an important argument, to the effect that traditional Marxism has paid too little attention to the forms of 'power' in daily life, assuming that power and state coincide—even though Engels in his own way was concerned with the family?

Foucault has made an important contribution to the analysis of the forms of bourgeois domination. This is a subject that is directly related to my own research interests. I too think that relations of power are incorporated in the least ostensive forms of communication, and that analysis of systematically distorted communication yields results analogous to Foucault's analysis of discourses. Themes of this type have already been taken up by the reform movement and the student movement in West Germany, and are now furnishing ammunition for the neo-populist movements. The real problem is to understand what is hidden behind intuitions like those, for example, of the ecologists. I think what is involved is a sense that areas which were still more or less the sites of free interaction are now being infringed. Similarly, in spheres of traditional life not yet completely penetrated by capitalism, comparable forms of interaction probably also existed. We must not limit our critique of relationships of power to those institutions in which power is overtly declared, hence to political and social power only; we must extend it to those areas of life in which power is hidden behind the amiable countenance of cultural familiarity. These questions were long ago intuitively understood and analysed by the Frankfurt School, above all in *Dialectic of Enlightenment* or in Marcuse's theses on the women's movement.

In effect, you are arguing for a widening of critical horizons, an enlargement of the terrain to be explored, to some extent beyond that traditional to Marxism. But this does not mean either abandoning Marx or reducing him to a foe of the open society, or a theoretician of totalitarianism.

Such an idea is pure idiocy. The generation of 'New Philosophers' who propound it thought ahistorically in 1968, and think ahistorically today, believing they are correcting an old error while merely committing it anew. They cannot see that the theoretical tradition of Marx and the practical-political tradition of the labour movement demand our affiliation in full historical consciousness. What they present as a great novelty—that there cannot be any socialism without a radical and coherent appropriation of the gains of the movements of bourgeois emancipation, of in effect the potential of bourgeois civic rights—is something that Western Marxism has always known, if we set aside the actions of Stalinist parties (including the PCI for a certain period). Instead of constructing an anti-Marxism, they should have learnt from Lukács, Korsch, Gramsci and the Frankfurt School that socialism and liberty are identical.

Hasn't the history of Marxism—its better variety—always been that of its revision and critique?

I consider the so-called New Philosophers to be a generational salon phenomenon. The least one could expect is that they realize criticisms of Stalinism did not begin with them.

Can we conclude with your views on a question which has remained suspended throughout our discussion, yet which presses most urgently on us today—the phenomenon of terrorism? A precipitate of all the elements of the structural, spiritual and institutional crisis that we have discussed, in some respects it also lends the problem of intellectuals and of new generations a frighteningly new cast.

Terrorism should be seen together with neo-populism as a reaction against the contraction of politics to administration on the one hand, and pure acclamation on the other. Reactions to this process of reduction can go in two directions. One of these directions is an attempt to introduce aesthetically expressive elements into politics, and the other to introduce more intransigently moral elements. Both have an authoritarian and an anti-authoritarian variant. The classical example of authoritarian attempts at the aestheticization of politics was fascism. An example of anti-authoritarian aestheticization can be found in certain forms of anarchism. The phenomenon of moralization is not dissimilar. The authoritarian version of an attempt to moralize politics leads to despotic-authoritarian forms of political revolt against the Welfare State. The anti-authoritarian response, which demands a *remoralization* of politics, points rather towards democratization, decentralization and socialist positions. If we accept the general schema, where do terrorist actions fit in? Here in Germany it is very fashionable to assert that the terrorists are the children of a misguided moralism. I don't believe this. Obviously, I am only speaking of Germany, where terrorist actions have had an extraordinary resemblance to a show, a performance of representation and self-gratification. That is to say, these actions do not really correspond functionally to their aims. If this is right, and if we take into account the remarkable degree of militarization, discipline and obedience within the terrorist organizations, then I would rather tend to interpret the 'terrorist game' under way in the Bundesrepublik as a counter-pole to fascism. In other words, I view it as an authoritarian version of the attempt to introduce aesthetically expressive elements into politics, like a small-scale underground. Terrorism does not fall from the sky. It is a structural phenomenon, and the fact that its most serious manifestations have occurred in nations like Germany, Italy and Japan can obviously be explained through the fact that in these countries political culture is less stable than elsewhere, historically less well anchored, and therefore more prone to extreme reactions to the same cultural phenomena than other countries. Although this may be a very unpopular view, I think we must say that terrorism is not an irrational phenomenon but should be categorized with other attempts to react against the same structural processes: in its own way, it is an attempt to reaffirm politics in the face of pure administration.

3

Political Experience and the
Renewal of Marxist Theory

*Herr Habermas, when the war ended you were sixteen years old; when
the Nazis first seized power you were barely four. Your socialization took
place for the most part under fascist domination. What influence did that
have on your political development?*

I'd rather not say terribly much about my youth. A true retrospective
can only be made at seventy, not fifty. I grew up in Gummersbach, in a
small town environment. My father was head of the Bureau of Trade
and Industry there. My grandfather was a minister and director of the
local seminary. The political climate in our family home was probably
not unusual for the time. It was marked by a bourgeois adaptation to a
political situation with which one did not fully identify, but which one
didn't seriously criticize either. What really determined my political views
was the year 1945. At that point the rhythm of my personal development
intersected with the great historical events of the time. I was fifteen years
old. The radio was reporting the Nuremberg trials, movie theatres were
showing the first documentary films, the concentration camp films that
we're seeing again today. These experiences undoubtedly helped
develop motifs which then further determined my thinking.

Weren't your parents shocked back then? Today a film such as Holocaust
*affects both young people and older ones as well. How can we explain the
fact that the earlier films you spoke of had no effect at all, since it is
obvious today that most people haven't assimilated their experiences
from that time?*

The reactions to the early films and the reactions to *Holocaust* are two
different things. I can only presume that the tremendous effect of
Holocaust rests in part on the fact that here, in the circle of the family,
where the television is, young people have been questioning their

parents about those events. We didn't do that. I think we were too inhibited at the time to covert our own personal shock into a direct family confrontation. I was in the Hitler Youth; at fifteen I was sent to man the western defences. Our situation was completely different from that of today's youth. Our own history was suddenly cast in a light that made all its essential aspects appear radically different. All at once we saw that we had been living in a politically criminal system. I had never imagined that before.

Does that mean that you weren't aware of what was happening to the Jews, that you didn't take the propaganda literally?

In 1939 I was ten years old, so I had no chance to get a particularly clear picture. But of course at that time we had the impression of a normality which afterwards proved to be an illusion. For us to see suddenly that those people were criminals—that had quite a different quality.

Given the background of these moral jolts, did you from the very beginning have a positive picture of the society which was then established, and which developed into the Federal Republic?

At first 1945 was a liberation, historically and personally. We had, as I recall, very fine weather then. I experienced all of this naively and intuitively as beautiful. At that time I was simply overwhelmed by a number of impressions. I devoured the first books from the Rororo newspaper series[1] and the ones from the Marxist-Leninist Library which were available in the communist bookstores. The first great political disappointments came with the formation of the government in 1949.

Why were you disappointed?

I'd started my studies in Göttingen. My first political disappointment came with the electoral meetings in Göttingen for the first Federal Parliament. I heard all sorts of people, among them Herr Seebohm, who belonged to the DVP. The party meeting was decorated with black-white-red banners and closed with the national anthem. I stormed out in an emotional furor—I just couldn't stand it. And this man became Minister of Transport. I thought to myself, it's just not possible that someone who embodies this historical continuity could be in the first cabinet. But the real political problem was rearmament. Heinemann

---

1. See note 2, p. 45 above.

(also a minister in the first cabinet) was against it. I myself had a very neutralist attitude at that period. The experience of the war had made me a pacifist. Heinemann's resignation made a deep impression on me at the time.

Was the situation ambiguous for you then—on the one hand the Nazi element, on the other a hope for the realization of bourgeois freedoms? For many (Abendroth, for example), it was very clear—the restoration of capitalism.

No, nothing was clear then. I was nineteen, and one is still very immature at that age. During my time at university, from 1949 to 1954, the politically dominant factors for me were first of all a strong moral reaction to the Nazi era, and secondly the fear that a real break with the past had not been made. I thought then what one cannot say today without criticism: if only there had been some spontaneous sweeping away, some explosive act, which then could have served to begin the formation of a political entity. After such an eruption we would have at least known what we couldn't go back to. There simply was no struggle. I think it makes a difference whether one says that looking forward or looking back.

Why did the German people have no possibility of creating a political identity?

What I mean, in concrete terms, is this: there was no spontaneous uprising either before or during the Allied invasion; no battles were fought; no one took a risk in order to put an end to the whole mess.

I myself am a product of 're-education', and not, I hope, an all too negative one. By this I mean that it was at that time that we learned that the bourgeois constitutional state in its French or American or English form is a historical achievement. This is an important biographical difference between those who experienced what a half-hearted bourgeois republic like the Weimar Republic can lead to, and those whose political consciousness was formed at a later date.

And the Republic after 1949 seemed more stable to you?

Of course. To me this state represented a real opportunity.

But in many ways you were in a negative frame of mind, didn't you just say?

I had no direct link to any particular party. Certainly not to the CDU. This party was founded right after 1945 by anti-fascists. But then you could see who went into it. In a small town you know right away what's going on. And social democracy—that's a difficult concept for the son of a bourgeois family. It's hard to imagine today, but the middle classes saw it as the re-emergence of the Social Democracy of the Weimar period. And what is more, it was then following the Schumacher line. He came out of the concentration camp obsessed with the idea that we had abandoned the national question to the Nazis in 1933. With that he ran directly into conflict with the mood of the general public. The idea that one should be 'national' seemed absurd to us. It made absolutely no difference to me whether the Saar was German or not.

You have to take into consideration the limited perspective which one had, being educated at a university that had remained essentially unbroken in its continuity since the 1920s. All the professors who had any importance for me were already professors before 1933 and, with one exception, namely Litt, remained in their positions. In a number of departments (philosophy, history, German, and psychology) it was an apolitical and almost ethnocentrically German university, with a consciousness that would have been justified in 1910, when great scientific achievements took place at German universities. In philosophy in Bonn, for example, the Anglo-Saxon currents were non-existent, as was the analytical philosophy which had been created by German emigrants, not to mention Critical Theory.

But in 1954 you too wrote a dissertation in this traditional sense. Were you able to free yourself very quickly from this tradition?

Until the appearance of Heidegger's *Introduction to Metaphysics* in 1953 my political and my philosophical 'confessions', if you will, were two completely different things. They were two universes which hardly touched one another. Then I saw that Heidegger, in whose philosophy I had been living, had given this lecture in 1935 and published it without a word of explanation—that's what really disturbed me. I then wrote one of my first articles about it for the *Frankfurter Allgemeine Zeitung.* I was terribly naive and thought, how can one of our greatest philosophers do such a thing? Of course one could have found out about that a lot earlier, but I hadn't been brought up that way. Around the same time, by the way, I read Lukács's *History and Class Consciousness*, which excited me a great deal.

How did you get hold of History and Class Consciousness *at that time?*

It was in the seminar library, which was relatively small. We were at home there; we practically lived there. We knew every book.

It was through Löwith that I first came into contact with the young Marx. That was why I later wrote an essay on the Young Hegelians as an introduction to my dissertation. I suppose I came across Lukács in that way, too. I thought, it's too bad one can't systematically revive these motifs. On the one hand, I was fascinated; on the other hand, I knew that nowadays it can't be done that way.

I was certainly politically moved by it at the time. And then memories began to return. I knew Marx of course from the bookstore in Gummersbach, but I had forgotten him in the meantime. I had the feeling that it would be good if all this could be taken up in such a way that a systematic argument could be developed from it. But I realized with a certain sadness that it wouldn't work with Lukács. And then—if I may leap ahead here—in 1955 I read Horkheimer and Adorno's *Dialectic of Enlightenment.* What fascinated me right away with those two was that they weren't engaged in a reception of Marx, that was not what they were up to at all—they were utilizing him. It was a great experience for me to see that one could relate systematically to the 'Marxist tradition'. Here were people who weren't writing a historical work on Aristotle, Kant, or Hegel; they were working out a theory of the dialectical development of present-day society, and in doing so they were proceeding from a tradition of Marxist thought. That was a tremendous thing for me. Of course I had been prepared for it on the basis of my reading of Lukács. At that point philosophical and political things began to come together for the first time.

Then you wrote Strukturwandel der Öffentlichkeit?

I first learned empirical social research, then came *Student und Politik* and finally *Strukturwandel der Öffentlichkeit.*

That book had a disillusioning effect on the younger generation's faith in democracy. It turned my political orientation, at least, completely upside down. The only alternative I could see after that was the SDS. Did you intend that kind of impact?

I always had a strong academic interest in the question. And of course I wrote *Strukturwandel* first and foremost as an attempt to clarify for myself the darker aspects and the flaws in our political system, whose merits I never doubted. A climate of social and political restoration dominated the time. This climate was so ingrained that I was startled when my friend Apel publicly called me a Neo-Marxist for the first time.

Then I thought it over and decided he was right. Today I value being considered a Marxist.

That was the background to my work on the 'structural transformation of the public sphere' as well. The question that interested me was: how can we get to the bottom of what is somehow wrong with this political system with regard to its political intentions, in spite of the Constitution. When the SDS was excluded from the SPD I was one of the three or four professors who, together with Abendroth, founded the Socialist League [*Sozialistischer Bund*]. We were sort of an 'old folks' section' of the SDS. I can't say that I wrote the book to guide people toward the SDS. I wrote the book to make it clear to myself and others that the political system of the Federal Republic has inherent weaknesses which can become dangerous.

As a question I'd like to quote Marx, who says that the limits of this system lie within the system itself. Do you see something similar here, that perhaps something is wrong with the basic liberal values? That this self-destruction is unavoidable? Or to put it differently: where do you get your optimism?

Optimism? We need to distinguish a number of things here. It is true that I do not share the basic premise of Critical Theory, as it took shape during the early 1940s, the premise that instrumental reason has gained such dominance that there is really no way out of a total system of delusion [*Verblendungszusammenhang*], in which insight is achieved only in flashes by isolated individuals. There is a contradiction here which irritates me even today. On the one hand, our social system is relatively stable (that applies to capitalist society in general, but perhaps to the Federal Republic in particular) and not just economically. It not only guarantees a relatively conflict-free mode of collective life, it has institutionalized political freedoms which must in the first instance be assessed and approved from a historical perspective. On the other hand, this society displays many symptoms which frighten me. On an intuitive level I'm quite convinced that something in this system is deeply amiss. That irritates me; it also motivates my theoretical efforts and is perhaps a reason for a certain oscillation. I'm not a Marxist in the sense of believing in Marxism as a sure-fire explanation. Still, Marxism did give me both the impetus and the analytical means to investigate the development of the relationship between democracy and capitalism.

But does that mean that you really are convinced that existing power structures can be broken by means of a theoretical analysis?

Yes, I'm firmly convinced that the Left in general, and the Marxist Left in particular, can claim one advantage over all other political forces. This is the belief in the possibility of introducing theoretical analysis with a middle- or long-range perspective into day-to-day politics. This is one tradition that should not be sacrificed. On the other hand, I also believe that now, more than ever before, we lack convincing analyses. That is perhaps one reason why for a time I clashed harder with the students than was perhaps politically necessary. At bottom, what I couldn't understand were the dogmas that prevailed even among the anarchist students. No doubt they were less dogmatic in their life styles and social relations ...

But your criticism at that time centred on another point, namely that the SDS was putting theoretical ideas into practice in such a direct and unreflective way. Certain charges against the SDS—and in this I certainly agree with the people who were critical at the time—have proved to have been justified. For example, it's a delusion to believe one can take over a society simply by hoisting a red flag in a seminar. But was it correct to make your criticism in that way at that time? Oskar Negt has accused you of a lack of solidarity in your actions, in the sense that on the one hand you helped inspire the student revolt, but on the other hand you distanced yourself from it and criticized it from the outside. Shouldn't there have been a discussion of social problems rather than a criticism using clinical concepts? Didn't you realize that by acting that way you would create an unbridgeable gap between yourself and the students?

I'd like to challenge one premise—that I placed myself outside the framework of the student movement. I never saw it that way; I never intended it so.

Weren't you trying to put a stop to discussion with your statements?

No, the discussion hadn't even begun when I made that rather out-of-place statement about left fascism. No, there can be no question of finality.

I made two public criticisms. The first was after the Benno Ohnesorg demonstration in Hannover.[2] What I meant there I later published in

---

2. Benno Ohnesorg, a West German student, was shot dead by a policeman during a demonstration against the Shah of Iran outside the Opera House in West Berlin, on 2 June 1967. A congress of the student Left held in Hannover on 9 June 1967, on the occasion of Ohnesorg's funeral, marked the moment at which the Berlin protest movement spilled over into the Federal Republic. Habermas's interventions at the congress can be found in his *Kleine Politische Schriften 1–IV*, Frankfurt 1981, pp. 213–215.

1969, in *Protestbewegung und Hochschulreform*. I still consider the substance of this statement to be correct. But I should have said it differently. The other time was at Pentecost, right after the withdrawal of the emergency regulations. The SDS had planned a conference for school and university students. Students came from all over the Federal Republic. A march was planned from the opera house to the university, which was occupied by the police. I considered it irresponsible and said so to the participants themselves. This can all be looked up. That was the time of May 1968 in France, and the students really thought the revolution was breaking out. That was the context of the situation.

As far as content is concerned, yes, but the manner ...

I know, I adopted a psychologizing standpoint, but for every sentence I could tell you a simple story behind it, explaining what led me to put it like that. You simply have to see how immediate and concrete everything was. Everyone was aware of it at the time. Today people read it in a different way. And at the time it was an *internal* critique of the methods of the protest movement. You ask me about my lack of solidarity. It's true that I didn't grow up in any organization—which one would it have been? So I did perhaps react a shade too much like a bourgeois intellectual. On the other hand, the impression the students had, that they were a living continuation of the tradition of the workers' movement, was equally false. So I don't think, even in retrospect, that I would have had a chance if I had stayed closer to the group.

Didn't that shake your faith in such political discussions, since you didn't have any influence on the events?

But I tried, I wanted to have an influence. The days when the SDS leadership spoke completely openly with me were gone by the middle of 1967. My attempt to have an influence had to take the form it did. Then people got the impression that Habermas really was setting himself apart from the protest movement. But even the introduction to *Protestbewegung und Hochschulreform* was a clear identification with the goals of the protest movement.

A representative of the other faction, Klaus Meschkat, has accused you of having a strange relationship to current events, because one could not tell from your speech in Frankfurt that May 1968 in France and the Easter demonstrations all over Germany had even taken place. Looking back, wouldn't you concede that there was more going on than you perceived at the time? Didn't much more happen then, in terms of people's conscious-

ness, than anyone could have perceived? The student movement marked, in a way, a point of no return.

But that's contained in my essays. Take a look at the last essay. It really does express optimism in regard to the protest movement.

Is that still your view today, that the protest movement was of tremendous importance for the development of the Federal Republic?

It brought about a certain rupture in the normative area, in attitudes, in the cultural value system.

Today people would probably assert the opposite, that students today are more willing than ever to submit to all sorts of restrictions.

No, there are studies which show through international comparisons that the value system of the population as a whole has changed. What Frau Noelle-Neumann characterized as a proletarianization of middle-class values can be described a bit more aptly.[3] What is reflected in this change is a distancing from the value orientations which shaped the culture of the 1950s in such an extreme way. Value syndromes that were instrumental, privatist, and competition-, career-, or family-oriented have become less fixed in parts of the population, as the shift from the 'old' to the 'new' politics shows.

But isn't it the case that where such attitudes are changed, no political change results? We can ascertain changes in attitudes, but people who change their attitudes drop out of the political system and become systematically under-privileged. So we don't have the values of the 1950s anymore—but what do we have instead?

We are only beginning to see the effects of the protest movement. Changes in family structure and child rearing had started earlier. In part, the protest movement was already a product of altered forms of socialization. One has to see that in a longer term perspective. But we're all agreed that the protest movement was effective in terms of cultural reorientations.

You're asking me what political results such changes have. Don't we have to be somewhat sceptical in that regard? You're pushing me more and more into the false role of an optimist. Here's how I see it at the

---

3. Elizabeth Noelle-Neumann is the head of the Allensbach Institute, a conservatively-oriented opinion poll organization in Germany linked to the CDU.

moment: new political potentials are being created which can have dysfunctional results and which can exercise a power of veto. This power could in the long run introduce a reorganization of the party system— and not necessarily of the kind which Strauss would like. But I don't want to make specific predictions. We're dealing here with historical trends that are hard to diagnose. I think there's a relatively large range of alternatives within which the party system can react to such challenges. If we had a rightist government that pursued, logically and thoroughly, a new economic policy in the manner of Milton Friedman—well, that would mean a dismantling of the welfare state. That in turn could lead to a revival of traditional class struggles. But I presume such a government also would be smart enough to weigh such risks.

I agree with you that the dismantling of the welfare state won't take place so quickly. On the other hand, what did trouble me (though I don't want to overestimate an isolated phenomenon) was this discussion with Kohl in Holland. There was tremendous uproar. Apparently the Germans, including Kohl, were more shocked by a certain framework of discussion being transgressed than by having to discuss sensitive topics. The fact that in a television interview the moderator and Kohl were not able to maintain control—that was extraordinary. The Dutch audience said, we'll decide what's an answer and what isn't. That shocked German viewers. I wonder whether there isn't a greater tendency in Germany than in Holland to regulate the shaping of the public sphere, whether what was revealed by such a programme isn't perhaps typical.

I didn't see the programme. But I assume it's symptomatic of corporatist restrictions of a functioning bourgeois pluralism. And such symptoms are, in my experience, more pronounced in Germany than in America or England. It isn't as though I only see clear skies ahead; quite the contrary. After the Schleyer kidnapping the politicians and the media (including nearly all of the press, not just the papers downmarket and to the right of the *Frankfurter Allgemeine Zeitung*) tore down the barriers of the political culture which had been so arduously built up during the first two decades after the war. In those years an official attitude was created which was far more liberal than the general attitude of the public. That healthy system of restrictions has been broken down. Suddenly it was OK to call for Böll's emigration, to consider shooting hostages, and so on. Those feelings exist, of course, but up to now it wasn't permissible to express them. In addition to that we saw public outrage that was bureaucratically orchestrated, along with attempts to turn the entire public into police assistants, and so on. I remember a press-conference where the League for Academic Freedom [*Bund*

Freiheit der Wissenschaft] read a list of names of professors and colleagues who were alleged to be terrorist sympathizers. I believe that the high degree of social integration in the Federal Republic is a deceptive phenomenon and has another side to it: strongly repressed emotions and attitudes which in extreme situations rise to the surface. They do, at any rate, when one of the major parties takes the lead. If the CDU hadn't joined in, we'd never have had a German Autumn.[4]

You created quite a stir at the time in your Spiegel *essay.[5] Many people were happy to see you publicly join in political discussion again. But nevertheless you didn't take part in the Russell Tribunal.[6]*

I'm afraid I miscalculated the effect of the first Russell Tribunal. I was afraid that afterwards the entire discussion of professional proscription would be driven into illegality. I thought that the institutional framework of the Russell Tribunal (which was in fact inappropriate for the Federal Republic) would discredit the whole affair so badly that the entire cause would be lost. Then I had the idea—you might say, a typical liberal intellectual idea—that we could get ten or twenty people together in Harheim to counteract the expected effect—we could say we didn't support the Russell Tribunal, but that what it brought to light was the real scandal. But I never got the group together. Anyway, they should have stopped after the first tribunal, because the second one had only a single issue, the *Kontaktsperre* law.[7] The cases in question were examples of real censorship, but censorship is no worse in the FRG than in any other Western country.

Take the Buback affair,[8] Paragraph 88a,[9] and students who avoid dealing with Marx in their examinations because they want to be teachers—aren't those things somehow typical for the situation in the Federal Republic?

---

4. The phrase 'German Autumn' refers to the right-wing backlash in autumn 1977 which followed the emergence of political terrorism in West Germany, and in particular the kidnap and murder of the president of the West German employers' federation, Hans-Martin Schleyer, in September–October of that year. In the course of this backlash left-wing intellectuals were accused of complicity with terrorism and threatened with legal sanctions.

5. 'Probe für Volksjustiz', *Der Spiegel*, 10 October 1977. Reprinted in *Kleine Politische Schriften*, pp. 364–7.

6. The Third International Russell Tribunal, concerned with aspects of human rights in the German Federal Republic, was held in Harheim, near Frankfurt, 28 March to 4 April 1978 and in Cologne, 3 to 8 January 1979.

7. The *Kontaktsperregesetz*, passed by the West German parliament on 30 September 1977, was intended to restrict the contact of terrorist detainees with each other, and with the outside world.

Of course!

This suppression of the formation of public opinion ...

Well, any liberal would answer you (and, I hope, with some justification) that we have the worst behind us. Mr Nixon, too, had to be deposed first of course. A democracy doesn't endure because of the things that pass through it, but because of the way it purges itself of them.

But there's something that needs to be mentioned in this context—the accusation of lack of loyalty that was lodged against the university teachers in Lower Saxony ...

What Pestel did there is a scandal, a resurgence of the McCarthy era. By the way, the fact that most of the professors signed the papers when it was demanded of them is also a scandal.[10]

That's an issue which concerns not just the Federal Republic, but also the smaller countries around it. The FRG has such a mighty economic power that it affects the political structure of its neighbours.

I've never been a fan of the idea of a 'unified Europe', even when it was fashionable, and I'm still not one today. But one does have to be glad to see a certain growing integration of the European nations.

About the confrontation with systems which place more value on political education and the formation of political opinion?

But also in a framework containing France, England and especially the Romance language countries with strong Communist parties. In the FRG, too, a stronger Eurocommunist party could be in many ways a

---

8. *Generalbundesanwalt* (general state prosecutor) Siegfried Buback, West Germany's leading terrorist-hunter, was shot dead in an ambush on 7 April 1977. An article published under the pseudonym 'Mescalero' in a Göttingen student newspaper, which expressed 'scarcely concealed joy' at the killing, resulted in police raids and legal action against the student union. In protest, it was republished in a dossier by a group of university teachers, generating a further political furore.

9. Paragraph 88a of the West German criminal code, introduced on 22 April 1976, made the advocacy, encouragement or approval of acts of violence illegal. It was revoked on 12 June 1980, against the votes of the opposition.

10. Eduard Pestel, CDU Minister for Culture in Lower Saxony in this period, forced eleven university teachers connected with the 'Mescalero' affair to sign a humiliatingly-worded 'oath of loyalty', declaring their abhorrence of violence and their active allegiance to the state.

liberalizing factor. Many things would be normalized. For instance, in this country you can't be a professor or a director of the Max Planck Institute and at the same time a Marxist. As long as that's the case the basis of political culture is not liberal.

One last question about politics—where do you see your own future political effectiveness?

I'm not sure whether I can still have any effect on the political consciousness of the Left in the FRG. That doesn't mean, of course, that one can't have the usual academic effect, on students, for example.

And your theoretical influence? Does your target group consist of young academics?

You could put it like that. But what does 'young academic' mean? There is something to the conservative outcry over the 'mediators of meaning' [*Sinnvermittler*], insofar as the normative horizon of our society has become more sensitive. It's no antiquated eighteenth-century Enlightenment illusion to contend that one can effectively alter the state of an argument by means of books. One can, if necessary, play a part in a change of attitude through articles in the daily press, a change which is not brought about intentionally, but for which interpretations are nevertheless important. Now I'll say something very old-fashioned: if one can illuminate somewhat a situation which nobody can really understand, then that has to touch the understanding, even the self-understanding, of broad social groups. That has to do with our extraordinarily effective media system. But at the moment I don't see any 'target group'. We have already spoken a bit about these new political potentials. My idea was to contribute something to the interpretation of conflicts which arise on the edges of over-legalized and bureaucratized areas of life. When someone correctly interprets an unclear situation, he or she not only has the success of advancing just a bit towards the truth, but may also influence a self-understanding which in the long run helps determine political orientations. On the other hand, heaven knows, I don't share the instrumentalist idea which is so widespread among our literary exponents of the new right-wing mood: that one can move the objective spirit to the left or right by means of ideological planning and a politics of language.

I have just one practical problem—getting across to students the problems contained in Communication and the Evolution of Society. *The massive synthesis of various theories causes students gradually to despair and say,*

*well, if we first have to begin fulfilling the sociological conditions and
then those related to the theory of evolution, and so on ...*

But we have to be allowed to write theory ...

*Right, of course, but I see the problem differently. I would also concede
that there are practical difficulties in conveying your theory. But the
difficulties are rooted in the material. Bloch always said he couldn't write
more simply about the material because the material itself was not
simple. For dogmatic Marxism this doesn't present a problem—they
shake an analysis of society right out of their sleeves. However, one
cannot cogently explain the present crisis with the crude instruments of
Marxist theory—for example, with the tendency of the rate of profit to
fall. For the object 'society', which is being analysed, is itself hard to
grasp. That is shown by other sociological theories which look around for
possibilities of combination with still further sociological theories in the
hope of getting a better grip on the object they're trying to analyse. I grant
you that it's a problem for students, trying to learn all those theories. But
if one pays due regard to the subject one can't get around it, or else I'm
getting my analysis of society on the cheap. That's precisely what I see in
your theoretical writings.*

I'm very sympathetic to what you're saying. But Herr van Reijen is
correct in one respect—what is mirrored in the difficulties of my texts is
of course my own lack of clarity on certain points. There's no question
about that.

*You just said you found what I was saying was sympathetic. Are you merely
sympathetic, or do you share that understanding of your own enterprise?*

Yes, I do.

*If you agree with that, then I have another question. Your theory is the
synthesis of various theories with differing paradigms, for example theory
of action, philosophy of language, Marxist theory, theory of evolution.
The discussions at the most recent sociology convention revolved around
the possibility of theory comparison and theory synthesis. Which criteria
do you use in your own syntheses? Can theories with such different
paradigms even be synthesized?*

I see things somewhat differently. If you were to ask me about the
possibility of a 'marriage' between behaviourist theory (for example
small-group research into the theory of learning, as developed in

America in the 1950s) and a sociology based on a theory of action (whether derived from Parsons or Marx), then I would have to say no, I don't think it's possible. Their basic concepts are mutually exclusive. In the first case one conceptualizes the object by eliminating the concept of 'sense'; in the other, one deals with intentional action, communicative action, or value-oriented action as a fundamental concept. Those are clear alternatives. I would never try to integrate such theoretical premises. On the other hand, I don't agree at all that there is such a wide variety of paradigms. That's more likely the artificial product of a scientific rhetoric that was unintentionally inspired by Kuhn. Throughout the history of sociological theory, insofar as it laid claim to being a theory of society (through Marx, Durkheim, Weber, up to Parsons, or whomever), the same problem has always existed in regard to fundamental concepts: how do we reconcile the systems paradigm with the action paradigm, or the systems paradigm with that of the life-world? Marx avoided the problem completely by accepting Hegel's fundamental concepts, because Hegel's conceptual apparatus is neutral, so to speak, with regard to such differentiation. This allowed Marx to develop a labour theory of value which served to translate the function-alist analysis of the process of realization of capital (systems analysis) into analyses based on class conflicts, on active subjects and groups. However, I don't consider the retention of the labour theory of value to be feasible. That's one of the reasons, by the way, why many people don't consider me a Marxist. Granted, there must be some systematic equivalent. In the course of his development, Parsons transformed his action theory into a systems theory, although there was something left over. That can be seen in the status of the so-called 'general frame of action', which was promoted to a general action system. I contend that the problem lies in relating the two paradigms to one another not merely rhetorically, but in a genuinely satisfactory manner. Only then can one deal systematically with the fundamental question posed by Marx. Loosely speaking, that is the question of how capitalist expansion (which must be systematically analysed) affects the structures of the life-world (first of the classes directly involved, today of more and more of the total population). The dialectic of objectified and living labour was supposed to explain how the destruction of traditional forms of life took place in the social strata from which the proletariat emerged. It was concerned with explaining the proletarianization of forms of life. That was Marx's practical impetus, and in that regard one can relate his thesis to our present circumstances. Our problem still consists in explaining how this capitalist economic system (whose growth rate isn't bad at all) destroys conditions of life which are so structured that they must be described in categories of action theory. As soon as one erases the infrastructure of life-worlds, through the use of systems theory, as soon as one admits on the analytical level only domains of social life which are systematically regulated—at that point we can no longer speak of socialized individuals; at most we can speak of Martians, of creatures that are so defined that one can no longer recognize under these descriptions socialized individuals and their problems.

Well, I can see from structuralist interpretations of Marx that there's no very great difference between systems theory and those interpretations. But can action theory and Marxist theory be synthesized so easily? As far as human actions are concerned, action theory cannot encompass all that goes on behind people's backs, and penetrate their consciousness. The silent compulsion of social relations falls right through the analytical net.

I think what interested Marx—the ability of objective life-circumstances to penetrate through the consciousness and action-orientations of the subjects involved—can be best reconstructed if one remembers that there is an idealism built into the basic tenets of action theory. In the most consistent theoretical versions of action theory, such as the linguistic (Winch), the phenomenological (Schütz) or the ethnomethodological (Garfinkel), society is basically defined as a life-world which is completely transparent. I would prefer instead to see it as consisting in systematically stabilized patterns of action of socially integrated groups. If we could succeed in conceptually linking paradigms of action theory and systems theory in the right way, then we could really begin to pursue the questions of Marxism instead of merely defining them out of existence, as both systems theory and action theory have done until now. So the variety of theories which I'm trying to integrate really isn't so large.

But that's another problem that has to be solved, in regard to your theory of emancipation. If I've understood correctly your ideal speech situation in a future society, doesn't that imply the idealistic hope that entire social systems will be altered through changes in the actions of single individuals, in the communicative actions of individuals? That idea must pursue you like the paradigms do Kuhn ...

That needs to be placed in perspective. I need the ideal speech situation in order to reconstruct the normative foundations of a Critical Theory. The communication theory which I envisage is based on a type of action oriented toward understanding, in which people involved use criticizable validity claims to gain an orientation. The level of understanding is determined by whether or not the validity claim which is raised by ego is accepted by the other. In this context I have to show what it means to raise and resolve criticizable validity claims—for instance, the truth-claim of an assertion. I believe that there are precisely two validity claims which can be dealt with only on an argumentative basis. That leads me to a 'discourse theory of truth', and in this context I have recourse to the general presuppositions of the ideal speech situation.

One should not imagine the ideal speech situation as a utopian model for an emancipated society. I use it only to reconstruct the concept of reason, that is, a concept of communicative reason, which I would like to mobilize against Adorno and Horkheimer's *Dialectic of Enlightenment.* Horkheimer and Adorno allow reason to shrivel down to the 'unreason' of mimesis. In the mimetic powers the promise of reconciliation is sublated. For Adorno that then leads to *Negative Dialectics*—in other words to Nowhere.

So the standpoint of identity wouldn't be acceptable to you either? The preservation of reason leads us to say that even in a future society there would remain a type of domination. One of Schelling's old problems. If the domination of reason remains in force, then there always remains a domination over objects. Schelling offered the one possible solution to this problem—identity.

I think that's a part of our conceptual heritage that can't be taken over as it stands. There is, if you wish, a bit of Kantianism in me. There remains something unreconciled in our relation to nature.

When we speak of reason, we aren't speaking of decisions concerning basic value postulates. We're dealing with unavoidable premises which are not at our disposition. The aspects of reason which, according to Max Weber, have separated out irreconcilably—the cognitive-instru-mental, the moral-practical, and the aesthetic-expressive aspects—these three continue to form a concept of reason which is internally differen-tiated. Max Weber is wrong, I would say, when he affirms that the autonomous moments of reason transform themselves, so to speak, into irrational powers of belief which compete with one another. No, they remain moments of reason, and the big question is: how can we describe with sufficient precision the way they fit together? What does this pattern of reason mean for the socialization of individuals who speak and work and, because they do those two things, can't help but reproduce their lives with the aid of this three-sided rationality? I certainly don't believe—and here Max Weber is right—that one can capture the unity of reason, the interrelation of the different aspects of reason, on the level of cultural systems of interpretation, in the form of a religious world-picture or a philosophy. That is what is meant, in Marxist terms, by the sublation of philosophy. Nothing is going to come together any more on the level of cultural systems of interpretation. However, the moments of reason fit together in social relations and in everyday communicative practice, albeit in a remarkably distorted way. That is also Marx's concern—the destruction of precisely these rationally based conditions of life through the backlash of an economic-administrative system which, in and of itself, has reached a high degree of system differentiation, yet is so constructed that it has destructive side-effects. It is these which pose the problem.

What constitutes the idea of socialism, for me, is the possibility of overcoming the onesidedness of the capitalist process of rationalization (to use Weber's terminology). Onesidedness, that is, in the sense of the rise to dominance of cognitive-instrumental aspects, which results in everything else being driven into the realm of apparent irrationality. With the overcoming of that system, these aspects would be shifted to their proper place, so to speak—not that there has ever been a previous phase when they did occupy their proper place. In socialism, too, one would have to live with an economic system which operates exactly like a partial system, a system which is separated out from the political context. But it would not direct this objective, covert, destructive force against communicatively-structured conditions of life. My criticism of Marx is that he failed to see that the capitalist production methods ushered in not only a new apolitical form of class domination, but a new level of system differentiation (as Luhmann would say). This differentiation had enormous evolutionary advantages over the level reached in state-organized societies of pre-bourgeois periods. Such evolutionary advantages, if we are to put it like that, are not something we can control. Marx imagined we could just destroy capitalism and the economy would dissolve back into the life-world under our control. He later assessed the matter somewhat more sceptically by separating the realm of necessity from the realm of freedom. Marx spoke of neutral forces of production. I wonder whether there are neutral increases of complexity, or whether this higher level of system differentiation which we have reached in the modern age was achieved only at the cost of some form of class domination. If the latter were the case, then there could be only regressive solutions for socialism. That doesn't necessarily make socialism less attractive, but it does leave it more or less without a future. What kind of condition would we be in if the majority of the population, in order to achieve more humane forms of collective life, were ready to pay the heavy price of a regressive economic system? But there are no a priori arguments for the pessimistic premise underlying that question. For this reason socialization, as a project which is capable of self-correction, undertaken on what could be called a fallibilist basis, is as essential today as ever.

4

The Dialectics of Rationalization

I
The Tradition of Critical Theory

Honneth: *To begin with, I shall summarize the topics we would like to address: First we want to concentrate on your position within the tradition of Critical Theory in order to, second, examine its deficiencies as you see them. The third and more systematic theme concerns the basic features of your theory, as developed in your latest book. I'm sure that will become very difficult and complicated once we have the comprehensive manuscript before us. In the fourth part our interest switches to the application of the theory to present-day political problems and conflicts. Finally, we'll want to address questions such as science as a vocation, the turning of Marxism and social theory into academic disciplines, and problems of the mode of production of Critical Theory. How can Marxism, which is caught up in an academic system, protect itself against a dangerous loss of experience and academic complacency? In other words: how can we rationally pursue critical scholarship today?*

That's not very clear to me either.

Honneth: *In a journalistic context you are perceived as the modern representative of Critical Theory. Do you accept this characterization?*

I've always felt myself over-estimated. After all, it was the older generation who produced Critical Theory in the 1930s. Lukács led me to the young Marx. Adorno played, shall we say, an absolutely electrifying role. It was he who taught me that one need not restrict oneself to a historical approach to Marx.

Knödler-Bunte: *But wasn't that really a philosophical reading of Marx?*

Neither an historicized Marx nor the theory of capitalism was of much importance to me at that time, in the 1950s, but rather the Marx of the *Economic and Philosophical Manuscripts*, of the *Grundrisse*—Marx as the theoretician of reification. Of course, there were also Lukács and Korsch. I didn't take Marx seriously as an economist until 1958, when I read Sweezy's *Theory of Capitalist Development*. Adorno always said, and this is a typically philosophical attitude toward the text: secondary literature is irrelevant. He considered Marx and Freud as classics. He also opened my eyes to the fact that one must first exhaust the primary texts, systematically exhaust them, before one explores their sequels. That was something new to me when I arrived in Frankfurt in 1950. He also led me to stop reading Marx from an 'anthropological' perspective. But, of course, I never considered Marx primarily an economist. He was also a political theorist who took up the traditions of the bourgeois revolutions and their theoretical treatments from the Jacobins to Thomas Paine.

Naturally, one can remain in such traditions only if one criticizes and transforms them. That is a hermeneutic commonplace. The traditions that survive are only those which change in order to fit new situations. The same is true of my relation to the older Frankfurt Circle. I am more than a generation younger than the 'old ones', if I may put it that way, and also come from a different background. For example, I am the first one who is not Jewish, who grew up in Nazi Germany and who experienced the fall of fascism quite differently than the others. For these reasons alone it is not possible for me to have an unbroken identification with Critical Theory. Besides, when I became Adorno's assistant in 1956, the intellectual past of the Institute for Social Research was not accessible to the new students.

Honneth: *What traditions were alive then, if the Critical Theory of the thirties was as good as unknown?*

My philosophical and literary response at that time was to the left traditions of the twenties. For example, I read Lukács very early in the course of my studies, although that wasn't yet a standard thing at the time. The turning point came with the young Hegelian critique as interpreted by Löwith, in an intellectual-historical but nonetheless extremely illuminating manner. The insights of the young Hegelian critique into that which sustains us all, into everything which took place between Kant and Hegel, including Hölderlin, were exciting. In retrospect, I sometimes have the impression that a student can recreate a segment of the critical theory of the thirties if he systematically works his way from Kant through Hegel, including Schelling, and then approaches

Marx via Lukács. I wouldn't want that understood as arrogance. If he were then confronted with Adorno in the late fifties and did not just read his writings but also heard him speak of Durkheim, Hegel and Freud, he could easily uncover the origins of this way of thinking, even without knowing the *Zeitschrift für Sozialforschung*. When this sunken continent later resurfaced—in the 1960s with the student protests—and entered the consciousness of us former assistants at the Institute, I didn't have the impression that what was occurring was entirely new.

Widmann: *When you got to Frankfurt didn't you sit down and look up the old papers in the Institute for Social Research?*

But they didn't exist.

Knödler-Bunte: *There was the* Zeitschrift *with the old essays ...*

That didn't exist. Horkheimer had a great fear that we would get to the crate in the Institute's cellar that contained a complete set of the *Zeitschrift*. Had we had a strong desire to, however, we would have been able to read all of it. I was told at the time, and it was true, that it could have been obtained from Carlo Schmidt at the Institute.

Knödler-Bunte: *How did you actually get to Frankfurt and what did you find there?*

When I arrived in Frankfurt, it struck me that Adorno and Horkheimer did not pay much attention to contemporary philosophy, which I had studied in Bonn. I never got the impression from Adorno that he had read Heidegger intensively. I don't know even today whether he just read isolated sentences. This selectivity—there was no Jaspers, no phenomenology—was something exotic. Only in the 1970s, after Adorno's death, as I read his inaugural lecture and the essay on natural history, did I become clearly aware of all the things Adorno had had in his head as a young man. Subjectively, I saw myself as someone who, in the face of a very narrow, almost dogmatic selection of acceptable texts, carried on philosophical and academic traditions in a less strict manner. Because of my—let us say—more systematic approach, I was also considered by my contemporaries in the philosophical seminar as a kind of foreigner. In addition, it became clear to me that the 1920s, in which I had lived theoretically during my student years, were, after all, the 1920s. That became a stimulus to become interested in American sociology, for example. Analytical philosophy came afterward. Categories such as 'bourgeois science' never meant much for me. In an established science there are either useful things or less useful ones. In principle, I considered worthwhile anything that had a cognitive, structural or hermeneutical element—anything that would allow one to open up objects from the inside.

Honneth: *What was the source of your—even pre-theoretical—affinity with Critical Theory?*

As I mentioned, I had read Lukács. Inspired by the young Hegelians, I looked at the transition from Kant to 'objective' idealism with great interest. Alongside all this were my very strong everyday political interests. I had read *History and Class Consciousness* both with fascination and regret that it belonged to the past. Then I read the *Dialectic of Enlightenment* and the first things published by Adorno after the war. That gave me the courage to read Marx systematically and not simply historically. Critical Theory, a Frankfurt School—there was no such thing at the time. Reading Adorno had given me the courage to take up systematically what Lukács and Korsch represented historically: the theory of reification as a theory of rationalization, in Max Weber's sense. Already at that time, my problem was a theory of modernity, a theory of the pathology of modernity, from the viewpoint of the realization—the deformed realization—of reason in history. So, naturally, the *Dialectic of Enlightenment* became a key. When I met Adorno and saw how breathtakingly he spoke about commodity fetishism and applied this concept to cultural and everyday phenomena, at first it was a shock. But then I thought: try to act as if Marx and Freud, about whom Adorno spoke with the same orthodoxy, *were contemporaries.*

Knödler-Bunte: *Where then did you see the deficiencies of Critical Theory?*

I didn't think of it that way at the time. For me there was no critical theory, no coherent doctrine. Adorno wrote critical essays on culture and held seminars on Hegel. He made contemporary a certain Marxist background. That was it. Only some clever young people in the late 1960s discovered early Critical Theory and made it clearer in my mind that a theory of society should be systematic. In retrospect, what appear to me to be weaknesses in Critical Theory can be categorized under the labels of 'normative foundations', 'concept of truth and its relation to scientific disciplines' and 'undervaluation of the traditions of democracy and of the constitutional state'. With questions about foundations one naturally becomes unpopular in all circles oriented to Adorno.

In the 1930s the old Frankfurt Circle still explicitly subscribed to a concept of reason and developed it in terms of the philosophy of history. This was achieved by means of an appropriation through ideology-critique of bourgeois philosophy. We find that in Horkheimer's book on the beginnings of bourgeois philosophy of history, and above all in the many essays in the *Zeitschrift*, including the articles by Marcuse and Horkheimer in 1937, in which both are convinced that bourgeois ideals, with certain limitations, are present in art as well as philosophy, survive as potentials. They could appeal to these potentials because, as Marxist social theorists, they could rely on political groups within the European working class movement—if not the proletariat in the Lukácsian sense—to unleash and realize historically the rational potential of bourgeois society, as a result of the ongoing development of the forces of production. This I call the philosophico-historical concept of reason.

In the 1930s, doubts began to arise about this among the Frankfurt theorists, and the results emerged in the *Dialectic of Enlightenment* and the *Eclipse of Reason*. What I consider Adorno's greatness, what gives him his position in the history of philosophy, is the fact that he was the only one to develop remorselessly and spell out the paradoxes of this form of theory construction, of the dialectic of enlightenment that unfolds the whole as the untrue. In this sense of critical insistence, he was one of the most systematic and effective thinkers I know. Of course, one can draw various conclusions from the results. Either one presses on in the illuminating exercise of negative philosophy, to the insight with which one is forced to endure that, if a spark of reason is left, then it is to be found in esoteric art. Or, on the other hand, one takes a step back and says to oneself: Adorno has shown that one must go back to a stage before the dialectic of enlightenment because, as a scientist, one cannot live with the paradoxes of a self-negating philosophy. If one takes Adorno's *Negative Dialectics* and *Aesthetic Theory* seriously and accepts them, and if one then wishes to advance just one step beyond this scene out of Beckett, then one has to become something of a post-structuralist to conceptualize it. Adorno never took this step. He would have considered it a betrayal of the rational heritage of Critical Theory. I don't think it is possible for Critical Theory in its strictest form to refer to any form of empirical or even discursive analysis of social conditions.

This is related to the second point of criticism, the philosophical concept of truth adopted from Hegel, which the old Frankfurt School never abandoned and which is irreconcilable with the fallibility of scientific endeavour.

The third point has become very relevant to me. On the level of political theory, the old Frankfurt School never took bourgeois democracy very seriously. Those are the three most important deficiencies of the Frankfurt School as I see them today.

II
Deficiencies of Critical Theory

Honneth: *I think we should move from this listing of systematic deficiencies in the tradition of Critical Theory to the constructive means you have employed in these three areas in order to overcome them. Thus, the question is: how have you corrected the normative deficiencies of Critical Theory? In what way have you transformed its concept of truth? How have you evaluated differently the achievements of bourgeois democracy? By what means is it possible to reach a better understanding on these three levels?*

Well, here I can only give some programmatic explanations. For the central intuition that I hope to have clarified somewhat in my *Theory of Communicative Action*, I am indebted to a reception of both the hermeneutic and the analytic strains of linguistic theory and, one could say, to a reading of Humboldt with the insight of analytic philosophy. This is the intuition that a *telos* of mutual understanding is built into linguistic communication. Along this path one comes to the concept of communicative rationality which, by the way, is also at the basis of Adorno's few affirmative utterances concerning the unspoiled [*nicht-verfehltes*] life. When in *Minima Moralia* Adorno actually tries to explain what he means by a mimetic association, not only with nature but also among people, he refers to Eichendorff's 'distant nearness'. So he has recourse to categories of intersubjectivity from which he abstains philosophically. So far this is an attempt to secure a concept of reason by means of formal pragmatics, that is, by means of an analysis of the general characteristics of a communication-orientated action. Naturally, that can only be a first step. The next step is to make the concept of communicative rationality applicable to social relations, to institutional-ized systems of interaction. Here one must be careful to avoid the pitfalls of foundationalism or linguistic transcendentalism. In the *Introduction to the Critique of Political Economy* of 1857, Marx established in what sense the category of labour is a universal concept applicable to all societies. He shows that only to the extent that the capitalist mode of production has become established are the objective conditions fulfilled that allow him, Marx, access to an understanding of the universal character of this category 'labour'.

With regard to such a theory of communication, one must use the same method to clarify how the development of late capitalism has objectively fulfilled conditions that allow us to recognize universals in the structures of linguistic communication, providing criteria for a critique which can no longer be based on the philosophy of history.

Honneth: *So the categorial means of correcting the normative deficiency of Critical Theory is a concept of communicative understanding based on linguistic theory?*

Yes, and now to the second point. I believe the Frankfurt School cling to a concept of theory—and also to a concept of truth—that was based on the emphatic concept of reason in the philosophical tradition. This is the same concept that reappears in an ironic fashion in the formulation 'instrumental reason'. 'Reason' is not meant to apply simply to truth-intentions, in the narrow sense in which we speak of the truth of utterances. Rather, reason should reveal the unity of the moments of reason separated out in all three Kantian critiques: the unity of theoretical reason with practical moral insight and aesthetic judgment.

When one does science and, within this framework, philosophy, one has only to do with truth claims in the narrower sense. This generates a dilemma. On the one hand, the conceptions of emphatic theory are tailored to 'truths' from which the moral and aesthetic-expressive aspects have not yet been split off. On the other hand, a critical social theory must also proceed scientifically: it can only make pronouncements with a claim to propositional truth. This is another way of formulating the awkwardness that Hegelianizing social scientists have always felt in relation to empirical procedures. If one doesn't follow Adorno towards a 'negative dialectics', which is a renunciation of the social sciences, it becomes necessary to use theories that specialize in questions of truth in the narrow sense. In this case, one must then see how it is possible, within the social sciences and, first and foremost, in the formation of philosophical theory, to bring into play the experiential domains of both the aesthetic-expressive and moral-practical without empiricist redefinitions, and without endangering the requirements of theoretical descriptions. That is the problem of *non-positivist approaches to theory in the social sciences.* Hermeneutic approaches ensure the connection to the realm of experience of everyday communicative praxis, which is virtually defined by the lack of differentiation between questions of truth, justice and taste (if you don't mind the Kantian divisions).

Freud's theory is another example. This finds inspiration in a concept of 'consciousness' or 'ego'—thus 'conscious control of drives', 'ego strength' and so on—which cannot be explained without simultaneously examining the moral-practical elements of Kant's (or Hegel's) concept of autonomy; and certainly not without referring to aesthetic-expressive elements of an 'id become ego'.

Just as non-objectivist research methods within the human sciences mobilize the standpoints of moral and aesthetic critique without endangering the primacy of basic questions of truth, we can find a similar counter-movement in ethics and aesthetics. Of course, cognitive ethics excludes problems of the good life, leaving over from what is good merely what is just. But the discussion of an ethics of responsibility and of conviction, and the more serious consideration of hedonistic factors, in turn bring into play viewpoints concerned with the consequences of action and the interpretation of needs, which lie in the realm of the cognitive and the expressive. Art, too, which has become autonomous, pushes towards an increasingly pure expression of basic aesthetic experiences. Today, however, post-avant garde art is characterized by a remarkable combination of realistic and politically engaged tendencies with authentic continuations of the classic modernism which had established the independent logic of the aesthetic. Thus, realistic and engaged art forms raise cognitive and moral-practical factors to the level of richness of form which was liberated by the avant garde. It seems as if such movements, which run counter to the radical singlemindedness of differentiated moments of reason, suggest once again a unity. This unity can only be acquired this side of the culture of experts—in a non-deformed daily practice.

The third deficiency—the theory of democracy—is connected with the question of developmental logics. Here I am of the opinion that one can show that the formal features of bourgeois systems of law and constitutions, of bourgeois political institutions in general, demonstrate a conceptual structure of moral-practical thought and interpretation which must be considered superior in relation to the built-in moral categories of traditional and legal political institutions.

Knödler-Bunte: *Superior in what sense?*

Superior in terms of the ability to answer moral-practical questions. This can be seen in the following way: if one reads Marx correctly, one can find certain ideas embedded in the institutions of the bourgeois state which belong to a heritage worthy of preservation in a socialist society. Naturally, one can say that the horizon from which the old critical theory derived its perception of contemporary history was so gloomy that nothing remained of anything that could be reclaimed as reason or—if you like—as utopian in Bloch's sense.

Knödler-Bunte: *Today, on the other hand, the critique of instrumental reason encounters a remarkably urgent situation marked by the expectations of doom and catastrophe-anxieties present in many movements. By contrast, your construction relies on a form of intactness of bourgeois society, at least insofar as it should be capable of developing certain structural mechanisms that bear the stamp of rationality. From a concrete standpoint, and without speaking philosophically, I believe that there are mechanisms which tend to make institutions independent, on account of their size, or through centralization, or by cutting off or obliterating possibilities for feedback. This sets a sort of uncontrolled machinery in motion and brings new risks which E. P. Thompson has called 'exterminism', the logic of self-annihilation.*

Yes, it makes a difference whether you see *any* kind of communicative rationality built into daily practice or the life-world, or into accepted traditional life-styles, or whether you simply just relinquish the criteria by which to criticize these tendencies towards independence, or leave these criteria diffusely in the background. It seems to me that the self-contradictions of reason went so far—from the perspective of the dialectic of enlightenment—that Horkheimer and Adorno (Pollock as well, with his theory of state capitalism) found political institutions, all social institutions, and daily practice as well, completely void of all traces of reason. For them, reason had become utopian in the literal sense of the word: it had lost all its locations and thus ushered in the whole problematic of negative dialectics.

For the moment, I simply want to recall that one should always explicate the conceptual structures used to criticize specific features, to avoid falling into embarrassment when the viewpoint, criteria, or context of this critique is challenged. The older Critical Theory fell exactly into this difficulty—even if Adorno was later able to articulate the dilemma fruitfully by recognizing it as such, and attempting to salvage the particular as the intangible, the injured, the victimized—that necessarily falls through the grasp of all discursive or identifying thought. Adorno asks this question but he did it in such a way that it no longer made sense truly to analyse the concrete social phenomena to which you refer, such as the autonomous dynamic of the arms race, economic growth, bureaucratization, and so on.

Honneth: *Even in the Marxist tradition it is not unusual to value the achievements of bourgeois-democratic institutions under the concept of formal democracy. Adorno's perspective, however, is more of a foreign perspective in Marxist theory in that it allows differences among political systems to fade under the pressure of fascism.*

Yes, one could describe that on a scale, to use a positivist device: on the one side are the Second International theorists of continuity, where progress becomes evolutionary in a sense that I wouldn't defend, and on the other side are Benjamin, Bloch, some anarchists—the theorists of total discontinuity. Although I have something against the Aristotelian virtue of moderation and of the mean, I do feel myself drawn to the middle in questions like this. In any case, one has to look at it as an empirical question: in which historical situations could and should fairly strong continuities be preserved with a declining social formation, and in which situations would almost everything have to be rejected to achieve even the smallest step toward emancipation?

III
Dialectics of Rationalization

Honneth: *Perhaps I can now ask the global question: how do these motifs fit together in your book due to appear this fall?*[1] *How do you tie together the different lines of thought you've been developing for the last ten years in the project of a theory of communicative action?*

Knödler-Bunte: *Adorno always used to say on such occasions: now say that in your own words.*

There are essentially four motifs that I have brought together in this monster. The first motif is an attempt at a theory of rationality. That is especially difficult today, when forms of relativism have the upper hand under the sign of a dubious revival of Nietzsche (or of irrationalism in general). I may be approaching this problem a little too 'straight', though certainly in a confrontation with important counter-arguments. For example, I discuss the rationality debate which took place in England in the early 1970s between some analytic philosophers and anthropologists. One side wanted to strengthen the hypothesis that every culture, every form of life, every language-game, constituted a self-enclosed totality with its own unique criteria of rationality. By connecting up with this kind of discussion I try to make my approach more plausible for all those who find such a theory of communicative rationality a shocking requirement, who cannot swallow such an awkward word as rationality without turning red. I am aware of the fact that the times are not favourable for this type of undertaking, since the tragedy Lukács described as *The Destruction of Reason* now reappears as farce in our liberal cultural weeklies. I develop the second motif (which is not quite

---

1. *Theorie des kommunikativen Handelns*, Frankfurt 1981, 2 vols. English translation *The Theory of Communicative Action* trans. Thomas McCarthy, Boston 1984 (vol. 1) and 1987 (vol. 2).

so untimely) in the form of a *theory of communicative action*, in order to deal with a series of more theoretical problems, such as the theory of argumentation. Above all, I want to demonstrate that beginning with understanding-orientated action is useful for purposes of social theory. It did not become clear to me until I was writing—which is why I kept throwing my first drafts away—that Anglo-Saxon discussions about action theory, language theory, and the theory of meaning have become independent as *l'art pour l'art*. One ends up with wonderful, pedantic, conceptually refined ideas of what social interaction is, but has forgotten for what purpose. This prompted me to stick more closely to the history of theory, for example to George Herbert Mead's theory of symbolically mediated interaction, in order to show that the pragmatic tradition already contained this concept of rationality. Further, I took up Durkheim and read him from the viewpoint of a theory of social evolution—which is rather unusual. With the aid of the concept of communicative rationality I decoded the perspective of development from mechanical to organic solidarity. Finally I went back to Max Weber to treat a substantial theme. For I did not just want to show how the theory of communicative action can be useful for social theory. I also had a third motif, namely, the *dialectic of social rationalization*. That was already the main theme of the *dialectic of enlightenment*. I wanted to show that one can develop a theory of modernity using communications-theoretical concepts which possess the analytic precision needed for socio-pathological phenomena, for what the Marxist tradition calls reification.

For this purpose I have developed—perhaps this is a fourth motif—a concept of society that brings together systems and action theory. Because Hegelian-Marxist social theory, developed in categories of totality, has decomposed into its parts, namely, action theory and systems theory, the present task now consists of combining these two paradigms in a non-trivial fashion—that is, not merely eclectically and additively. Thus, one can give new form to the critique of instrumental reason which could not be pursued further using the methods of the old Critical Theory. The appropriate form is a critique of functionalist reason.

Honneth: *Why a theory of rationalization? There would seem to be other ways to a critical social theory, for example, a theory of capitalization, or a theory of specific degrees of the division of labour. Why do you take up the motif of rationality? Why is rationality the key to a critical social theory?*

I could make the answer easy and say that, after all, Adorno and

Horkheimer already used the concept of instrumental reason to re-formulate the theme of reification. I suggest we first look at the background, in the sense of the psychology of research. The fact that I finally sat down at the end of 1977 to deal seriously with the matter has to do with the following—I'll get back to the theme of rationality later. The tense German political situation, which was becoming more and more like a pogrom following Schleyer's kidnapping in 1977, drove me out of the theoretical ivory tower to take a political stand. For the first time I took seriously neo-conservative ideologies which had become fashionable since about 1973. I did not just shrug my shoulders as if experiencing a sense of *déjà-vu.* Rather, I considered the appearance of these militant late liberals—who followed above all Gehlen and Carl Schmitt in Germany—as signifying a broader change of climate. I attempted to clarify the concept of modernity implicit in these con-siderations, and the departure from modernity, a departure from radical democracy and enlightenment—those ideas which had given rise to the Federal Republic. That was one side. The other side was that for the first time I felt I better understood the meaning of the new potentials for protest, the new movements with which I had no intrinsic relation. If you take these two phenomena together, you will perhaps understand that at this time the interpretive scheme was formed which guided my concluding observations, if not the whole book. Perhaps I should explain that a little better. Both sides, the neo-conservatives and the critics of growth, the one with greater articulation, the other more diffusely, offer conflicting interpretations of the state into which Western societies have got themselves, with Reagan and the Lady at one end, Mitterrand at the other, and Schmidt in the middle—three decades after the last disaster. Both understandings, ideologies, interpretive schema—whatever you want to call them—manipulate unfortunate consequences of an other-wise successful stabilization of internal conditions. This stabilization was attained on the basis of the welfare-state compromise, of what is in a broad sense a social democratic compromise, as Dahrendorf puts it.

Honneth: *What do you mean by that?*

It is only a catch-word. The mass democracy of the welfare state and state interventionism form a system that maintains to some degree the dynamic of capitalist growth. From this growth it finances compensa-tions in line with the system (money, leisure time, and so on), pacifying traditional class conflicts without disturbing the sanctity of private investment, the structure of private wealth, and so forth. This machine is not running so well at the moment, either *economically* or *socio-psychologically.*

Economically: Some try a refurbished neo-neo-Keynesianism, while others try Friedman and the monetarists, and what results is a fluctuating shift of unsolved problems from the marketplace onto the state, from the state onto the marketplace, and back again. The participants in this zero-sum game have somehow not grasped that the poles 'state' and 'society' are only two sides of the same coin—if viewed from the historical perspective of modernization—namely, systems of action which have become differentiated through the steering media of exchange value and administrative power. These systems have been consolidated into a monetary-administrative complex, and having been disconnected from the communicatively structured life-world (with private and public spheres), have apparently grown *overcomplex*. The state and the economy will necessarily become more complex with economic growth (this is what the neo-conservatives do not see). Connected to this are conflicts that today take a more socio-psychological form: the defence of life-styles threatened by internal colonization. We must also consider the drastic, only temporarily repressed, military dangers of the instability between super powers, with the whole absurdity of the arms race. The conflicting interpretations that have assumed sharper and sharper contours in the last five or six years react against all of this. What most directly interests me is that both sides turn against the heritage of what Weber calls Western rationalism. The one side does this in the name of a robust post-modernism with curiously regressive characteristics—regardless of whether one evokes the social romanticism of pioneering capitalism, as the American neo-conservatives do, or mobilizes the counter-Enlightenment, as in Germany. The other side does it mostly by summoning up anti-modernist emotions. My fear is simply that the two competing and conflicting syndromes are racing toward the destruction of all that I consider deserves to be saved in the substance of Western traditions and inspirations. The post-modernists would like to hold onto the capitalist blueprint of social rationalization at any price—in fact, rather rabidly. They give economic growth priority over the welfare state. This policy attempts to dampen its negative effects on socially integrated areas of life, upon the family, school, political sphere, and so on, by returning to a Biedermeier culture, to uprooted but rhetorically re-harnessed traditions. Luhmann's talk of ideology planning was never as true as today. However, the displacement onto the market of problems which have been shifted with good reason from the market onto the state since the nineteenth century can hardly provide an answer. The problems will survive being shoved back and forth between the media of money and power. And I do not know how one could renew the cushion of tradition that supported capitalist societies for centuries, which was consumed without being regenerated, indeed how traditionalism in any sense could be renewed by a historically enlightened consciousness. The only resource we can still creatively draw on—cultural modernism—is rendered despicable in this perspective.

But this gives rise to an unfortunate convergence with the anti-modernist critique of growth. The demanded de-differentiation is obviously no solution unless clear distinctions are made. One must distinguish between the restraint of the monetary-administrative-military complex and the rolling back of the structural differentiation of life-forms. Modern life-worlds are differentiated and should remain so in order that the reflexivity of traditions, the individuation of the social subject, and the universalistic foundations of justice and morality do not all go to hell. Hopefully, this is not leading to an ironic division of labour; between apologetic neo-conservatives who want to give their celebrated functionalist reason a traditionalist twist, and young conservatives who increasingly combine their awareness of the high risks of contemporary history, their important and courageous defence of threatened life-forms, and their exploration of new ones with a kind of post-structuralist renunciation of reason itself.

To return to the point of departure: my real motive in beginning the book in 1977 was to understand how the critique of reification, the critique of rationalization, could be reformulated in a way that would offer a theoretical explanation of the crumbling of the welfare-state compromise and of the potential for a critique of growth in new movements, without surrendering the project of modernity or descending into post- or anti-modernism, 'tough' new conservativism or 'wild' young conservatism.

Honneth: *So, in your opinion, the neo-populist potentials fall prey to a misunderstanding of themselves as long as they follow the critique of modernity offered by post-structuralism or* Lebensphilosophie?

I think so. In any case, you must not get the impression that this book is directly political. It is a very theoretical attempt above all to discover how much better the political intentions of these critique-of-growth movements could be understood, if they were separated from critiques of modernism in general. That is first of all a theoretical problem, and when you read the book you will notice that it has become hopelessly academic.

I wanted to take up the systematic problem again, the question of the normative foundations. Is it not possible—*pace* Adorno—to explicate a concept of communicative reason that can stand against Adorno's negativism, so that it contains what Adorno believed could be made visible only indirectly, by implication, through continual and consistent self-negation? Adorno would certainly not have agreed. All that would have been too affirmative for him. But when one is as involved in scientific research as I am, one must stay away from positions with one foot in post-structuralism; one must seek a theoretical approach that permits connections to productive scientific approaches, in order simultaneously to retrieve the claim of the older Critical Theory and do it justice. What this generates may appear to be a return to positions once aimed for by Critical Theory in the 1930s. Naturally, 'return' must have many quotation marks around it, for I want to make this return without adopting Critical Theory's background in the philosophy of history. That was a rather long-winded answer to your short question: why critical social theory as a theory of rationality?

Honneth: *Two more questions on that: what is communicative rationality and how does it allow an interpretation of the structure of contemporary society?*

As I said, I am trying to work out the normative content of the idea of understanding present in language and communication. That leads to a complex concept that implies not only that we understand the meaning of speech acts, but also that mutual understanding is produced between participants in communication regarding facts, norms, and also experiences. (Each of us has privileged access to experiences, and must reveal them through expressive self-presentation before an audience if they are to be regarded as one's own.)

Here we find the three dimensions contained in the concept of communicative rationality; first, the relation of the knowing subject to a world of events or facts; second, the relation to a social world of an acting, practical subject entwined in interaction with others; and finally, the relation of a suffering and passionate subject (in Feuerbach's sense) to its own inner nature, to its own subjectivity and the subjectivity of others. These are the three dimensions that come into view when one analyses communication processes from the participants' perspective. To these should be added the life-world, however, which stands behind the back of each participant in communication and which provides resources for the resolution of problems of understanding. Members of a social collective normally share a life-world. In communication, but also in processes of cognition, this only exists in the distinctive, pre-reflexive form of background assumptions, background receptivities or background relations. The life-world is that remarkable thing which dissolves and disappears before our eyes as soon as we try to take it up piece by piece. The life-world functions in relation to processes of communication as a resource for what goes into explicit expression. But the moment this background knowledge enters communicative expression, where it becomes explicit knowledge and thereby subject to criticism, it loses precisely those characteristics which life-world structures always have for those who belong to them: certainty, background character, impossibility of being gone behind.

Widmann: *In this context, alternative life-styles must be of interest to you. Here it is precisely the life-world that is to be criticized. From discussions of personal relations to questions of varying tolerances of uncleanliness, an attempt is being made rationally to discuss questions which are otherwise inaccessible to criticism.*

Knödler-Bunte: *And don't these experiences prove that rational discussion and criticism do not necessarily destroy the life-world, but that new life-worlds can develop?*

Well I certainly do not believe that attempts to develop alternative life-styles result in the destruction of life-forms. I simply think that one can label as a life-world only those resources that are not thematized, not criticized. The moment one of its elements is taken out and criticized, made accessible to discussion, that element no longer belongs to the life-world. I also think it is impossible to create new forms of living by talking and talking about things. One element of these alternative life-styles does appear to differ clearly from more strongly traditional life-styles. That is the wider horizon of what *can* be thematized. That is also very characteristic of what I have called, perhaps using too harsh a term, the 'rationalization of the life-world'. I mean that in a thoroughly positive sense.

One thing you must not forget in any case: for every element of the most explored, well-worn and well-tried life-world that is changed or even consciously accepted, there are untold masses of elements that, even in the course of the most radical weighing of alternatives, never even crossed the threshold of thematization. The life-world is so unproblematic that we are simply incapable of making ourselves conscious of this or that part of it at will. The fact that certain elements of the life-world become problematic is an objective process. It depends on the problems that press in on us from outside in an objective way, by virtue of the fact that something has *become* problematic behind our backs.

Knödler-Bunte: *Do you postulate also, as Agnes Heller does, an ontology of structures of the everyday world that every person has?*

There Agnes Heller is somewhat too anthropological for my taste. I also believe, however, that there are general structures which are essential for life. But they are present only as infrastructures in historical life-forms, which can only exist in the plural—besides which they change in the evolutionary dimension.

One more thing about the problem of thematizing the life-world. The demands of the student movement, that formal rules and institutions, which up till then had been taken for granted, should be questioned, cannot be simply transferred, in my view, to the life-world context in general.

Widmann: *But* Authority and the Family *was after all the theoretical foundation of the alternative schools movement . . .*

Without taking account of what one could have learned about the radically altered life-situation, compared with the twenties and thirties, from the seminars which Oevermann and I were giving at the time. But let's leave that on one side, I don't want to play the professor.

Honneth: *So far the subject has been the concept of communicative rationality. What do you mean, however, by the concept of rationalization? If I understand it correctly, this is supposed to bring a dynamic point of view into the analysis?*

First of all, where history of theory is concerned, Max Weber was my point of departure. What he terms processes of social rationalization—essentially the institutionalization of purposive-rational action, above all in economic and administrative systems—can be understood as the advance of an institutional embodiment of complexes of rationality. Weber himself analysed this on another level, that of culture, predominantly in the sociology of religion. Social rationalization means, then, that a society remoulds its basic institutions in order to make use of—so to speak—culturally ready-made structures of rationality. In Weber's view, the capitalist economic system could only arise because there was a class of entrepreneurs to be recruited from the puritanical sects, who brought with them the ethical and motivational presuppositions for a methodically rational conduct of life; on the other hand, the capitalist means of production could not have been established and stabilized if a legal system had not been institutionalized, which was tailored to subjects of private law, acting strategically, purposive-rationally, each following his or her own goals. The cognitive structures of a mode of thought governed by principles of an ethic of conviction are embodied in the modern legal system. These structures are embodied by these institutions in the same way that they are 'anchored' in the motives of the strata bearing the spirit of capitalism.

Honneth: *Thus far Weber. But a concept of communicative action would also have to provide another basis for the concept of rationalization.*

Schematically described, my critique of Weber is as follows: he does not see the selectivity in the pattern of capitalist rationalization. He does not see that in the development of capitalism those elements are repressed that he himself analysed under the heading of the 'ethics of brotherhood'. Nevertheless, for Weber, also, there are moral-practical potentials here which came into play in the radical religious movements, the Baptists, for example, in the attempt to create institutional forms that were not just simply functional for the emerging capitalist economic system. And precisely these potentials did not enter into the dominant institutional pattern of capitalist modernity. It is just these ethical visions—which push towards communicative forms of organization—that are excluded in capitalism.

On the basis of Mead and Durkheim, I attempt to develop an evolutionary perspective for the increasing reflexive fluidity of world-views, for a continuing process of individuation, and for the emergence of a universalistic moral and legal system through the simultaneous detachment and liberation of communicative action from institutionally frozen contexts. Further, I sharply distinguish between the more or less differentiated or 'rationalized' life-worlds that are reproduced by way of communicative action and, on the other hand, formally organized systems of action based on steering media.

Today economic as well as administrative imperatives are encroaching upon territory that the life-world can no longer relinquish. To grossly oversimplify the case, until now the processes of destruction that have paved the way to capitalist modernization have occurred in such a way as to give rise to new institutions. These new institutions transferred social material from the realm of sovereignty of the life-world into realms of action steered by the media and organized by formal law. This went well as long as it only touched on functions of material reproduction that need not necessarily be organized communicatively. In the meantime, however, it seems that system imperatives are encroaching on areas which are demonstrably unable to perform their tasks if they are removed from communicatively structured domains of action. This is true of tasks such as cultural reproduction, social integration and socialization.

The battle lines between life-world and system thereby acquire a new relevance. Today economic and administrative imperatives embodied in the media of money and power encroach on areas that somehow collapse as soon as they are broken off from communication-orientated action and transferred to interactions steered by these media. These are processes that no longer fit into the scheme of class analysis. But one can demonstrate a functional connection between the central conflicts of the life-world and the requirements of capitalist modernization. I have shown this with examples from social, educational and family policy, and also to a degree from the new protest movements.

Honneth: *We have now already entered a new complex of issues. How are the terms of a theory of communicative action used to describe the constitution of contemporary society? Perhaps we should first pose questions of classification. I would like to have the following question answered: whether it is not more useful to begin with collective agents, with social groups and their organizations, rather than with systems and the logic of institutions?*

From the methodological standpoint my suggestion has the advantage that one can take over something from both structuralism and systems theory. It is worth considering that these two research traditions might have good reason for leaving the realm of action theory. I believe there are such grounds. If one wants to analyse steering crises in the economy, for example, one must bring systems-theoretical methods to bear. We have no choice, since the objective dialectic and the concept of totality of Hegelian theory no longer inspire confidence. What was once bound together is now split asunder: systems theory and action theory.

Widmann: *Fine, what you have said is: here is a sophisticated arsenal of tools, of conceptual means that can be applied. But what domains of reality are revealed by your approach? What cognitive gains do you hope to make?*

One cognitive gain is that the normative contents of a humane social life can be introduced in an unsuspicious way by means of a communication theory, without the need to smuggle them in secretly by way of a philosophy of history. With a theory of communication, there is no obligation to proceed only according to action theory, to speak only of agents and their fate, acts and consequences. It becomes possible also to speak of the characteristics of life-worlds in which agents and collectives or individual subjects move. For instance, it is possible to trace the uprooting of a plebeian lower class from a traditional world dating from the time of early industrialization. What are the ideas with which those who have resisted capitalist modernization for centuries have identified?

Well into the nineteenth century it was not so much with the ideals of bourgeois emancipatory movements and certainly not with the ideas of socialism. Instead, such movements drew strength mainly from the potential of traditional ideas, from religious ideas, from religiously-anchored natural law, and so on. I don't mean just the Peasant Wars, rather this extends far into the artisans' movement of the nineteenth century. These movements are driven by directly provoked feelings of injustice as well as the need for spontaneity and expression. But such impulses do not become a historically effective reality if they cannot be publicly expressed. There must be leaflets, there must be someone who will speak out, with whom one can identify. Now, for example, the limits that a traditional life-world places on political movements that objectively aim beyond these life-worlds cannot be comprehended hermeneutically in the intentions and motives of single agents. It is not enough to ask what the agents were thinking of, what their motives were, what they talked about, although these questions have again become perhaps justifiably fashionable in the name of a historiography of everyday life. This is very useful in itself but, as Adorno would have said with more pathos, it is somewhat lacking in concepts. For this reason, a structural analysis of life-worlds, based on communication theory, can be useful if one does not wish simply to load the material from outside with economic interests, political power struggles, and so on. Otherwise, one is swimming in a sea of historical contingencies. Just as a sort of grammar emerges in art through the organization and unfolding of a style, so also differentiations of the life-world can be described from within without recourse to the level of action. What does it mean, for example, when a stable system of institutions, which encapsulates pre-formed patterns of action, differentiates and separates itself, first, from interpretive world-views, which can now also take over functions of legitimation—that's to say, deception—and, second, releases itself from networks of interaction which are now left to the self-definition of individual actors?

Honneth: *I can see that this 'structuralist' element of social analysis does guard against an under-conceptualized approach to social processes. My only reservations are that such analyses may no longer translate back into the field of social conflicts between collectives and agents. Once one has divided up the different dimensions of modern rationality in this way, we must ask what paths of rationalization are pursued by specific collective agents. For instance, one must ask how accumulated knowledge is monopolized by power elites and how social strata themselves are thereby constituted. Doesn't social reality divide in this way into social confrontations in regard to monopolies of rationality?*

There you are sketching a programme that I have no reservations about, although I'm sure we would agree that it still requires an extremely long period of development.

Knödler-Bunte: *But must everything really fit together in one theory, as you would have it? Why can't one accept that there are differing types of theories, each with its strengths and weaknesses? Their powers of expression compete with each other, and at times they leave room for whatever has as yet found no clear methodical approach? After all, is it possible to imagine one social theory, founded on evolutionary theory, that can incorporate the pattern of universal history as well as concrete analysis of objects and situations?*

One can be satisfied with a respectable historiography that is candid about its own hermeneutic relativity. But is that enough? One would also like to have a situational analysis, which, if we are lucky, allows us to understand more than a generalizing historiography can. The latter can make it clear to us why, here in Germany, we have such a deformed political culture. It reveals to us the lines of tradition: the empire, Wilhelminianism, the Nazis, the only half-completed bourgeois revolution, and so on. On the other hand, we have theories of language, morality and cognition. All this would just remain in mid-air, without telling us very much, if social theory could not develop the focusing power of a kind of magnifying glass, and throw a bright spotlight on the present.

Knödler-Bunte: *But this bright spotlight could also come from such a view as Benjamin's, which combines disparate contexts in order to make specific, shocking revelations about ourselves.*

If one uses such an approach from the start, one has relinquished a scientific attitude and has gone over to an aesthetic view of history. Let me explain again my own procedure. Naturally, I am somewhat self-conscious about the approach of evolutionary theory. One is plagued on the one hand by the Second International, and by Luhmann on the other, and perhaps even by the ghost of a naturalistic philosophy of history. This must be avoided. But I also see what can be gained from a theory that tries to work out a logic of development. Such an evo-lutionary perspective is dangerous if one wants, thus heavily armed, to produce a respectable work of social or cultural history, unless one tempers it to the degree I believe is necessary. As far as evolutionistic assumptions are concerned, I restrict myself to certain modes of interpretation for the infrastructure of possible life-worlds, according to general, genetic-structuralist categories.

I have yet to carry out an historical analysis with these instruments of evolutionary theory, but I can imagine that they could reveal new dimensions even of a field as well-researched as the Peasant Wars. One has to give it a try. It is somewhat simpler where the present is at issue. In that context we just let ourselves be guided by everyday intuitions. We are all armchair sociologists who put Hegel's 'realist's morning prayer' into practice, that is: the reading of the newspaper.

Honneth: *Because of the way your conceptual framework is set up, your analysis of the present limits itself to the perception of horizontal frictions in the social system, namely frictions between the life-worlds and the systematically integrated partial systems. By contrast the dimensions of a vertical analysis get short shrift—although not necessarily, since I can easily imagine that one could rework Marxist class theory with your categories, in a way which would reveal more of social reality than can be found in the newspapers.*

One would probably have to produce a combination of class theory and analysis of subcultures, in order to explain the current shifts in areas of conflict and forms of consciousness, but I didn't attempt that in my new book. And as long as this isn't done, one has no way of testing the viability of the approach.

IV
Crisis Theories and Social Movements

Widmann: *In a certain sense, this combination of class theory and analysis of subcultures already exists. Or at least the beginnings of such a combination. Almost nothing is discussed in the ecology movement on a theoretical level as much as the relation between classical Marxist crisis theory and the new crises of complexity evident, for example, in the mechanisms which render the technical and military apparatus autonomous.*

I find it more elegant and plausible to give capitalism credit for being what it is—for what it has actually achieved thanks to its level of differentiation and its ability to control social processes. Let's give our Marxist hearts a shock: capitalism was quite a success, at least in the area of material reproduction, and it still is. Granted, it has indulged from the beginning in an enormous plunder of traditional forms of life. But today the imperatives built into the dynamics of capitalist growth can only be fulfilled through a substantial growth in what we call the monetary-bureaucratic complex.

As a consequence, we now observe, and feel, and suffer an 'overspill', an encroachment by the system on areas no longer at all related to material reproduction. These areas of cultural tradition—social integration through values and norms, education, socialization of coming generations—are, however, ontologically speaking, held together by their very nature through the medium of communicative action. Once the steering media such as money and power penetrate these areas, for instance by redefining relations in terms of consumption, or by bureaucratizing the conditions of life, then it is more than an attack on traditions. The foundations of a life-world that is already rationalized are under assault. What is at stake is the symbolic reproduction of the life-world itself. In sum, crises that arise in the area of material reproduction are intercepted at the cost of a pathologizing of the life-world. I developed this thesis in my book, and I believe that in this way some problems can be solved.

Honneth: *I am more interested in questions that again touch on the conceptual distinction between subsystems, but I would like to begin with empirically oriented questions. Isn't what you have just been saying too much centred on West Germany? Beyond our western borders there are conflicts of a much more profoundly threatening nature, and which can hardly be explained by recourse to a crisis theory of system and life-world. I am thinking of the quite traditional conflicts that today arise mainly from structural unemployment resulting from capitalist accumulation, and from a tremendous wave of rationalization which is approaching us and whose consequences we can only speculate on.*

Where will these conflicts be precipitated as long as the safety net of the welfare state holds up?

Widmann: *When the president of the Swedish association of Savings Banks predicts that the Western industrial nations will lose one quarter of both their blue-collar and white-collar jobs in the next 15 years, I don't see any safety net of social services that can deal with that. I don't believe crises are automatic, but I see the approach of huge problems that have nothing to do with a conflict between system and life-world.*

The analysis I have worked out presents this alternative: on the one hand, the conditions necessary to the welfare state compromise may be fulfilled—continuous, albeit restrained, economic growth. Then problems would arise that I would place under the heading of colonization of the life-world, an erosion or undermining of realms of communicatively-structured action. On the other hand, the dynamics of growth may not be maintained; then we would see some variant of traditional conflicts.

Widmann: *Can conditions be determined that would once again set off traditional class conflict? Isn't what you have just outlined therefore a theory of the exceptional case?*

Well, first of all, I don't believe in the 'law' of the falling rate of profit ...

Widmann: *That was the exceptional case.*

But it would be absurd to attempt to exclude the possibility of economic crises. At this very moment we are getting lots of material which illustrates my friend O'Connor's thesis concerning the fiscal crisis.

Knödler-Bunte: *Put quite simply, our problem was this: precisely because we face new zones of conflict, isn't it necessary to reconstruct the old theory of class in light of new experiences, without weakening the concepts of class and class struggle beyond recognition? Don't we need new theoretical approaches that can point out to us the interrelation between traditional zones of conflict and new potential for resistance? The crisis theory assumptions concerning system and life-world remain irrelevant if at the same time new interpretations aren't given to the older problems of class-specific oppression and inequality of cultural opportunity and life-chances. I believe that a theory of social movements, including the classical theory of revolution and class-struggle, must be much more historicized, and must be disconnected from the determinations of political economy, and from conceptions of a universal history. What we know as the workers' movement arose in a specific phase of capitalist industrial development, with many internal time-lags and contradictions. The workers' movement became most radical where the transitional situation, in which it found itself in Germany in the second half of the nineteenth century and the first quarter of the twentieth, was experienced most dramatically. Large parts of the working class could not return to agricultural production or to small artisanal enterprises, but neither were the conditions present which would have permitted an integration into bourgeois culture. This basic outlook can be reconstructed with the model of system and life-world, except that—in contrast to today—the life-worlds of workers were organized in a much more traditional way by shared schemas of interpretation. These were later eroded under the pressure of the internal differentiation of both proletarian and bourgeois culture, up to the point of the present privatization of life-worlds. I've outlined all that in a very general way, but I don't see such a sharp break between the traditional lines of conflict of the working-class movement and the social movements of today.*

It could be that radicalization came about through an influx of cultural conflicts. You said it yourself: there is no comparison between the world of the Social Democrats of 1890 or 1910 and that of today. That was still a political party which provided a sense of identity. It also had no stabilizing function comparable to social democracy today. The old Social Democratic Party was truly an 'enemy of the *Reich*'.

Honneth: *But since there is no such thing anymore as the working-class movement in its traditional form, we have to confront problems that didn't even exist in, say, the time of the Weimar Republic. I just think that the potential for conflict and protest that you speak of in terms of 'neo-populist movements' has to be seen in a different light. One could say that these are the potentials for protest which are given publicity enough in the press these days, but that they are the tip of an iceberg rising out of a broad spectrum of persisting class-specific problems and conflicts. These, however, do not find an appropriate voice because a working-class movement that previously provided cultural means of expression no longer exists.*

That would be a decisive point only if the groups that today present the medium of resonance and articulation for the now questionable class-specific base were to react to some kind of class-specific problems.

Honneth: *The first thesis would be that there are states of conflict and potential for protest that are or have been forced to remain voiceless, for different historical reasons and for reasons traceable to cultural repro-duction. The problems that accumulate here and which are related to class-specific conditions of life ...*

But why then should the class-specific problems of workers forced into silence find their voice precisely in the complaints of the sons and daughters of the bourgeois strata?

Honneth: *No, no, that is a misunderstanding of my thesis. I simply suspect that next to these explicit protest formations, which of course have also been encouraged by the press, there exists another, more traditional set of conflicts, which does not have this kind of cultural means of expression. Your thesis of cultural impoverishment could therefore be taken seriously in another way. I admit that in order to name such forms of conflict one certainly cannot rely on what you referred to as empirical data. One therefore can't rely on questionnaires, that privilege certain economic . . .*

I wonder if that isn't an ahistorical view. Isn't it true that you can discover these deficiencies because you belong to an entirely different current of protest? Isn't it so, that with your completely different background and socialization, you experience the imperatives—of consumption, administration, bureaucracy—that penetrated into highly differentiated life-worlds from the outside as a conspiracy? Aren't you ascribing your viewpoint to someone who sees things differently?

Honneth: *Yes, it is always difficult to answer the objection that one is projecting one's own sensibilities onto social groups and strata that may not be affected by them. I believe one can avoid this by hypothetically testing the type of conflict or experience of deprivation that is in question, and by being able to show that this has nothing to do with one's own sensibilities and experiences. The core of what I could expect here would be a repressed and culturally silenced potential for protest in dimensions of social respect and social recognition. Those may be antiquated concepts, but they are still capable of recording a persistent experience that we really do have of the deprivation of social respect. I don't believe that is a projection. There would be no historical indices of that, which a new historiography of the working-class movement would have to investigate. Precisely this motive of the 'struggle for social recognition' is perhaps a central and also always latent impulse.*

Knödler-Bunte: *I would also say that it is in parts of the middle class that the psychological framework for sensitization, for experiencing cultural disenfranchisement, finds its breakthrough point, so to speak. That still says nothing about the genesis and the validity of these conflicts, although it does oppose the thesis of a suspended class struggle, in which the working class is considered culturally integrated. Is it actually true that the entire proletariat has been bound to the system by internalizing the norms of abstract labour? Or is it not the case that in truth large portions of the proletariat, the majority of the working population, have simply not participated to a great extent in this system—bourgeois culture as a structuring of the subject? Perhaps they have not subscribed, after all, to the normative concepts of bourgeois ideology along with its self-understanding and its world view, but have kept it at arm's length, always conscious that in very basic issues the system operates independent of their own wishes and needs. That is the question as I see it, whether the 'alternative movement' does not to a degree continue this experience in a non-class-specific way. Within the dominant system it, too, finds no cultural recognition, no way of establishing a satisfying organization of its own life.*

All right, you know the scene better than I do. Earlier, at least, it was simpler to see the student movement as a catalyst providing energy for the real class struggle. Perhaps one should now realize that the 'alternative scene' arises from the sensibilities of those who are able to experience as deprivations things which a middle-aged Social Democrat worker or employee would not experience in that way.

Knödler-Bunte: *There I would still disagree with you, for several reasons. First, as I see it, the predominant type of person in the 'alternative scene' is by now no longer someone from an educated bourgeois family and often has not completed any programme of higher education. For such a person, to drop out is less symbolic as an experiment with new living patterns than it is as an alternative to life in a factory or office, with clear and concrete advantages and disadvantages. The aesthetic stylizations come from outside, from the culture apparatus (also on the Left), which projects onto the 'alternative scene' its own wishes and fears. Within the workings of 'alternative' projects there are few illusions about what one is doing, and many concrete experiences of the difficulty of organizing life and work. That brings me to a second point. Recently, I have taken part in many discussions between young unionized workers and members of 'alternative' projects. It was remarkable how quickly and directly the two groups understood each other. And that is actually not surprising, since both have to deal with similar problems of the work situation—division of labour, hierarchies in the workplace, and the right to work. Only the possible solutions are different. The need to live and work differently, therefore, seems to extend far into the core of the industrial workers' community. 'Alternative' projects would be attractive to many young workers if concrete dialogue would take place and if 'alternative' projects could make certain guarantees regarding income, continuity and social services. Finally, a third point. Your criticism is aimed too high, because you assess our argument by very traditional standards. You apply a concept of class struggle and class analysis that in recent debates, especially in social history, has long since been opened up and expanded. Perhaps the theory of class we have ascribed to Marx has itself become historical, applicable at best to a short phase of industrial capitalism in the second half of the nineteenth century. Fine, you say, that is a cultural reinterpretation of the theory of class. But I think that one must analyse social conflicts in a widened spectrum of cultural theory, without letting the concept of class lose its expressive power.*

Honneth: *I would ask if it is possible to define the dimensions of social class relations on the basis of the concept of the social life-world, which is what you are actually doing. I am thinking here not only of the dimension of class-specific living situations and certain, let us say, biographically central sets of problem. These can be empirically observed in specific opportunities for social mobility, opportunities for securing an identity, risks to life and damage to health. But I am also thinking of the dimensions of cultural reproduction—a concept that is also central to your model—that is, a socially stratified system of cultural opportunities for expression and rights to social definition. Can what Gramsci describes with the concept of cultural hegemony—the elevation of one social class's form of expression by means of a culturally prescribed network of dominant forms of expression—simply be separated from the idea of cultural reproduction? To put it simply, what can be learned for the concept of the social life-world from this cultural turn in Marxism? Can one simply exclude it?*

No, of course not. But Lukács had already used reification as a general term for deformations of consciousness. In Critical Theory's critique of mass culture this is even more pronounced.

Widmann: *I tend more to the opinion that your model is to a certain extent a general theory, of which the theory of class struggle describes a particular sharpening at a certain point in time. The theory of class struggle would then be a special case of the antithesis of system and life-world, which permeates all of history.*

You mean that the classical conflicts between peasants, proletariat and bourgeoisie also reflect a defensive reaction against the destruction which was caused by capitalist modernization. I can accept that without hesitation. The only thing which is missing from this picture is the transformation of the life-world itself. Marx could not sufficiently distinguish between traditional life-worlds, which are worn away through modernization processes, and a structural differentiation of the life-forms which are today threatened in their communicative infra-structure. As a result of capitalist modernization disruptions occur, which imply the downfall of traditional forms of life. Where modern societies arise this breakdown is indeed always unavoidable. This does not mean that one should bring it about intentionally or consider it as morally acceptable.

Knödler-Bunte: *I agree with that. The question is only: can the destruction of life-worlds by the imperatives of a capitalist system in each case only be constructed on the basis of concrete historical material, or is there something like a logical progression of steps for the differentiation of life-worlds? There I am very sceptical.*

Well, there are certainly communicative structures, which all life-worlds have in common. These are very formal elements like the relation of personality structures to social institutions and to contexts of tradition. The dimension of developmental logic concerns only how these elements differentiate themselves and how the differentiation passes through individuation processes, through the abstraction and generalization of norms and through the increasing reflexivity of cultural traditions. That is what Durkheim or Mead described. That does not mean that these processes are irreversible, but just that they take place when any form of modernization begins.

Honneth: *I do not believe that one can introduce the above mentioned categories in a class-neutral fashion. One cannot argue on the basis of an internal evolutionism that asserts a linear destruction of the life-world. Is it not more the case that when one looks at the family, for example, then the proletarian family is a product of the historical conflicts surrounding the shortening of the working day?*

These communicative life-relationships should therefore not be seen as remnants of a precapitalist life-world, which was untouched by the constraints of capitalist rationalization, but rather as a product of social conflicts and not as a remainder of a precapitalist form of production which will gradually be corroded by capitalism.

That is also the case.

Knödler-Bunte: *I also believe that destruction and deformation are interfaced with new growth and new formations.*

Widmann: *It makes a difference, however, whether one understands the current protests as a form of reaction of a closed life-world to administrative and monetary intervention or whether one conceives of the life-world itself as functional for the administrative system, so that in the course of development both spheres must determine anew their relation to one another and thereby also their inner structure. From this perspective an intact life-world does not simply stand opposed to the capitalist system. Instead, today's conflicts are a medium through which a new balance must be found between these spheres and within themselves. Thus, they fulfil the same function as the classical crisis of capitalism. It did not signal the collapse of the system, but rather the mechanism by which the system maintained itself through change. That is a different view, a different perspective, than yours. According to you the communicative life-world is a block against which capitalist rationalization scratches.*

Yes, I really do believe that it is a question of injecting communicative everyday praxis into institutions. This was once a conservative view.

V
Science and Life-Praxis

Knödler-Bunte: *I admit that I have the most difficulties with the structure of your theory and with the attitude that I surmise is behind it, and considerably fewer problems with your political programme and your political and theoretical self-understanding. What libidinous images does a theory evoke, which is so abstract and which stands under an unbelievable compulsion to synthesize? Where in the intellectual work linked to it are the moments of happiness, of satisfaction, without which one can hardly understand such effort? In your explanations of your concerns the word anschlussfähig [making connections] appears again and again: one's own intellectual work must connect with the standards and expectations represented by the academic system. But how do you justify the centrality of this academic system that is practically your only reference point? The other—historically alternative—reference point, namely a proletarian political organization, has since disappeared from the scene, but are there really only these two possibilities? The scientific-educational system and the organized labour movement have one thing in common, that they have made themselves institutionally autonomous and have isolated individuals from exactly those experiences which they require for intellectual stimulation. As a result, the best that the tenured academic and the political functionary can still offer is a kind of ethic of craftsmanship. That is, if it has not already been buried by industriousness and officiousness, and by the accommodation to short-term requirements which maintains the system and keeps things going. Radical attitudes and scientific innovations require changes in life-praxis, a restructuring of the priorities according to which one structures one's life. Can a social theory such as you propose also prove that this confidence in the ability of the academic system to produce results is objectively justified?*

There are two questions here. The first has to do with the impulses and motives behind my work, and the second with a certain, shall we say, faith in science. Concerning the first question I have a conceptual motive and a fundamental intuition. This, by the way, refers back to religious traditions such as those of the Protestant or Jewish mystics, also to Schelling. The motivating thought concerns the reconciliation of a modernity which has fallen apart, the idea that without surrendering the differentiation that modernity has made possible in the cultural, the social and economic spheres, one can find forms of living together in which autonomy and dependency can truly enter into a non-antagonistic relation, that one can walk tall in a collectivity that does not have the dubious quality of backward-looking substantial forms of community.

The intuition springs from the sphere of relations with others; it aims at experiences of undisturbed intersubjectivity. These are more fragile than anything that history has up till now brought forth in the way of structures of communication—an ever more dense and finely woven web of intersubjective relations that nevertheless make possible a relation between freedom and dependency that can only be imagined with interactive models. Wherever these ideas appear, whether in Adorno, when he quotes Eichendorff, in Schelling's *Weltalter*, in the young Hegel, or in Jakob Böhme, they are always ideas of felicitous inter-action, of reciprocity and distance, of separation and of successful, unspoiled nearness, of vulnerability and complementary caution. All of these images of protection, openness and compassion, of submission and resistance, rise out of a horizon of experience, of what Brecht would have termed 'friendly living together'. *This* kind of friendliness does not exclude conflict, rather it implies those human forms through which one can survive conflicts.

Knödler-Bunte: *My questions were rather concerned with what kind of impulse, what structure of experience underlies this explicit self-under-standing. Perhaps I can illustrate this by a contrast of extremes. I can have the basic feeling that, fundamentally, the world is in order as it is, and for this reason I can relate to individual domains of reality in an experimental and adventurous way. Chaotic multiplicity does not disturb me at all, because I can relate to it from an affectively secured distance. I detect this attitude in the typical Brechtian gesture, Brecht being, so to speak, a virtuoso of radicalized adaptation. The other fundamental structure consists in experiencing chaos as threatening, and in therefore attempting to structure it by means of conceptual systems, in order to have some firm ground under one's feet. This type would rather correspond to that of the surveyor, who must first create structures before he begins to move.*

Well, I do not have this primitive trust in my environment, but neither do I have the attitude of someone who must bring a satisfying order into chaos. There is nothing at all to which I have an unambivalent attitude, at least apart from very rare moments. For this reason even my naive connection to social relations is not really naive, but profoundly ambivalent. This has to do with very personal experiences, which I would rather not speak about, but also with critical moments—for example with the coincidence of great events and my own puberty in 1945. I am also ambivalent because I have the impression that something is deeply amiss in the rational society in which I grew up and in which I now live. On the other hand, I have also retained something else from the experience of 1945 and after, namely that things got better. Things really got rather better. One must use that as a starting-point too; and I then go on to look for a prehistory which is too lightly disposed of with the concept of 'Enlightenment'.

Now for the question about confidence in the established system of scientific knowledge. I am myself still not certain whether what I truly intend and what intuitively directs my work can be accommodated in its essential elements within this system. When one grows up as we have, one tries somehow to do something in life into which one can bring, and in which one can clarify, one's basic intuition. For me, this occurs through the medium of scientific thought or philosophy. When one is oriented to questions of truth and does not misunderstand oneself in the process, then one should not try, as Heidegger and Adorno both did, to produce truths outside of the sciences and to wager on a higher level of insight, on the thinking of Being or on a mindfulness of tormented nature. It is my deep conviction that one should not do that when one ventures on thinking.

Widmann: *Why not?*

If one wants to live and write from a fund of ultimate, self-evident truths, then one should not try to achieve what one would like in a tenured professorship or at a research institute. That reminds me of experiences I have had at the rostrum or in the seminar room. When I realize that students are totally uninvolved emotionally with what I am doing, what we are doing together, then I am dissatisfied because I know that all learning depends on the formation of deeper motives. On the other hand, when I realize that students can no longer stand back from their emotions, that a symbiotic relationship is being developed, then I become tremendously nervous. I want to preserve a sense that questions of truth can be isolated, to keep a sense for discourse alive in a situation which objectively forces one not to mix questions of truth with questions of justice or taste. That is a stubbornly Kantian way of putting things; but I have accustomed myself to this neo-Kantian jargon in recent years, and I am somehow relieved that I can say it so casually. I have never before dared to say it in this manner—'this bureaucratic departmentalization of moments of reason', Adorno would have said. Precisely this, however, is the mark and the thorn in the side of modernity. How we cope with this situation is perhaps the problem.

In what I intend—one never really knows what one is up to—I meet Max Weber half-way by trying to keep various spheres separate: first of all these political-journalistic things, then 'real' philosophizing (which paradoxically I can only pursue intermittently, even though it is here that my intentions are most consistently realized). After that, scientific work in a narrower sense; and finally teaching and, when the time is ripe, a political praxis which goes beyond journalism. In the last ten years I have also had to play the role of institutional director. I keep these various kinds of work separate, but I am not saying that this is the kind of division of labour in which one thing has nothing to do with another, or in which it is a matter of a combination of various roles. I would much rather play each of these roles in such a way that the others remain visible at the same time. What annoys me terribly, what gets to me, is the aggressivity of people who do not see the role-differentiation in me, let alone respect it, and mix everything together. I have experienced that again in the last few weeks. I am not speaking about the routine persecutory articles, about the degenerate products published under the editorial direction of the Bavarian minister for culture in the *Rheinische Merkur*; I mean the sheer opportunism of the so-called liberal mileu.

I would like to maintain a certain differentiation, and indeed, if it does not sound too lofty to say so, for moral reasons—or perhaps also out of fear? In contemporary society there are certain criteria that separate responsible from irresponsible minds. As a professor or scholar, with the authority of one who examines questions of truth, one should not say things that affect other people without at least trying to bring one's work up to the standards set by institutionalized research.

Widmann: *Don't the reasons for this lie much more in yourself? Namely, that you would not like to be caught holding on to something against all reason?*

There is also a dogmatic core to my convictions, of course. I would rather abandon scholarship than allow this core to soften, for those are intuitions which I did not acquire through science, that no person ever acquires that way, but rather through the fact that one grows up in an environment with people with whom one must come to terms, and in whom one recognizes oneself.

Widmann: *Why do you consider the geographic site of the university to be the place where rational argumentation and meaningful analytic procedure are guaranteed?*

I only think like this when I get annoyed with people who persist in talking about 'bourgeois science', as if they had commandeered a sweeping insight. Theories can in any case no longer be sorted out according to such criteria. But that is only a genetic explanation. With that one has not yet said why exactly the choice of the university ... But is there then another location?

Widmann: *You always link up with dominant theories or good outsiders ...*

Perhaps what you mean by that is: are you not a coward who always makes himself secure by means of authorities and what is currently in vogue? It is certainly true that in the 1960s and 1970s, and this annoys the empiricist crowd, I played a large role in bringing certain theoretical methodologies into discussion, which others still had to work through— such as Wittgenstein, Piaget, Chomsky, Kohlberg, Searle, and so on. The difference is only that I still hold on to what I have learned from all of them, even when academic fashion has moved on. When I have learned something from someone I remain to a certain extent faithful to him in this respect. I do not follow the fashions of the academic industry. I do not know whether this answers your question.

Widmann: *Do you have the feeling that you need these constructs, this speaking in different tongues, this terrific willingness to be receptive, in order to articulate your own concerns?*

I think I make the foreign tongues my own in a rather brutal manner, from a hermeneutic point of view. Even when I quote a good deal and take over other terminologies I am clearly aware that my use of them often has little to do with the authors' original meaning. What is then the peculiar pleasure to be had in the process? Even if I sweat a lot over my work and use a lot of my life history for it, I enjoy it when I have the impression: 'Ah, you have seen something. There you can further develop something with arguments'. Then I am satisfied because I think that it is the only way. Those are certainly small joys. The thinker as lifestyle, as vision, as expressive self-portrait is no longer possible. I am not a producer of a *Weltanschauung*; I would really like to produce a few small truths, not the one big one.

When I have found an interesting flower or herb I try to figure out how it will fit together with others, whether it can create a bouquet or pattern. This is constructive puzzle-work. I take over other theories. Why not? One should accept others according to their strengths and then see how one can go from there. One thing should support another, for theoretical truths actually exist only in the form of plausibilities.

For my own part, in any case, I have said goodbye to the emphatic philosophical claim to truth. This elitist concept of truth is a last remaining piece of myth, and you know that I do not want to return to where the *Zeitgeist* is leading today.

Knödler-Bunte: *Are there experiences of happiness and of satisfying situations in your intellectual praxis?*

There are minds which are more analytic and minds which are more synthetic, and I certainly belong on the synthetic side. As a result, my satisfactions lie more in a synthesis of argumentation. Earlier, I used to enjoy fabricating texts. This aspect of the 'pretty tongue', as Grass once said about Adorno, has retreated more and more. More recently, I have put up with rougher discourse in order to develop something even when a text is not the result. You can see it in my new book. Of course, there is still the ambition that there should be a text with introduction, exposition, interpolations, and so on, but the setting up of perspectives on problems is now more important.

I experience the problems that occupy me at any given moment in an almost physical way, so I am happy when something seems to be working out for me. I am very seldom euphoric ... I must have paper in front of me, blank paper, written-on paper, books around me, but I am not someone who works with card indexes. One needs to invest oneself in the work, and then the problems begin to move with the writing. This way, having problems is a matter of personal history. It disrupts your life, and then you are happy, when you have found a solution and can carry on writing.

Knödler-Bunte: *What is the next mountain you need to climb?*

Hills, only little hills. I might go to the University of Frankfurt, and I do not know how much time my responsibilities there will leave me. I am planning a series of lectures about theories of modernity. That will certainly be fun. With colleagues from other disciplines I would like to practise what I always insist on, the cooperation of philosophy with the individual scientific disciplines. It must be possible to show with empirical material that one can introduce reason into science. The other aim would be once again to write something like *Strukturwandel der*

Öffentlichkeit, from my current perspective. So much fog lies around everywhere today. I am not giving up hope that this fog can be lifted. It would be nice if I could still make a contribution to this task.

5

Conservative Politics, Work, Socialism and Utopia Today

In recent decades philosophy has increasingly contented itself with a defensive position. This is a role which you justified in your 1971 essay, 'Does Philosophy Still Have a Purpose?'[1] Today, it is true, you once more entrust it with bigger tasks—and yet there is a growing chorus which laments or even invokes the 'end of philosophy'. There are certainly reasons for, and indeed a long tradition behind, this attitude. With the Enlightenment philosophy consciously forfeited its power as a positive world-picture. Later, as a means of interpreting the world, it lost out more and more to the individual sciences.

You have always defended a concern with the linking of philosophical and scientific—in particular sociological—thought, with proving them and testing them against each other, in the intention of holding onto philosophical goals which can no longer be straightforwardly defended in their own terms. For a good ten years you were the Director of the Max Planck Institute for 'Research into the Life Conditions of the Scientific-Technical World' in Starnberg. The activities of the Institute included both research into theoretical foundations and empirical programmes.

What opportunities does such a demanding linkage open up for philosophy, against the background of such a fragile situation; where does its impulse derive from; what cannot be relinquished in this tradition?

Philosophy today is no longer in possession of metaphysical truths. It is involved, almost to the same extent as the sciences, in the fallibilism of a research process which takes place on the shaky ground of argumentation which is never immune to revision. Nowadays it is philoso-

---

1. Jürgen Habermas, 'Does Philosophy Still Have a Purpose?' in *Philosophico-Political Profiles*, London 1983, pp. 1–19.

phizing animal behaviour specialists, or physicists, who push towards popular syntheses which have something of the character of world views, and with regard to which philosophers are unable to conceal a certain scepticism. To this extent the traditional roles have rather been reversed. On the other hand, philosophy still retains a more intimate relation to common human understanding and to the life-world than do the sciences. It still has to play the role of an interpreter in the exchange between autonomized cultures of experts and everyday life.

Because science, morality and art have acquired a considerable independence as specialist cultures and developed an institutional life of their own, the need—in reaction to this splitting-off—to mediate theory and practice, morality and customary ethics, art and life, has become ever more urgent—in this context it is the same reference point of everyday communicative practice which is intended under different titles such as 'practice', 'customary ethics', or 'life'. At an earlier stage this was called the need for enlightenment, for enlightenment concerning collective interests and one's own; and philosophy still seems better equipped for this purpose than other disciplines. Furthermore, philosophy can play the role of a stand-in within the human sciences, holding open possibilities of universalistic questioning, encouraging bold theoretical strategies, and contributing to the analysis of the rational foundations of knowledge, speech and action.

In recent years we have seen certain philosophical currents exert a more powerful influence on the life-world, not only in France, with its stronger cultural traditions, but also in Germany. Here what is at stake are questions of how one should live one's life, questions of the significance and the dangers of reason. It is quite astonishing that in many of these projects, which are also controversial in other respects, Nietzsche plays an important role. In 1968, as editor of a volume of Nietzsche's epistemological writings, you remarked laconically that Nietzsche was no longer contagious [2] ...

... I was mistaken there ...

Doesn't this Nietzsche renaissance awaken extremely ambivalent memories, for example of the history of his influence within National Socialism, even though it was already noted at the time that a few Nietzschean motifs had been substituted for the 'whole Nietzsche'?

---

2. See 'Zur Nietzsches Erkenntnistheorie', postscript to Friedrich Nietzsche, *Erkenntnistheoretische Schriften*, Frankfurt 1968. Reprinted in Jürgen Habermas, *Kultur und Kritik: Verstreute Aufsätze*, Frankfurt 1973, pp. 239–263.

It is through the reception of authors such as Foucault and Derrida that Nietzsche has once more become a virulent influence on ways of looking at the world, for the first time in the history of the Federal Republic. Of course, he has always been present on the academic scene in recent decades, but now he is influential not through particular insights in the domain of epistemology or the critique of ideology, but as the author of *Zarathustra*, above all as the author of *The Birth of Tragedy*, in other words as the Dionysian thinker who settles accounts with the West. How far the Nietzsche of *The Will to Power*, or rather of the aphorisms from the *Nachlass*, which could certainly only have had the historical effects they did in the compilation prepared by Elizabeth Förster-Nietzsche, how far this ideologically exploited Nietzsche is playing a role today I would not venture to judge. Presumably a few of the old Nietzsche fans are creeping out of their holes, and now publicly expressing the elitist phantasies which they always had in their heads. But the Nietzsche who comes to us mediated through France is rather the aestheticist, playful Nietzsche, thoroughly critical in posture, even if the implications are ultimately hostile to reason. This, of course, is a different Nietzsche from any the Nazis could have lived with. I take this reception of Nietzsche entirely seriously. This is one of the reasons why I am about to begin a series of lectures in France on the 'discourse of modernity', in which I want to engage with French colleagues, who have indeed been extremely productive. During the last ten years of my life in a research institute, I have not taken all this as seriously as I should have. But that was a mistake.

The question of the possible influence of philosophy can also be posed from another, more primitive, but not necessarily less effective angle. After and in addition to the abandonment of universal interpretations of the world, there is a further test for critical thought: the new conservatism which—along a broad front, above all in the Federal Republic—expresses its wish to revoke the claims of the Enlightenment through what are at times militant demands, and would prefer most of all no longer to permit any critical understanding of problems—whether in everyday life or in science—at all. The strivings of this counter-enlightenment are directed towards a ban on thought. Critical thought is seen as a kind of sickness, a pathology, which always appears whenever people no longer think in conformity with the rules.

Such turnarounds in the intellectual climate, of the kind which have taken place in the whole Western hemisphere since the mid-seventies, are not autonomous developments, but rather reflections of shifts in the political and social order.

What arguments are employed in this context to stake out the terrain of permissible thought?

There are extreme examples. I remember the autumn of 1977, when the 'League for Freedom in Science' made public a list of names of university teachers, who were denounced, in phantasy terms, as being liable to establish links with the terrorist underground. Such things serve as an aid to the *Verfassungsschutz*, which neo-conservatives generally provide with somewhat more subtle means, and in less dramatic circumstances than at that time. Furthermore, the neo-conservative theses which have become influential through the press are tailored to justifying the form of life created by capitalist modernization. The ideology-planning which is envisaged for this purpose has been summarized by Peter Sloterdijk as: a halt to reflection and solid values [*Reflexionsstopp und feste Werte*]. I find it difficult at the moment to warm over this whole theme, which I have in fact treated extensively elsewhere.

Let me ask what the change of regime in the Federal Republic means, about the social and political background to these neo-conservative trends. Is it an alteration of social attitudes which is expressed here, an alteration of political orientation? What kind of explanation can we give for the slide to the right in parliament?

First of all, it has to be said that changes of regime in periods of major economic difficulties are perfectly normal. Without Strauss's candidature, the changeover would probably have taken place two years earlier. What is more interesting is the weakening of the Social Democratic Party. I do not consider its internal divisions at all reprehensible. It is the only one of the established parties whose sense-receptors are still open; it is still sensitive to the kinds of problems which agencies concerned simply with acquiring and retaining power push to one side. The weakness of the SPD is also a consequence of its democratic strength, which consists in the fact that it does not hush up a central social conflict, but at least experiences it in its own body, even if it cannot resolve it. In one respect, the SPD represents the successes of post-war development in the Federal Republic, insofar as—with its right hand—it stubbornly defends the welfare-state compromise, which has indeed secured internal peace in a practical way during the last three decades. In another respect it is doing penance for the unwanted side-effects of these successes, insofar as—with its left hand—it even intensifies the neo-conservative critique of the welfare state, without being able to counterpose a productive answer to the false prescriptions of the other side. I don't have any answers either, by the way. But let me at least attempt to explain the problem as clearly as possible.

From the subjective perspective of the economically active citizen, the welfare-state compromise consisted in the fact that one earned enough and received sufficient social security to come to terms with the stress of more or less alienated labour, with the frustration of a more or less neutralized political role as a citizen, with the paradoxes of mass consumption—for example during an annual holiday spent as a tourist—and with the uneasiness of a client relationship to the bureaucracies. This compromise is at present endangered from two directions. It is obvious that neo-Keynesian economic policies are no longer sufficient to ensure the growth which is necessary to secure full employment, and to inhibit conflicts over distribution. A loss of real income for the mass of the population, unemployment and poverty for a growing minority, the collapse of companies, and at the same time improved conditions for investment, even rising rates of profit, for a small minority—these are the obvious signals of the abandonment of compromise. In a less obvious way, however, the welfare-state compromise is also being abandoned from another direction.

What I am thinking of here are the problems which have been taken up by the Greens, in the counter-cultures, and in the new social movements—namely the costs of capitalist modernization, and the breakdown of a policy of war-prevention based on strategic calculation rather than on the generalization of consensus. These two things are more and more experienced as *absurd* threats, as *bewitched* dangers, the more each grows and grows and grows: both the forces of production and abstract wealth, as well as the forces of destruction and the stockpile of weapons. This seems all the more absurd, the more our experiential capacities, our fantasy, our imagination, our sense of responsibility, our understanding, our feelings—the range from love to hate for example—lag behind our technical power to control and destroy nature, and behind the complexity of the mesh of social relations. When the substance of the foundations of life, which had up till now been taken for granted, comes into question, whether in nature, in the urban environment, in the family environment, or in the school, then phenomena of withdrawal and experiences of deprivation result, around which new lines of conflict emerge.

Thus, the welfare-state compromise is being put into question from these two directions—and Social Democracy, as both the advocate of this compromise and the diagnostician of its growing costs, is being pulled in different directions. It must either justify a defiant continuation of these policies—that is the perspective of the conservative apparatchiks in the SPD; or it must find a productive answer—without relying on the patent remedies of Reaganomics or Thatcherism. Let me add a couple of words about this.

Instead of too much state, a return to a bit more market—how could the problems suddenly be shifted back onto the market, when the long-term trend of increasing state income and state expenditure is only the symptom of a successful policy for the pacification of class conflict?

So are the old prescriptions to be taken up again, against new problems like unemployment, conflicts over distribution, the possible outbreak of class conflict, against the threatened disintegration of mass loyalty and the safety net of welfare? What shape are these prescriptions in?

The old prescriptions, which our present regime is working its way through more and more energetically, basically require four additions. *Firstly*, a demand-oriented economic policy, which must be able to cope with mass unemployment, even in the long term. This could lead to a new segmentation of society into 'ins' and 'outs', in which the 'ins' are composed of socially privileged minorities, who form a majority over against those who have been expelled from the labour-process. The mentality of a majority of basically middle-class character, which is prepared to exclude a severely underprivileged minority, will one day only be describable in the vocabulary of social Darwinism, a vocabulary which even today has acquired a surprising new lease of life in the enthusiasm for elites, and in the invocation of a readiness for competition and for making one's own way.

The *second addition* consists in a traditionalism which—in the domains of cultural, educational and family policy, but not in media policy, which directly affects economic interests—backs secondary virtues, the positive features of the past, common sense, unbroken historical consciousness, conventional religiosity, in short which backs the natural order of things [*Naturwüchsigkeit*], a halt to reflection and solid values. Cultural modernity, by contrast, is experienced as subversive. Spiritual-moral renewal means a return to before the eighteenth century, which is seen as promising a wondrous regeneration of certainties, a cushion of tradition—in other words—which can take the strain wherever monetary and bureaucratic forms of direction break down.

The *third element* is, as it were, the opposite of Willy Brandt's slogan, 'Dare more Democracy'—not a direct dismantling of democracy, but attempts to free the state from the onerous constraints of legitimation, attempts to contract the circle of themes of public debate, to de-problematize the political consciousness of the populace, to disburden it of socio-political questions, with which either negative or utopian investments of future perspectives could be connected. The limitation of the right to demonstrate which has just been decided on must be set in this context. *Fourthly*, there belongs to this prescription, if not a deliberate sharpening of international tensions, at least the stimulation of the awareness of a growing external threat. Of course, the defence policies against outer and inner enemies must work in tandem. Both are dramatized at the same time: the threat posed by the Red Army, and by the troublemakers within the country. Nervous journalists in our country have been busy for months assimilating the forms of non-violent protest to the same legal status as the use of violence.

What chance do you think such a strategy has?

I would not dare to make a definitive judgement as to whether and to what extent such a neo-conservative politics can be successfully implemented. In the last decade and a half a remarkable change of attitude has taken place, not only among marginal groups, but also among the mass of the population. For example, the difficulties which Herr Genscher ran into during the change of regime can only be explained by the fact that demands for legitimacy are being made which are different from those of the fifties.[3] A change of regime which took place legally was not experienced as legitimate. The resistance to the census was a similar symptom.

The question of possible strategies for a solution can basically be posed in the context of a different set of themes: as a question of what socialism means under contemporary conditions, in a high-technology society with structural unemployment. Socialism, particularly in its Marxist version, made not only ethical and socio-political, but also scientific and historico-philosophical claims. In the nineteenth century there was an obvious basis for this, which made socialism's pathos and its force effective: an excess of available labour, new technologies, the setting up of factories, the breaking-down and mechanization of the labour process, and so on. This made necessary the uprooting of workers from the context of their daily lives, and led to a visible impoverishment of human beings. The pitiless exploitation, the brutality of factory and machine, the increase of labour time, without even the guarantee that the basic

---

3. Hans-Dietrich Genscher, the leader of the Free Democrats and Helmut Schmidt's coalition partner, switched his support to Helmut Kohl in September 1982, bringing about a change of regime without an election for the first time in the history of the Federal Republic. The result was a split in the Free Democratic Party, and the resignation of its general secretary, Günther Verhengen.

necessities of life would be provided, the extremely low life expectancy, injuries caused by negligence—all this reveals the dark side of immiseration very clearly. Socialism as the revolutionary solution to these grievances was obvious, and needed no additional justification: only proletarian revolution could offer the workers the prospect of securing their own survival through the control of production. This transparency of the whole system entered into Marx's theory. The experience of misery forces the exploited and deprived into solidarity, and brings it about that oppression becomes an educative process.

The contemporary situation is not only the outcome of different developments, but shows that the conflicts have been held in check, the class struggle frozen. Disagreeable labour is tied up through the welfare system with more than just the satisfaction of primary needs; consumerism beckons in the form of a range of goods which package happiness and satisfaction for every need.

Today we also face the menace of another development which strikes at the basis of such a clear opportunity for socialism: work is becoming increasingly scarce, is itself becoming redundant, and with this the model of the oppressed worker, who is forced into an educative solidarity, dissolves. Unemployment due to increases in productivity and automation, a stabilized international division of labour, which more and more 'exports' disproportions and inequalities—these developments in the highly industrialized societies force us to consider more precisely what socialism means at the level attained by modern standards of living, and their attendant dangers, against the background of much increased 'free time', and of the unmistakable consequences of industrialization, of forms of economy whose necessary growth has never been truly or fundamentally challenged by Marxists. Are there new forms of solidarity? Is there an indignation which is aroused not by conditions of material need, but by the total moral condition of such an economy? Or do we quite simply face the threat of a forcible and violent—albeit controllable—division of society, centred on the sharing out of a limited supply of work, and the privileges generated by a new scarcity?

The substance of those expectations which were connected with the concept of socialism in the workers' movement has not been realized. But one should only say that when one has taken note, with due respect, of what has nevertheless been achieved historically. Merely because we have the side-effects of a terribly brutal process of modernization before our eyes, we should not forget what have today become trivial acquisitions—by this I mean not only the level of subsistence of the masses, but also the democratic and constitutional achievements of citizens. Indeed, the fact that one only becomes aware of these acquisitions when they are threatened is a circumstance which merits philosophical attention. What I am thinking of is the peculiar tracelessness of a particular type of progress, as a result of which progress does not become something bad, but rather something subjectively unreal. Material improvements—for the generations who lived through the economic upswing of the post-war period, these have a biographical obviousness of course—bear, so to speak, the sign of a loss of historical memory on their brow. Thirty days annual holiday or the first car once meant an eminent increase in private mobility and satisfaction—they were goals for the sake of which we accepted struggle, even sacrifice. But a level of satisfaction, once attained, eliminates, as it were, the traces of the history of its own appearance. Specific achievements, real emancipation from constraints of nature or society, must obviously be symbolically preserved if they are to be snatched from the fate of forgetfulness, of absorption into the stifling, ahistorical, 'bad' present of an endless pressing forward. Utopias are important, perhaps we will even speak about this later; but memory is just as important, anamnesis, ever if not in such a demanding sense as Benjamin's anamnetic solidarity. We need a symbolic form of representation for those things for which we have fought, for which a collective effort was required. What is terrifying about material progress, even about political and constitutional progress among people who have not fought through a revolution, is this traceless disappearance of the historical path. It is terrifying both for past suffering and past sacrifice, which, without the possibility of a reconciling rememoration, is as good as lost, and for the identity of those who come later, who, without an awareness of the heritage which they have entered into, can have no idea of who they are.

The work-based society [Arbeitsgesellschaft] prioritized the development of labour as a technical system. The solidarity acquired through shared experiences is disappearing more and more, and is replaced by other domains organized on technological lines (for example, consumerism, the mass media). And yet it is still the case that the problem of progress is explained either in terms of the compulsion peculiar to technology, or simply in terms of inadequate control, so that technology then appears as a neutral force which merely needs to be applied in a rational way in order to have a liberating effect. What you are saying points towards an unexplored and unconsciously functioning domain: that progress is achieved through the extinction of remembrance, and is consolidated by means of it. In this sense there would be no 'neutral' technology.

Yes, 'extinction of remembrance' is a good expression. In the list of questions you sent me, you spoke about the 'lack of images of happiness', and asserted that 'on the iconographic level, images of happiness are not to be found in the industrial, but only in the artisanal and the familial domains.' This is perhaps a key to the extinction of remembrance in all societies based on industrial labour. Industrial labour is haunted by the telos of its own abolition. If you go into the assembly-shop of a factory which produces television sets nowadays, you will see that the few tasks which are still carried out by (female) labour power are already moribund—a residue left over from the tempestuous advance of technical rationalization. And you can also already identify the tasks which, in a few years' time, will no longer be carried out by living labour. Where the physical movements of the human organism become appendages of electronically controlled installations, tasks are performed in the anticipation that they will disappear without trace. Perhaps human labour has been confronted with the prospect of its own elimination ever since the first breaking-down of labour processes in manufacture. This objective state of affairs will probably only enter the consciousness of the broader public v hen not only sociology conferences, but the mass media, tackle the fact which Dahrendorf has reduced to a pregnant formula: that work is disappearing from the work-based society. At the last German sociology conference in Bamberg Claus Offe addressed this question. He demonstrated very convincingly that the facts of work, production and income are less and less determining the state of society as a whole.

Is the sphere of work and production losing its structurational force? Can one say, despite the continuing wage-dependence of the overwhelming majority of the population, that, on the individual and on the global level, work is losing its central significance?

If, like Offe, you give a positive answer to this question, then there are consequences for the theory of society, which has in fact been centred, since Marx, around concepts such as praxis and labour. It is for this reason that I have proposed the use of the concept of communicative action as a key to theory-construction, so that we can get a better grip on the structures of the life-world. And above all on the menacing of this life-world by bureaucratic and economic imperatives, dangers which arise from the fact that ever more personal relations, services and phases of life are being transformed into objects of administration, or into commodities. Even what the Greek philosophers once honoured as the founding elements of nature—water, earth, air, sun and shade—one must buy for oneself, as a tourist, by the slice.

The end of the work-based society, if I can use this slogan, is throwing up problems which so far have not been properly analysed. But they are experienced as problems by everyone.

I have already mentioned the first problem. Two colleagues, Herr Esser and Herr Fach, have indicated developments which suggest that the Federal Republic is moving towards a 'split' society, with a productive core of the employed, and an expanding margin of the poorly fed and neglected, who are forced into subcultures and ghettos. The decisive political question of the next few years will be whether this process can be kept out of the public gaze, or will become the focus of political confrontations—and which side, if the problem is explicitly dealt with, will win out: the selfish interests of a majority which is prepared to defend its possessions tooth and nail—we have had a foretaste of this in the struggle around the maintenance of the tripartite school system in recent years,[4] or in the doctors' protest in Paris; or rather the solidarity of those who are still on the inside with those who have been left out. This will also—and perhaps in the first instance—depend on whether the trade unions go in for a 'closed shop' policy on the American model, or whether they take up the solidaristic traditions of the workers' movement. In this case, too, political culture could be more important than political economy. Will our society insist on preserving its existing structures, and prefer to put up with what Gorz calls a 'non-class of non-workers', or—as Marx puts it—'to feel at ease in alienation'? Or has the rat-race society, has capitalism, through the unleashing of competitive struggle, of an orientation towards achievement, and of self-assertive energies, fulfilled its historical mission—namely, the creation of an ensemble of productive forces which has long ago surpassed the utopian imaginings of the last century?

What is crucial here is how one analyses this set of questions. The *second problem* is therefore of a more theoretical nature. Is the potential for development of the work-based society in the advanced industrial countries of the West also exhausted in the sense that the process of transforming traditional domains of activity into organized occupational systems with monetary rewards is coming up against a critical limit? Curiously enough, up till now there have always been domains where capitalism has not intruded—thus, for example, the professionalization of the role of mother or housewife could monetarize the enormous domain of childcare and housework within the family. And yet one has

---

4. Up until recently, secondary education in the Federal Republic has been divided between three types of school, with selection at the age of ten: the *Volksschule* for those destined for manual trades, a *Mittelschule* for those likely to take up clerical jobs, and the *Gymnasium* preparing pupils for higher education. Attempts to alter this system, mainly in social-democratic *Länder*, through the introduction of a *Gesamtschule*, have encountered middle-class resistance.

rather the impression that the mechanism of the labour market is breaking down in the face of the social need for certain types of activity. At present, for example, we have neither too few teachers, nor too many superfluous teachers, but too few paid teachers, who are able to do the work they would like to do, and which is also needed. This picture can quickly alter as a result of demographic developments. But the problem remains. For one thing, the need for socially necessary labour seems to be shifting into domains which are unfamiliar with activities modelled on industrial labour, which rather demand communicative interaction with persons; for another, this need is shifting into domains which do not fit into the organizational forms of industrial and administrative enterprise.

Here I am thinking of social and educational tasks, also political ones, which cannot be transposed into formal occupational structures, because they do not offer a profit; but which also cannot be organized as services, because this would deliver up the life-world even more to the clutches of experts. Nowadays, for example, we speak of work concerned with relationships, also of 'political work'—just think of the time-consuming, highly intensive decision-making processes which would be needed in tenants' associations, in neighbourhoods, in communes, in order to arrange the collective life of different gener-ations—for example—in such a way that the negative effects of nuclear family structures, whose advantages we would not wish to abandon, could be compensated for—in relation to the elderly, to children, to the handicapped and frail, to those afflicted by loneliness, and so on. I mean this in a quite unsentimental way: I doubt whether the market is still appropriate for identifying the work which is really needed, and for satisfying this need within socially recognized forms of labour.

What has up till now been productive labour from the capitalist standpoint, therefore, stands opposed not only to social recognition, but also to the value of social activities which no longer fit into the available forms of recognition and evaluation.

This is connected with the *third problem*, the revaluation of activities. So called 'free time' [*arbeitsfreie Zeit*] is increasing, not only on a weekly basis, but also over the span of the individual's life-history, and yet the areas of life which lie outside of formal occupations are still only defined privately, in relation to a sphere of labour which is becoming more and more obsolete. How can society be reconstructed from the foundations up so that, not only from the perspective of the economy as a whole, but also from the standpoint of the individual life-history, a shift of emphasis can take place? As Offe suggests, what counts as productive labour is above all remunerative activity in an economic enterprise, which takes the form of a processing of things, and can be divided up into abstract operations. In contrast to this, one should consider the type of 'work' in which energies of which we are scarcely aware, and yet which are not inconsiderable, take on a meaningful form, of the kind which today come together in a women's group, for example, or in a local social democratic party, where—despite all good intentions—they tend to be damped down, in other words, both canalized and neutralized.

So, different and differently characterized forms of distribution would be necessary, another basis for the social recognition of necessary and neglected activities. What does socialism mean, then, when its strategy can no longer start from production, as was obviously necessary in an earlier period?

I have the impression that, judged in terms of real needs and capacities, the allocation mechanisms for the distribution of socially recognized labour are no longer working. Nor do I have any answers which could be treated as recipes. I merely think that one can only achieve a clear image of socialism under present conditions when one thinks such questions through. Socialism used to mean making an attempt, which was as fallibilist and as open to self-correction as possible, to at least reduce identifiable suffering, identifiable injustice, avoidable repressions, in other words, to resolve through collective efforts, and from a specific perspective, problems which have to be dealt with and resolved as one goes along anyway. This perspective can be easily characterized in abstract terms: namely, to arrest the destruction of solidaristic forms of life and to generate new forms of solidaristic collective life—in other words, life-forms with possibilities for expression, with space for moral-practical orientations, life-forms which offer a context within which one's own identity and that of others can be unfolded less problematically, and in a less damaged way. This is a perspective which has emerged from the self-criticism of the life-forms which were established by capitalist modernization, and which are predominant today.

Well, there is at least a long tradition of decisions concerning development based on different convictions: the utopias. It is precisely socialism, however—particularly in the scientific forms defended by followers of Marx—which has had a broken and negative relation to the utopian. Eventually technological development, the state of the productive forces, overlook the images of utopia. Even Herbert Marcuse has pointed to the 'end of utopia' in this context. Our relation to utopias is characterized in both these respects by a kind of prohibition of images. More recently, however, the necessity of utopian orientations has been increasingly appealed to, and from an irritating variety of directions. Utopian thought is recommended as a form of correction, although with regard to such corrections it is difficult to know whether the utopian image has a right to be tested through an attempt to put it into practice. What kind of function does the drawing up of utopias have today?

Utopias have a practical function to the extent that they enter into social movements in the form of orientations. Bloch, for example, used the formula 'walking tall' with the gaze of a utopian. Society should be such that everyone can walk tall, even the long-suffering and the heavy-laden, the deprived and the degraded. In this context the use of utopian image serves to introduce a precisely defined concept, namely that of human dignity. Dignity was once, of course, a feudal category. Dignity meant that one possessed a certain status within a hierarchical order, and behaved in a manner appropriate to this status—it is in this mediaeval sense, for example, that the Pope has dignity. Compared to this, one could perhaps characterize the show-business style of an itinerant tamer of the masses as undignified.

By contrast, human dignity has been more abstractly conceived in rational natural law, and in modern philosophy in general. Every individual should be unmolested in his or her autonomy, protected in his or her physical and spiritual integrity. This universalistic concept can be derived from the metaphor of walking tall through a process of conceptual sharpening. This is an example of the critical function of promissory images in theoretical contexts. Promissory—dignity must be taken over from the feudal world where only representative figures walk tall, and transposed into the bourgeois and socialist world, where even the deprived and heavy-laden may walk tall, here and now, and not just in the beyond.

Ernst Bloch always said that utopia gets a bad press. Today we are rather confronted with a inflationary use of the word . . .

. . . by Ernst Bloch, amongst others . . .

. . . which is not made conceptually viable, but which apparently links up with new forms of sensibility. A sensibility, for example, for what you term the dessication of life-worlds and communicative traditions. On the other hand, it is becoming clear how insidious appeals to utopia can be. Utopia is taken as justifying the individual's projection of phantasy worlds, which aim at nothing less than a boundless whole. This seems to be something different from the critical, and therefore self-critical, potential of utopian thought.

In specific historical moments, where we can recognize a real social movement, real historical struggles, we also become aware that people do not fight for abstractions—despite the three great and ineradicable goals of the French Revolution. People do not fight *for* abstractions, but *with* images. Banners, symbols and images, rhetorical speech, allegorical speech, utopia-inspired speech, in which concrete goals are conjured up before people's eyes, are indeed necessary constituents of movements which have any effect on history at all. Everything else, by comparison, is re-working and stasis.

Even in conceptual thought, however, most obviously in the domains of philosophy, of the social and human sciences, but even in physics, the language of theory is not free of pictorial, metaphorical, or indeed mythical elements. There is no language which is exclusively conceptual. This is what could be called the mythical kernel of even scientific discourse, although here the image is conceptually tamed. A philosopher like Bloch can then make out a strong case for the necessity of moving back and forth between theoretical language, where the intention is to proceed purely discursively, simply because there are problems to be solved, and a receptivity to the pictorial language which is more central to everyday life, which is at any rate rooted in everyday experiences.

When constructive utopian thought aims at the interpretation of totalities, there remains a lingering critical suspicion that this totality covers over deficiencies and side-effects. Doesn't this critique, in its emancipatory intention, turn against the very idea of utopia?

There are good reasons for that, I think. Utopias are often depicted forms of life. In other words, they are outlines of totalities. As such, they cannot be theoretically retrieved. I do not believe there are any theoretically-based utopias. Whenever one portrays totalities, whole forms of life, whole life-histories, whole areas of life in their concretion, and suggests that these can be directly politically realized, the result can easily be the kind of consequences which our neo-conservative friends have indicated. This is why, in the socialist tradition, a certain abstinence has been practised with regard to the depiction of concrete forms of life. One should only speak of socialism in the sense of an attempt, in the historical conditions in which one finds oneself, to indicate the necessary conditions which would have to be fulfilled in order for emancipated life-forms to emerge—whatever they may be. Totalities only appear in the plural, and this pluralism cannot be anticipated in theory.

Is an understanding of utopia sufficient for this purpose which aims at a system of freely developed conceptions of the good life, at a kind of minimal state which allows individuals to realize their own utopias, and to enter into agreement with one another by way of regenerative life-forms?

Those are liberal ideas, which have an honourable history. I would in fact retain an element of this tradition. That degree of legal equality should be achieved which will allow at the same time the greatest possible measure of individualism, and this means space for individuals to shape their own lives. However, one cannot simply forget the kinds of criticism of these individualistic constructions of law which have been brought forward ever since Hegel. Freedom, even personal freedom, freedom of choice in the last instance, can only be thought in internal connection with a network of interpersonal relationships, and this means in the context of the communicative structures of a community, which ensures that the freedom of some is not achieved at the cost of the freedom of others. Interestingly, abstract right is not sufficient for this purpose. One must make the effort to analyse the conditions of collective freedom, which remove the dangers of individual freedom, its potential for social-Darwinistic menace.

The individual cannot be free unless all are free, and all cannot be free unless all are free in community. It is this last proposition which one misses in the empiricist and individualist traditions.

6

A Philosophico-Political
Profile

I

Could you tell us something of the sequence of the principal intellectual influences on your work? You are often represented as an heir of the Frankfurt School who gave its legacy a 'linguistic turn', with a move from a philosophy of consciousness to one of language. Is this an accurate image—or did your interest in, at least, the American pragmatism of Dewey and Peirce actually predate your encounter with the work of Adorno and Horkheimer? In what period did you start to reflect on the ideas of Wittgenstein or Austin? Similarly, in the social sciences, was your concern with Weber or Parsons subsequent to an earlier, primarily Marxist, orientation—or did these coexist from the outset? What were the seasons of your engagement with the phenomenological tradition of Schütz, or the genetic psychology of Piaget and Kohlberg?

Apart from the summer semester in Zurich, I studied in Göttingen and Bonn between 1949 and 1954. As far as my areas of study were concerned, there was an almost unbroken continuity of subject-matter and personnel stretching back through the Nazi period to the Weimar Republic. It is not at all the case that the German universities were opened up to outside influences immediately after the War. Thus, from the academic standpoint, I grew up in a provincial German context, in the world of German philosophy, in the form of a declining Neo-Kantianism, of the German Historical School, of phenomenology, and also philosophical anthropology. The most powerful systematic impulse came from the early Heidegger. As students we were familiar with Sartre and French existentialism, perhaps also a few works of American cultural anthropology. While working on my dissertation on Schelling I naturally read the young Marx. Löwith's *From Hegel to Nietzsche* encouraged me to read the young Hegelians; Lukács's *History and Class*

Consciousness also made a strong impression on me. These first intrusions of 'left-wing literature' did have the result that I rounded out my dissertation, which was strongly influenced by Heidegger, with an introduction setting late German Idealism in relation to Marx. Directly after my studies I became familiar with industrial sociology. I was then given a grant to do work on the concept of ideology—this gave me the chance to penetrate somewhat deeper into Hegelian Marxism and the sociology of knowledge, and I also read Adorno's *Prisms* and the *Dialectic of Enlightenment.* In Frankfurt, from 1956 in other words, Bloch and Benjamin were added, along with a few articles from the *Zeitschrift für Sozialforschung,* Marcuse's books, and a discussion— which was very lively at the time—around the so-called philosophical and anthropological Marx. A little later I tackled *Das Kapital* seriously, and in this connection I also read Dobb, Sweezy and Baran. I also learned sociology in these early Frankfurt years; above all I read empirical things on mass communications, political socialization, political sociology. At this point I first came into contact with Durkheim, Weber, and very cautiously with Parsons. More important than this were the Freud Lectures in 1956—since hearing the international elite, from Alexander and Spitz to Erikson and Binswanger, I have considered psychoanalysis, despite all the dire predictions, as something to be taken seriously.

During these years as Adorno's assistant, between 1956 and 1959, there evolved what later crystallized in the empirical investigations of *Student und Politik,* and in my first two books (*Strukturwandel der Öffentlichkeit* and *Theory and Practice*)—the attempt to continue the Hegelian and Weberian Marxism of the nineteen-twenties with other means. All this remained within the context of a very German tradition, or at least of one rooted in Germany—even though at the time, through my contact with Adorno and Horkheimer, and later with Abendroth and Mitscherlich, I lived with a sense of having grown into different, decisively broader horizons of experience, of having been freed from provincial narrowness and a naively idealistic world.

In Heidelberg, from 1961 on, Gadamer's *Truth and Method* helped me to find my way back into academic philosophy. Hermeneutics interested me, on the one hand, in connection with questions of the logic of the social sciences, and on the other in comparison with the later philosophy of Wittgenstein. This was the period, therefore, of my first more intensive involvement with linguistic philosophy and analytical philosophy of science. Encouraged by my friend Apel, I also studied Peirce, as well as Mead and Dewey. From the outset I viewed American pragmatism as the third productive reply to Hegel, after Marx and Kierkegaard, as the radical-democratic branch of Young Hegelianism, so to speak. Ever since, I have relied on this American version of the philosophy of praxis when the problem arises of compensating for the weaknesses of Marxism with respect to democratic theory. This inclination was also the basis of my later friendship with Dick Bernstein. In any event, when I returned to Frankfurt to take up Horkheimer's chair in 1964, I had a firm enough footing in Anglo-Saxon discussions to be able to distance myself from an overstrained concept of theory derived from Hegel.

In the mid-sixties Cicourel and ethnomethodology led me back to Schütz. At that time I viewed social phenomenology as a protosociology, carried out in the form of analyses of the life-world. This idea connected up with influences from another direction: I was fascinated both by Chomsky's programme for a general theory of grammar, and by Austinian speech-act theory, as systematized by Searle. All this suggested the idea of a universal pragmatics, with the aid of which I wanted above all to deal with the awkward fact that the normative foundations of the critical theory of society were entirely unclarified. Having rejected the orthodoxy of the philosophy of history, I had no wish to lapse back either into ethical socialism, or into scientism, or indeed into both at once. This explains why I hardly read Althusser. In the second half of the sixties, thanks to collaboration with accomplished co-workers like Offe and Oevermann, I worked my way into specific areas of sociology, primarily socialization and family research on the one hand, political sociology on the other. In the process I got to know Parsons better. I was already reading Piaget and Kohlberg, but it was only at our Starnberg Institute, that is, after 1971, that I became an adherent of genetic structuralism. It was also here that I first began a more intensive study of Weber.

So you can see that from the outset my theoretical interests have been consistently determined by those philosophical and sociotheoretical problems which arise out of the movement of thought from Kant through to Marx. My intentions and fundamental convictions were given their stamp by Western Marxism in the mid fifties, through a coming-to-terms with Lukács, Korsch and Bloch, Sartre and Merleau-Ponty, and of course with Horkheimer, Adorno and Marcuse. Everything else which I have made my own has only acquired its significance in connection with the project of a renewal of the theory of society grounded in this tradition.

In the twenty-five years since Strukturwandel der Öffentlichkeit, *you have produced a very large body of work, of increasing complexity and range, with impressive continuity of direction. At the same time, your thought has obviously also undergone certain alterations of substantive emphasis or conviction during this period. What do you regard as the most important such changes?*

The books which I published at the beginning of the sixties implicitly express the conviction that the things I wanted to do could be accommodated more or less within the inherited theoretical frame-work—in this respect I felt a special affinity with the existentialist, i.e. the Marcusean, variant of Critical Theory. What is more, Herbert Marcuse, with whom I became friends in the nineteen-sixties, felt the same way. I still remember the day when he dedicated a copy of *One Dimensional Man* to me with a flattering quote from Benjamin—'to the hope of those without hope'. However, the engagement with analytical philosophy, and also the positivist dispute, then reinforced my doubts about whether concepts of totality, of truth, and of theory derived from Hegel did not represent too heavy a mortgage for a theory of society which should also satisfy empirical claims. At that time, in Heidelberg and then back in Frankfurt, I believed that this problem was an epistemological one. I wanted to do away with it through a methodological clarification of the status of a doubly reflexive theory (reflexive with respect to its context of emergence and of application). The result was *Knowledge and Human Interests*, which was written between 1964 and 1968. I still consider the outlines of the argument developed in the book to be correct. But I no longer believe in epistemology as the *via regia*. The critical theory of society does not need to prove its credentials in the first instance in methodological terms; it needs a substantive foundation, which will lead out of the bottlenecks produced by the conceptual framework of the philosophy of consciousness, and overcome the paradigm of production, without abandoning the intentions of Western Marxism in the process. The result is *The Theory of Communicative Action*. In a brilliant article soon to be published in Britain,[1] Dick Bernstein expounds the particular problems which have forced me immanently to make repeated changes of position—away from 'know-ledge and human interests' to 'society and communicative rationality'.

What is your sense of the current intellectual conjuncture in the West? In 'Does Philosophy Still Have a Purpose?' you suggested that Germanic philosophical intensity and originality were migrating to the United States, while Europe relapsed into a placid 'Swissification'.[2] Would you

---

1. 'Introduction', in R. J. Bernstein, ed., *Habermas and Modernity*, Oxford 1985, pp. 1–32.
2. *Philosophical-Political Profiles*, London 1983, p. 8.

still hold to this judgement? More generally, most of your references in recent years have been along a German-American axis of comparison— as lately in your criticism of the different forms of neo-conservatism in the two countries. Is this due to biographical reasons, or does it express an underlying judgement about the predominance and relevance of these two cultures for the West as a whole in the late twentieth century? Would one be right in thinking that France and England, for example—central poles of reference in your treatment of bourgeois civilization in the eighteenth and nineteenth centuries in Strukturwandel—*have lost salience in your subsequent work?*

The reasons for this orientation towards developments in the USA are undoubtedly trivial—it is typical for the post-war generation of German philosophers and sociologists in general. Of course, there is also a background in power politics: the Federal Republic has come so close to being the 51st State of the Union that the only thing we still don't have is the right to vote. This total dependence has never before appeared so undisguisedly as it did in autumn 1983, with the stationing of missiles that was forced upon us. Nevertheless, I do in fact prefer a political culture which, like the American, dates from the eighteenth century. I marvel at the intellectual openness and readiness for discussion, this mixture of impartiality and engagement, that I find in American students more than here in Europe. For a German of my age and outlook there may also be the fact that in American universities we could follow very readily in the footsteps of German emigrants who had acquired a considerable reputation. In addition, the Institute for Social Research, where I have worked, eventually returned from the USA. And those members of the Institute who did not return—Marcuse, Löwenthal, Kirchheimer, Neumann and others—have made a big contribution to the dense web of personal and academic ties between here and over there. Today this web is in fact extending to a third generation of younger scholars.

Speaking of the younger people, it is evident that the influence of the French has been growing steadily for the last ten years or so. In questions of social theory, the most inventive impulses are coming from Paris—from people like Bourdieu, Castoriadis, Foucault, Gorz, Touraine and so on.

Finally, so far as England is concerned, you yourselves admit that I have been influenced by analytical philosophy. However, I would not wish to deny that there is a certain difference of climate between England and the Continent. There are no deep elective affinities between the spirit of empiricism, which is still dominant in your country, and German Idealism. A fermenting agent is lacking in the philosophical metabolism, which could mediate between the two mentalities—as pragmatism does, for example, in America. I believe I can detect this estrangement in basic philosophical convictions. For example, I observe a certain incomprehension in the way in which distinguished colleagues like Quentin Skinner or W. G. Runciman, even my friend Steven Lukes, write about my concerns. In their case the ontology of empiricism has become second nature. Of course there are also counter-examples such as Tony Giddens.

Recently you have argued that Horkheimer and Adorno can only find resistance to a totalized purposive rationality in the irrational mimetic powers of art and love, or in the 'impotent rage of nature in revolt'.[3] *Although these strictures do pinpoint a certain tendency of classical Critical Theory, it is not clear that they can be applied without qualification to the thought of Adorno, who always remained conscious of the danger of appeals to an unmediated nature. Is it possible that in your desire to distance yourself from an unremitting negativism, and to rehabilitate the collaborative and constructive conception of Critical Theory current during the 1930s, you have been led into polemical exaggerations, and have underplayed the extent to which Adorno remained fundamentally committed to the ideals of autonomy and enlightenment, even at his most desperate?*

I agree with you: at no point does Adorno and Horkheimer's critique of reason darken to a renunciation of what the great philosophical tradition, and in particular the Enlightenment, once intended, however vainly, by the concept of reason. Like Nietzsche, they both radicalize the critique of reason to the point of self-referentiality, in other words until this critique begins to undermine even its own foundations. But Adorno differs from the followers of Nietzsche, from Heidegger on the one hand and Foucault on the other, precisely in the fact that he no longer wishes to break out of the paradoxes of this critique of reason, which has now become as if subjectless—he wishes to endure in the performative contradiction of a negative dialectics, which directs the unavoidable medium of identifying and objectifying thought against itself. Through the exercise of endurance he believes himself to be remaining most nearly faithful to a lost, non-instrumental reason. This forgotten reason, belonging to prehistory, finds an echo only in the powers of a wordless mimesis. The mimetic can be circled around by negative dialectics, but it cannot—as Heidegger suggests—be revealed. The mimetic does allow

---

3. *The Theory of Communicative Action*, vol. 2, p. 333.

one to sense what it is performing the role of stand-in for, but it permits no knowledge of a structure which could be characterized as rational. To this extent, Adorno cannot appeal to any structure heterogeneous to instrumental reason, against which the force of totalized purposive rationality must collide. In the passage that you mention I am in the process of pinning down such a resistant structure, namely the structure of a rationality which is immanent in everyday communicative practice, and which brings the stubbornness of life-forms into play against the functional demands of autonomized economic and administrative systems.

Can Adorno, in his evocations of reconciliation, justly be accused of surreptitiously employing categories of intersubjectivity from which he abstains philosophically, and can what he terms 'love towards things' be simply reformulated in terms of undistorted communication? One might consider, for example, the following passage from Aesthetic Theory, *where Adorno seeks to evoke a reciprocal relation between nature and human technology, without in any way suggesting that nature could be legitimately viewed as a subject: 'After the abolition of scarcity, the expansion of the productive forces could occur in a dimension which is different from the quantitative increase of production. There are intimations of this in functional buildings that have been adapted to forms and lines in the surrounding landscape; or in old architecture where the raw materials for buildings were taken from the surrounding area, and fitted in with it, as is the case with many castles and châteaux. What is called "culture landscape" in German is beautiful as the schema of this possibility. A rationality which took up such motifs could help to close the wounds of rationality.'⁴ In the light of such passages, would it not be plausible to suggest that there is a relation of complementarity— rather than of substitution—between Adorno's explorations of the subject-object relation, and your own theory of communication?*

If I may say so, I find your suggestion, that Adorno's *Aesthetic Theory* and my theory of communication should be viewed simply as supplementing each other, a little too innocuous. On the other hand, neither can one theory simply replace the other, if for no other reason than that I have said very little about aesthetic matters.

Albrecht Wellmer, who has a far more thorough understanding of these questions, has shown, in an outstanding discussion of 'Truth,

---

4. *Aesthetic Theory*, London 1984, pp. 69–70 (translation modified).

Illusion and Reconciliation',[5] how Adorno's aesthetic utopia 'turns sour', so to speak, once its connection with the philosophy of history of the *Dialectic of Enlightenment* is dissolved. If this is done, Adorno's aesthetic insights become independent of the metaphysical thesis that, with every new advance of subjectification, humanity becomes ever more deeply entangled in reification. To this negative view belongs the perspective, extended into a positive, of a reconciliation of human productivity with nature, which you recall in your quotation. Adorno's appeal to '*die Liebe zu den Dingen*' is not without irony, and yet in earnest. This love is a utopian counter-image to the despairing belief that subjectivity 'works towards its own extinction by the force of its own logic'. A theory of communication which breaks with the conceptual framework of the philosophy of subjectivity undermines this 'logic', this apparently indissoluble internal relation between emancipation and subjugation. More specifically, it discovers that there is already a mimetic moment in everyday practices of communication, and not merely in art. Allow me to put this in Wellmer's words: 'This must remain hidden to a philosophy which, like Adorno's, understands the function of concepts in terms of the polarity of subject and object; it cannot recognize, behind objectifying functions of language, communicative performances which are the condition of its own possibility. For this reason, it can only understand mimesis as the other of rationality ... In order for the prior unity of the mimetic and the rational moment in the foundations of language to be recognized, a paradigm-shift is required ... For if intersubjectivity of understanding, communicative action are no less constitutive of the sphere of mind than the objectification of reality in contexts of instrumental action, then the utopian perspective which Adorno seeks to elucidate with the concept of an unforced synthesis derived from the philosophy of consciousness, migrates into the sphere of discursive reason itself: undamaged intersubjectivity, the unforced togetherness of many, which would make possible a simultaneous nearness and distance, identity and difference of individuals, indicate a utopian projection whose elements discursive reason derives from the conditions of its own linguisticality.'[6]

In a number of recent essays you have passed sharp judgements on post-structuralism, suggesting that the French post-structuralists must be seen as 'Young Conservatives' who 'on the basis of modernistic attitudes ...

---

5. L. v. Friedeburg, J. Habermas, eds., *Adorno-Konferenz 1983*, Frankfurt 1983, pp. 138 ff.
    6. Ibid., p. 150.

justify an irreconcilable anti-modernism'.[7] *Could you expand on this assessment, if necessary drawing distinctions between different post-structuralist thinkers? And could you explain the discrepancy between your condemnation of post-structuralism, and your comparatively friendly reception of the work of Richard Rorty, which provides parallels to, and has in some cases been directly influenced by, post-structuralist themes?*

As you will see from my lectures on the philosophical discourse of modernity, which are due to appear shortly, 'condemnation' is not the appropriate word for my attitude towards post-structuralism. There are, of course, many similarities between negative dialectics and the procedures of deconstruction on the one hand, between the critique of instrumental reason and the analysis of formations of discourse and power on the other. The playful-subversive element of a critique of reason which is conscious of its own paradoxical self-referentiality, and the exploitation of experiential possibilities which were first revealed by the aesthetic avant-garde—these two things characterize a Nietzschean style of thought and presentation, which founds the spiritual kinship of Adorno with Derrida on the one hand, and with Foucault on the other. What separates him from these two figures, as from Nietzsche himself— and this seems to me to be politically decisive—is simply this: Adorno does not merely bale out of the *counter*-discourse which has inhabited modernity ever since the beginning; rather, in his desperate adherence to the procedure of determinate negation, he remains true to the idea that there is no cure for the wounds of Enlightenment other than the radicalized Enlightenment itself. Unlike Nietzsche and his disciples, Adorno has no illusions about the genuinely modern origins of aesthetic experience, in whose name modernity falls victim to a levelling, undialectical critique.

As far as Richard Rorty is concerned, I am no less critical of his contextualist position. But at least he does not climb aboard the 'antihumanist' bandwaggon, whose trail leads back in Germany to figures as politically unambiguous as Heidegger and Gehlen. Rorty retains from the pragmatist inheritance, which in many, though not all, respects he unjustly claims for himself, an intuition which links us together—the conviction that a humane collective life depends on the vulnerable forms of innovation-bearing, reciprocal and unforcedly

---

7. 'Modernity versus Post-Modernity', *New German Critique* No. 22, Winter 1981, p. 13. Reprinted as 'Modernity—an Incomplete Project', in Hal Foster, ed., *Postmodern Culture*, London 1985, p. 14.

egalitarian everyday communication. This intuition is even more alien to Derrida and Foucault than to Adorno (who also remained a romantic of course, and not just as a composer).

The question of post-structuralism has an obvious importance at the present time, given the increasing penetration of this style of thought into the Federal Republic. What do you consider to be the reasons for this success, and what are your feelings about the repatriation of the thought of Nietzsche and Heidegger in post-structuralist form?

The influence of post-structuralism on the German universities is undoubtedly also connected with the situation in the academic job-market. The horizon of expectations of the younger intellectuals has become so gloomy that a negativistic mood has become widespread, which in part even flips over into apocalyptic anticipations of revival. Social reality is doing something further: it is not miserly in the creation of ever new dangers which, even on calmer consideration, appear as side-effects of purposive-rational action, thus as dangers which we have brought upon ourselves. For this reason theories which grasp the whole as the untrue, and offer the affirmation of the impossibility of escape as the only affirmation possible, not only match the mood of the critique of civilization—they also have an increasing reality-content. After all, how ought one to respond to the spectacle of the last American election, in which all levels of reality triumphantly intermingled: in which a play-actor president reveals to an enraptured public that, despite all asseverations of leadership and he-manship, he is merely playing at being president, and is promptly returned to office? To that kind of thing one can only reply with the cynical antics of the deconstructionists.

The situation is a little different with Heidegger, who still tends to inspire a holy terror in this country. The latest return of a felicitously de-Nazified Heidegger is, of course, based on the ahistorical reception of Heidegger in France and America—where he stepped on stage after the War, like a phoenix from the ashes, as the author of the 'Letter on Humanism'.

The suspicion of system in philosophy is characteristic of many currents in twentieth century thought. Scepticism about the possibility of philosophy as an ordered body of truths is characteristic of thinkers as diverse as Wittgenstein, Merleau-Ponty and Adorno. How would you defend the need for, and possibly of, systematic philosophy against these deeply rooted objections?

Since Hegel's death philosophical systems are no longer to be had with good conscience. Any thinker who, in the twentieth century, has asserted and practised the death, the supersession, the end, or the disbanding of philosophy, has therefore simply been belatedly carrying out a decree which was issued by the first generation of Young Hegelians. Ever since then philosophical thought has sought to step over into another medium. In this respect we have all remained contemporaries of the Young Hegelians—all post-modern ambitions notwithstanding. 'After Philosophy'—the title of a collection of essays which Tom McCarthy is planning—characterizes a situation which, for me, has become so self-evident that I consider the grand gestures of the anti-systematists to be pretty superfluous. Any philosophical work implicitly renounces thinking in systems which weaves itself into the ramified network of the human and social sciences, without fundamentalist claims and with a fallibilistic consciousness, in order to contribute something of use whenever the problem of the presumptively universal features of knowledge, speech and action arises.

One of the most obvious general developments in your work has been the increasing prominence of the arguments and procedures of analytical philosophy. Could you explain the reasons for this transformation? What resources are offered by analytical philosophy which cannot be provided by other traditions, including the major German traditions?

In general, the example of analytical philosophy has been a salutary force in post-war German philosophy for no other reason than that it demanded a higher level of explicitness. I have learned most from Wittgenstein, Austin and Searle—as you know, I find instruments in their work for the investigation of general pragmatic presuppositions of the use of propositions in utterances.

One of the most prominent developments in English-speaking philosophy over the last ten years or so has been the emergence of new, substantive works of political philosophy (Rawls, Nozick, Dworkin, Walzer) and of a widespread debate around them. How significant do you consider this development? And do you feel that it would be appropriate for you to make a more direct intervention into this debate than you have so far, given that the concerns of these thinkers in many respects overlap with your own?

Besides speech-act theory, I could also have mentioned moral philosophy, at least the line of thought (from Baier and Singer to Rawls) in which the substance of Kantian ethics is retrieved in a certain way in terms of linguistic philosophy. More recently, I myself have explained the discourse ethics approach, which Apel and I favour, more thorough-ly.[8] This approach is an attempt to reconstruct Kantian ethics with the help of the theory of communication. The suggestions which I have reworked in this process derive above all from Rawls and Kohlberg. When I initiated a discussion of civil disobedience last year, in response to contemporary events, the work of Rawls and Dworkin provided the most important points of reference. If you are under the impression that I have not been sufficiently engaged on this front, this may be the result of my somewhat restricted understanding of the task of philosophical ethics.

According to my conception, the philosopher ought to explain the moral point of view, and—as far as possible—justify the claim to universality of this explanation, showing why it does not merely reflect the moral intuitions of the average, male, middle-class member of a modern Western society. Anything further than that is a matter for moral discourse between participants. Insofar as the philosopher would like to justify specific principles of a normative theory of morality and politics, he should consider this as a proposal for the discourse between citizens. In other words: the moral philosopher must leave the sub-stantive questions which go beyond a fundamental critique of value-scepticism and value-relativism to the participants in moral discourse, or tailor the cognitive claims of normative theory from the outset to the role of a participant. In this way we gain a larger space for the contribu-tion of social theory to the diagnosis of the present. Admittedly, ethical considerations are frequently of great methodological value in the construction of such theories. I have discussed this question in *Legitima-tion Crisis*, in connection with the problem of distinguishing particular from universal interests.

In your own recent writing stylistic considerations appear to have retreated in favour of a more functional mode of expression, a shift which seems to be correlated with the increasing importance of analytical philosophy in your work. Given your remarks, in 'Does Philosophy Still have a Purpose?', about the end of 'great philosophy', the transformation of philosophy into a branch of 'research', and the demise of the 'style of philosophical thinking tied to individual scholarship and personal representation',[9] would you consider a concern with style in the work of a contemporary philosopher to be a diversion or a regression? Is what is of value in a philosophical position always susceptible to direct statement?

8. 'Discourse Ethics: Notes on a Program of Philosophical Justification' in *Moral Consciousness and Communicative Action*, pp. 43–115.
   9. *Philosophical-Political Profiles*, pp. 1–2.

The type of text changes in accordance with purpose, addressee, place and time—according to whether I am dealing with the theme of the *Berufsverbot*, or of civil disobedience in the public-political sphere, or whether I am giving a speech in honour of Gadamer, polemicizing against Gehlen, writing an obituary for Scholem, or whether I am attempting to justify a moral principle or to classify speech-acts. The rhetorical constituents vary in relation to these different purposes. We are now well aware, since Mary Hesse at the latest, that even the language of the sciences is shot through with metaphors; this is plainly true of the language of philosophy, which can never of course be entirely absorbed into its role as a stand-in for scientific theories with strong universal claims. But one cannot, like Derrida, conclude from the unavoidably rhetorical character of *every* kind of language, including philosophical language, that it is all one and the same—that the categories of everyday life and literature, science and fiction, poetry and philosophy, collapse into each other. For Derrida all cats are grey in the night of 'writing'. I would not wish to draw this conclusion. The use of language in the practices of everyday life stands under different restrictions from the language used in theory or in art, which is specialized for the solving of problems, or for an innovative disclosure of the world.

How would you summarize your present conceptions of truth? If any adequate approach to truth should include a theory of evidence and a theory of argument, would it be fair to say that your work so far has given much more attention to the latter than the former? Today, would you still maintain the categorical separation between 'objectivity' and 'truth',[10] the experiential and the veridical, of the postscript to Knowledge and Human Interests?

The core of the discourse theory of truth can be formulated by means of three basic concepts: *conditions of validity* (which are fulfilled when an utterance holds good), *validity-claims* (which speakers raise with their utterances, for their validity), and *redemption* of a validity-claim (in the framework of a discourse which is sufficiently close to the conditions of an ideal speech situation for the consensus aimed at by the participants to be brought about solely through the force of the better argument, and in this sense to be 'rationally motivated'). The basic intuition, then, is simply this. Validity-claims are explicitly thematized only in non-trivial cases, but it is precisely in these cases that there are no rules of

---

10. *Knowledge and Human Interests*, London 1978, pp. 360–366.

verification available which would make it possible to decide directly whether certain conditions of validity are fulfilled or not. When claims to truth or justice become really obstinately problematic, there are no neat deductions or decisive pieces of evidence which could *enforce* an immediate decision for or against. Rather a play of argumentation is required, in which motivating reasons take the place of the unavailable knock-down arguments. If one accepts this description, it becomes clear that the following difficulty arises in the attempt to explain what it means to say that an utterance is valid. An utterance is valid when its conditions of validity are fulfilled. According to our description the fulfilment or non-fulfilment of conditions of validity, in problematic cases, can only be ascertained by means of the argumentative redemption of the corresponding validity-claims. The discourse theory of truth, then, explains what it means to redeem a validity-claim by an analysis of the general pragmatic presuppositions of the attainment of a rationally-motivated consensus. This theory of truth provides only an explication of meaning, it does not provide a criterion; in the end, however, it undermines the clear distinction between meaning and criterion.

To what extent is the notion of an ideal speech situation as a regulative principle of truth a circular one? If truth is defined as the consensus that would be reached by the speakers in an ideal speech situation, how could the existence of such a situation itself ever be truthfully ascertained? In other words, isn't the idea susceptible to the same kind of critique that Hegel made of Kant's theory of knowledge, and you of Hegel's, in Knowledge and Human Interests—*the 'aporia of knowing before know ledge'*[11] *Perhaps one could reformulate such a criticism another way. How could any speech situation be ideal, save in terms of the symmetry and sincerity of its speakers? But even at their most perfect, these conditions could normally only yield agreement rather than truth—that is, in abstraction from evidence, the opportunities for which can themselves never be ideal, since they always depend in some measure on historically changing techniques. Even the most flawlessly democratic and equal community of classical Greeks could not have discovered the laws of thermodynamics in the absence of modern optics. Isn't this one of the limits of any consensus theory of truth?*

The discourse theory of truth only claims to reconstruct an intuitive knowledge of the meaning of universal validity-claims which every competent speaker has at his or her disposal. 'Ideal speech situation' is

---

11. *Knowledge and Human Interests*, p. 21.

somewhat too concrete a term for the set of general and unavoidable communicative presuppositions which a subject capable of speech and action must make every time he or she wishes to participate seriously in argumentation. In answering your previous question I wanted to recall the fact that this intuitive knowledge of universal presuppositions of argumentation is linked with the pre-understanding of propositional truth and moral truth (or rightness). Of course, we know from philosophy and from the history of science that these ideas can be operationalized in very different ways; what counts at any given time as a good reason, as a proof, as an explanation, obviously depends on historically-changing background convictions, and also, as you suggest, on the associated techniques for controlling and observing nature; in short, on changing paradigms. But the paradigm-dependence of theories can be more readily harmonized with a discourse theory of truth than with a realist theory. The discourse theory is only incompatible with a Feyerabend-style paradigm-*relativism* because it sticks to the idea that paradigm-dependent ideas of truth and rightness nevertheless point towards a universal core of meaning.

How do you conceive the relation between philosophical and scientific truth-claims? Are philosophical truth-claims cognitive claims, and would a rational consensus ultimately guarantee the truth of the consensus theory of truth itself?

This is an interesting question, on which I have been working for a good while, although so far I do not have a conclusive answer to hand.

What is your attitude to psychoanalysis today? In Knowledge and Human Interests *you eloquently present it as the paradigm of a critical science serving an emancipatory interest. At the same time, you remark that Freud's metapsychology was a misunderstanding of his own project, whose instinct theory has never yielded 'a single statement that has ever been tested experimentally'.*[12] *But how far does this stricture apply to the main body of analytic theory itself? Even if the evidential weaknesses— widely aired—of psychoanalysis are set aside, doesn't the theory in fact present peculiar difficulties for a consensus theory of truth, insofar as the transactions between analyst and analysand are inherently confidential— i.e. non-extendable to others? In the gap between the 'clinical' and the 'ideal speech' situations, isn't there a temptation in your original account to fall back on essentially a pragmatic justification of Freud's theory—*

---

12. *Knowledge and Human Interests*, p. 253.

*whose test becomes a change in the conduct of the patient, a 'continua-
tion of the self-formative process' indeterminable in direction or
duration? This could seem close to the kind of Deweyan instrumentalism
that you reject in the postscript. But the success rate even in these terms is
not very high. In sum: isn't there much more question about the
scientificity of many of Freud's claims, scrutinized in a large literature,
than you allowed in the late sixties?*

My friend Mitscherlich once summed up his experience as a psycho-
analyst in the following terms: therapy often achieves 'no more than the
transformation of illness into suffering, but into a suffering which
enhances the status of *homo sapiens,* because it does not extinguish his
freedom'. I would like to make use of this statement to express my
scepticism about critiera based on statistics of so-called success.

It certainly seems to be the case today that psychoanalytic research
has come to a standstill, not only in Germany but on an international
scale, and that intelligent young people prefer to go into other disciplines. But how definitive is this? Many disciplines have survived similar
periods of stagnation. Even sociology is going through thin times at the
moment. I have not done any work myself on Freud's metapsychology
since the end of the sixties. But I find the attempts to bring Freud and
Piaget together, which have been undertaken in various contexts, both
exciting and fruitful. Beyond that, my interpretation of Freud in terms of
communication theory still seems to me to be plausible. I cannot entirely
accept your objection. I have never understood the therapeutic discourse
as discourse or argumentation in the strict sense, because of the
asymmetries between doctor and patient which are built into it. Of
course it is inhabited, so to speak, by the *telos* of working to remove
those asymmetries. For these reasons the patient also acquires in the
end, at least in the ideal case, a freedom to say 'yes' and 'no' which
immunizes him or her against the suggestive obtrusion of functional
interpretations, which are, in a superficial sense, 'life-assisting'. What
should be involved is, of course, the continuation, made possible
through reflexive insight, of an interrupted, neurotically-inhibited
process of formation of the self.

The Theory of Communicative Action *contains a fascinating reconstruction and critique of Weber's account of 'rationalization' as a world-
historical process. In it, you tax Weber with abandoning his own
starting-point—the advent of substantive reasoning with the major
religions—in his final focus on formal rationality alone, as the necessary
matrix of modern capitalism; and you also point to significant lacunae in
his regional theory of the origins of capitalism—his omission of the rise*

of modern science, and more generally its bearers during the Renais-
sance. These are compelling demonstrations. What is not so clear, on the
other hand, is whether you accept the main thrust of his thesis concerning
the importance of the Protestant Ethic itself, as the engine of a rational-
ized life-world and so motor of early capitalism. Many historians have
been highly sceptical of Weber's claims for Calvinism—one need only
think of a critical survey of the evidence like Kurt Samuelson's Religion
and Economic Action, *or Trevor-Roper's essays on Erasmianism. Did*
you feel that these doubts fell outside the province of your treatment of
Weber?

I did indeed neglect the wide-ranging discussion around the question of whether and to what extent Weber's analysis of capitalism has proved correct. There were, above all, practical reasons for that—it would have required, if not another book, at the very least an additional chapter. It is also for these reasons—to reduce the burden of work—that I planned *The Theory of Communicative Action* as an intertwining of history of theory with systematic investigations. In Weber's case this had the additional advantage of illustrating a favourite idea of mine. Weber perceives with great acuity the narrowness of the Calvinistic doctrine of grace, and the repressive traits of the forms of life which bore the stamp of this doctrine; but Weber refuses to see this protestant ethic as a *one-sided* exploitation of a potential which was built into the universalist ethics of brotherhood. In fact, it is the selective model of capitalist rationalization as a whole which is mirrored in the protestant ethic.

Of course, such interests attached to the form of presentation should not be allowed to get the upper hand; otherwise one would become cynical about questions of truth. Insofar as I am familiar with the literature, I believe that Weber's thesis must be expanded and revised with regard to *other* social strata who were bearers of early capitalism. However, I doubt whether such revision would be forced to tamper with the general correlation of an ethics of conviction, worldly asceticism, and economic behaviour.

More generally, what is your view of the position and contribution of
history as a discipline within the social sciences? You have always argued
that 'history as such is not capable of theory', because it is always a
retrospective narrative—'whereas theoretical statements allow the deriva-
tion of conditional predictions of events that will occur in the future'.[13]
You contrast this incapacity for theory and prediction with the compe-
tence in these respects of sociology or evolutionary discourses. This

---

13. *Zur Rekonstruktion des historischen Materialismus,* Frankfurt 1976, pp. 204, 207.

distinction seems quite close to the neo-Kantian dichotomy between ideographic and nomothetic sciences. But is it warranted? It is difficult to see why historians like Taylor or Hobsbawm should be unable to make forecasts at least as reliable—to put it no higher—as those of sociologists like Bell or Dahrendorf, whom you cite as valid diagnosticians of the time. Don't warnings of the increasing dangers of nuclear war, for example, have a special weight when they come from a historian of the authority of Edward Thompson? Once such a sharp division is made between 'history' and 'theory', aren't the effects on historical materialism itself necessarily paradoxical—in the sense that to reconstruct it as theory, it has to be drastically reduced as history, in the evolutionary version presented in Communication and the Evolution of Society? *It would appear prima facie more plausible to imagine that Marxist (and other) historians would have more to contribute to the enterprise of reconstructing historical materialism than child psychologists. Couldn't one cite your* Strukturwandel *against yourself here, as a memorable example of a work at once and indivisibly historical and theoretical, and diagnostic to boot?*

The prognostic capacity of social theories was and is very limited—that could hardly be otherwise, given the high level of abstraction at which these statements concerning complex states of affairs are formulated. Nor do I doubt that a shrewd and politically-seasoned historian, with his or her experience-steeped intuitions, often judges contemporary developmental tendencies with an astonishing sureness of touch. It is for methodological reasons that I have insisted on a distinction—but not a distinction of rank—between historiography and social-scientific theory. If one introduces the viewpoint of social evolution into history without mediation, it is easy to fall victim to patterns of thought familiar from the philosophy of history, above all the danger of thinking in terms of historical teleology, which Marxists in particular have often enough succumbed to. The reflections which you refer to belonged in the context of the critique of historical objectivism, and of its unfortunate consequences for the political practice of so-called vanguard parties. I am not in any sense opposed to the necessity of theoretically-guided historical research. Theories, especially those of Marxist inspiration, ultimately only prove their worth by making a contribution to the explanation of concrete historical processes. I myself find it unfortunate that for the last two decades (if one disregards some shorter political writings) my interest has been taken up exclusively with problems which can be characterized in a broad sense as problems of theory construction. I must accept the criticism which, most recently, Tom Bottomore has directed at me in this respect.

What are the methodological grounds for the homologies you postulate between individual growth and social evolution? In The Theory of Communicative Action, *you remark that most adults in* all *societies can achieve the higher levels of moral and cognitive competence, as described by Piaget and Kohlberg.*[14] *If this is so, how can the maturational sequence they posit help to explain the huge differences* between *such societies, when arrayed along a scale of rationalization of the world-views they exhibit?*

Empirical investigations come out strongly against the idea that all adult members of a society, even of modern Western societies, have acquired the capacity for formal-operational thought (in Piaget's sense) or for post-conventional judgements (in the sense of Kohlberg's theory of moral development). I maintain only (for example, with reference to tribal societies) that individuals can develop structures of consciousness which belong to a higher stage than those which are already embodied in the institutions of their society. It is primarily subjects who learn, while societies can take a step forward in the evolutionary learning-process only in a metaphorical sense. New forms of social integration, and new productive forces, are due to the institutionalization and exploitation of forms of knowledge which are individually acquired, but culturally stored and capable of transmission and so, in the long term, accessible to the collective. However, the process of social implementation only takes place as a consequence of political struggles and social movements, of the outrider-role of innovative marginal groups, and so on. Thus I start from the trivial assumption that subjects capable of speech and action cannot help but learn, and use this to support the assumption that ontogenetic learning processes acquire pacemaker functions. However, this thesis is contested by Klaus Eder in his *Habilitationsschrift* on the development of German constitutional law since the eighteenth century. He traces the innovative impulses back directly to *social* learning processes in the framework of new forms of association, namely to new experiences of egalitarian social relations, initially in the Masonic lodges, secret societies and readers' unions, later in the early socialist workingmen's associations.

Can a theory of emancipation avoid the idea of progress? You stress in The Theory of Communicative Action *that we cannot judge the worth of societies by the degree to which their life-worlds are rationalized, even in the sense of an 'encompassing' rationality that is not only formal but*

---

14. *The Theory of Communicative Action*, vol. 1, p. 44.

substantive; suggesting that at best we can speak perhaps of the relative
'health' or 'sickness' of a given social order.[15] *Earlier, however, in*
Legitimation Crisis, *you criticized the use of such terms, drawn from*
biology, as fundamentally inapplicable to society.[16] *Have you definitely*
changed your views here, or is this still a relatively unresolved issue for
you? The difficulty seems to be to resist historical triumphalism—an
Enlightenment complacency that devalues all anterior or alien social
forms—without falling into political agnosticism. For if all epochs and
societies are equally close to God, in Ranke's sense, why fight for a better
one? A consistent cultural relativism must be conservative. In what
direction do you think a solution to these dilemmas is to be looked for?

I have not revised my conception in this respect, but continue to think
that statements concerning the level of development of a society can
only relate to *single* dimensions and to *universal* structures: to the
reflexivity and complexity of social systems on the one hand, and to the
social forces of production and forms of social integration on the other.
One society may be superior to another with reference to the level of
differentiation of its economic or administrative system, or with reference to technologies and legal institutions. But it does not follow that we
are entitled to value this society more highly *as a whole*, as a concrete
totality, as a form of life. You know that, in relation to objectifying
knowledge and moral insight, the position I represent is one of cautious
universalism. We observe tendencies towards a 'progressive' rationalization of the life-world—not as a law, of course, but as a historical fact.
Again and again those tendencies have been confirmed which distinguish modern societies from traditional ones—the increasing reflexivity
of the cultural tradition, the universalization of values and norms, the
freeing of communicative action from tightly circumscribed normative
contexts, the diffusion of models of socialization which promote
processes of individuation and the formation of abstract ego-identities,
and so on. But all these 'advances' concern the universal structures of
life-worlds in general; they say nothing about the value of a concrete
way of life. This value must be measured by other things, of the kind
which we look for in clinical judgements: whether people in such and
such circumstances have a 'hard' life, whether they are alienated from
themselves. For the intuition of an unspoiled life we apply yardsticks
which are valid in the first instance in the context of our culture or
plausible in the context of our tradition, which in any event cannot be

---

15. Ibid., p. 73.
16. *Legitimation Crisis*, London 1976, pp. 175–177.

generalized in the same way as the standards which we use in judging processes that involve learning—knowledge of nature or moral and legal ideas, which, despite their paradigm-dependence, are not *entirely* incommensurable. So far I have no idea how the universal core of those merely clinical intuitions—if indeed they have one at all—can be theoretically grasped.

Can a morality of enlightenment skirt a commitment to happiness? If not, what is the bearing of a 'discursive ethics' on it? In your essay on Benjamin, you evoke the possibility of a society at once freed of domination and devoid of meaning—rationality without felicity. Doesn't such a prospect undermine the argument that every truthful statement is 'an anticipation of the good life'?[17] Another way of putting the question would be this: you have argued on a number of occasions that ethics is a 'reconstructive science'—while elsewhere you define such sciences as those, in contradistinction to critical theories, which are without practical effects on the conduct of agents.[18] But isn't the idea of a post facto *ethic, an anodyne codification of existing practices, virtually a contradiction in terms?*

Let me start with a couple of general propositions. Morality has certainly to do with justice and also with the wellbeing of others, even with the promotion of the general welfare. But happiness cannot be brought about intentionally, and can only be promoted very indirectly. I prefer a relatively narrow concept of morality. Morality refers to practical questions which can be decided with reason—to conflicts of action which can be resolved through consensus. Only those questions are moral in a strict sense which can be answered in a meaningful way from the Kantian standpoint of universalization—of what *all* could wish for. At the same time, I prefer a weak concept of moral theory. We have already touched on this: it should explain and justify the moral point of view, and nothing more. Deontic, cognitive and universal moral theories in the Kantian tradition are theories of justice, which must leave the question of the good life unanswered. They are typically restricted to the question of the *justification* of norms and actions. They have no answer to the question of how justified norms can be *applied* to specific situations and how moral insights can be *realized.* In short, one should not place excessive demands on moral theory, but leave something over

17. *Philosophical-Political Profiles*, pp. 115–158; *Knowledge and Human Interests*, p. 314.
18. *Knowledge and Human Interests*, p. 378; *Theory and Practice*, London 1974, p. 23.

for social theory, and the major part for the participants themselves—
whether it be their moral discourses or their good sense. This merely
advocatory role sets narrow limits to theory: whoever takes a risk upon
him or herself, must be allowed to make his or her *own* decision. But
now to your questions.

Moral theory proceeds reconstructively, in other words after the
event. Aristotle was right in his opinion that the moral intuitions which
theory clarifies must have been acquired elsewhere, in more or less
successful socialization processes. However, I would also expect a
critical theory to perform the task of making possible enlightening
interpretations of situations, which affect our self-understanding and
orientate us in action. Even social theory would overstep its competence, however, if it undertook to project desirable forms of life into the
future, instead of criticizing existing forms of life. In so doing, it can
refer to historically superfluous repressions, and to that untapped
potential for rationality which can be read off from the state of the
productive forces, the level of legal and moral ideas, the degree of
individuation, and so on. For this reason Marxist theory cannot cash out
the expression 'socialism' in terms of a *concrete* form of life; at most it
can indicate necessary conditions under which emancipated forms of life
would be possible today.

*How far is the realm of 'inner nature' a source of potential values for
you? You've written of a necessary 'fluidification' of this nature in any
post-conventional morality or society, and have suggested that art has a
particularly significant role to play in such redispositions.*[19] *Could you
give some examples of the kind of process you have in mind?*

Our needs are only ever accessible to us in an interpreted form. In other
words, language is constitutive for needs, in the light of which situations—which are always affectively tinged—are disclosed to us. Up till
now the transformation of evaluative, need-interpreting languages has
taken place in a nature-like manner; the changing of this vocabulary has
taken place as part of the changing of linguistic world-pictures. To the
extent that art and literature have become differentiated into a sphere
with a logic of its own, and in this sense have become autonomous, a
tradition of literary and art criticism has been established which labours
to reintegrate the innovative aesthetic experiences, at first 'mute', into
ordinary language, and thus into the communicative practice of
everyday life. In the medium of this criticism the formerly sluggish,

---

19. *Communication and the Evolution of Society*, London 1979, p. 93.

nature-like process of revaluation of our evaluative vocabulary, our world-disclosing and need-interpreting language in general, becomes more and more reflexive; the whole process becomes, as it were, discursively fluidified. Central concepts such as the happiness, dignity, integrity of the person are now changing as if before our very eyes. Diffuse experiences, which crystallize out under transformed life-circumstances produced by changes in social structure, find their illuminating, suggestive, visible expression through cultural productivity. This is what Castoriadis means by 'imagination'. Benjamin, for example, investigated through Baudelaire those experiences of a mobilized, concentrated, metropolitan life-world which surfaced like a new conti- nent in nineteenth-century Paris, the 'capital of the nineteenth century', as he called it. Kafka and Musil can be seen as literary exemplifications of the experiential space of the collapsing Austrian Imperial and Royal Monarchy, Celan and Beckett of a world transformed by Auschwitz. Our moral-practical reflections and discourses are affected by this productivity, precisely to the extent that it is only in the light of such innovations that we can say what we *really* want, and above all: what we *cannot* want. Only in this light do we find a precise expression for our interests.

In recent years you have polemicized against theories of post-modernity, associating them with concepts of post-history and with the neo- conservative implications of post-structuralism. It is not entirely clear, however, whether you intend to deny that there are any developments to which the concept of post-modernism corresponds, or whether you are merely contesting the appropriateness of the designation. Would you deny, for example, that the shift away from the esotericism of high modern art to fusions of high and mass culture is a development to which the term 'post-modernism' could be applied? In The Theory of Communicative Action *you hint at the emergence of a 'post-avant-garde art' which would be 'characterized by the simultaneity of realistic and engaged tendencies with the authentic continuation of that classical modernity which separated out the distinctive meaning of the aesthetic'.[20] What examples would you give of works of art which are moving in this direction? And, given your refusal to deny all progressive potential to mass culture, would fusions of high and mass culture be one aspect of such a 'post-avant-garde art'?*

Peter Bürger sees post-avant-garde art, art after the failure of the

---

20. *The Theory of Communicative Action*, vol. 2, p. 397.

surrealist revolt, the contemporary scene in general, as being characterized by the juxtaposition of styles, which draw either on the formalist
languages of the avant-garde, or on the inheritance of realistic or
political-didactic styles and literatures. You can find examples in the
museum of any large city. This juxtaposition also includes the by now
ritualized forms of the '*Aufhebung*' of esoteric art. I would not interpret
the contemporary scene in the sense of so-called post-modernism as a
sign of the exhaustion or the 'end' of modernism in art and architecture.
Our situation testifies, rather, to the fact that the aesthetic experiences
revealed by the twentieth century's avant-gardes find no access to a one-
sidedly rationalized everyday practice, but circle around restlessly before
its portals in split-off specialist cultures. I share Adorno's reservations
about mass culture, against Benjamin's overhasty hopes for its 'profane
illuminations', only to the extent that the fusion of high and trivial
culture has, up till now, fallen short of its programmatic goal. Desublimated mass-art does not penetrate in a transforming, illuminating
and liberating way into life-forms reified by capitalism, and deformed
and distorted by consumerism and bureaucracy, but rather helps to
advance these tendencies. It was not the hopes of the surrealists which
were false, but their path—the *Aufhebung* of aesthetic illusion—was
counter-productive.

*One of the significant developments in your work over the last decade has
been the progressive attenuation of the claims made for the 'ideal speech
situation'. In* The Theory of Communicative Action *you admit the
utopian nature of the project of an ideal speech community, and you have
also emphasized that the procedural rationality of argumentative
grounding cannot provide the substance of a form of life as such. Even
after having made the concessions, however, there might still be a tension
between the telos of universal consensus and the human (and epistemological) value of conflict and diversity. It is this kind of tension to which
Mill, whose conception of truth in some ways resembles your own,
reveals himself to be sensitive when he writes, in* On Liberty : 'The loss of
so important an aid to the intelligent and living apprehension of truth as
is afforded by the necessity of explaining it to, or defending it against,
opponents, though not sufficient to outweigh, is no trifling drawback
from the benefit of its universal recognition.' In* Strukturwandel *you
suggest that Mill disguised his 'resignation before the rational insolubility
of competing interests in the public sphere' by means of a 'perspectivist
theory of knowledge'.*[21] *However, as the above quotation makes clear,*

---

21. *On Liberty*, Harmondsworth 1982, p. 106; *The Structural Transformation of the Public Sphere*, Cambridge, Mass., 1989, p. 135.

this is not entirely accurate. Mill does not doubt that truth ultimately entails consensus, but nevertheless perceives unanimity as purchased at the cost of other human values. Are you at all susceptible to this kind of consideration?

I think I am—after all, my Marxist friends are not entirely unjustified in accusing me of being a radical liberal. I can only repeat what I have already stressed elsewhere. 'Nothing makes me more nervous than the imputation that because the theory of communicative action focuses attention on the social facticity of recognized validity-claims, it proposes, or at least suggests, a rationalistic utopian society. I do *not* regard the fully transparent—let me add in this context: or indeed a homogenized and unified—society as an ideal, nor do I wish to suggest any other ideal—Marx was not the only one frightened by the vestiges of utopian socialism.'[22] The ideal speech situation is, as I have said, a description of the conditions under which claims to truth and rightness can be discursively redeemed. In communicative action these validity-claims remain for the most part implicit and unproblematic, since the intersubjectively shared life-world holds in reserve a solid background of culturally self-evident truths, taken-for-granted assumptions. The action-coordinating role of processes of reaching understanding, which proceed by means of the criticism of validity-claims, does not conflict therefore with the pluralism of life-forms and interest. The fact that modern societies are differentiated in terms of life-forms and interest-positions, and are becoming increasingly differentiated, is a fact which does not put action orientated to reaching understanding out of service; of course, the need for understanding, which increases in step with this process, must be satisfied at higher and higher levels of abstraction. For this reason the consensual norms and principles become ever more general.

There is also another way of meeting a need for understanding which goes beyond the available possibilities of reaching consensus; this need in fact disappears entirely as soon as socially-integrated domains of action are switched over to system-integration. That is precisely what happened to many areas of life in the wake of capitalist modernization. Money and power—more concretely, markets and administrations—take over the integrative functions which were formerly fulfilled by consensual values and norms, or even by processes of reaching understanding. Of course my thesis, which I develop in the second volume of

---

22. 'A Reply to my Critics', in J. Thompson and D. Held, eds., *Habermas—Critical Debates*, London 1982, p. 235.

The Theory of Communicative Action through a discussion of Parsons' theory of media, is this: that those domains of action which are specialized for the transmission of culture, social integration or the socialization of the young rely on the medium of communicative action and cannot be integrated through money or power. A commercialization or bureaucratization must therefore generate—this is the thesis—disturbances, pathological side-effects in these domains. But here I am straying from your question about the rights of pluralism.

In your discussion of the structures of domination typical of capitalism, you stress the way in which these act to occlude and suppress 'generalizable interests', as opposed to 'particular interests' which they themselves covertly represent. You argue that the difference between these two kinds of interest can in principle be established by a species of thought-experiment you call 'simulated discourse'.[23] *Could you give an illustration of how this might work? One of the problems the distinction seems to raise is the status of interests that are not generalizable but are nevertheless perfectly valid—in other words, the question of the 'natural' heterogeneity of interests, even in socialist society, in which different agents or groups will have a plurality of specific needs or exigencies, all in their own terms quite legitimate—regional, occupational, generational, and so on. How would your proposed model of 'discursive will-formation', which appears to put a premium on consensus around generalizable interests, arbitrate conflicting demands of this sort?*

The model of repressed generalizable interests is of course only a proposal for a way of criticizing interests which unjustly pass themselves off as general interests. This goal is also pursued by Marx in his critique of bourgeois legal forms, or in his critique of the doctrines of Smith and Ricardo. The model which I propose is designed to demonstrate the non-generalizability of interests which are presumed to be general. For example, an argument which arouses this suspicion today often crops up in social-democratic pronouncements: such and such a stimulus must be given to investment 'in order to secure jobs'.

Your objection is directed against an assumption which I do not in any way make. In no sense do I begin from the basis that in all, or even in the majority of, political decisions, legal or administrative regulations, a general interest is at stake. Modern societies are not like that. Often, maybe in the majority of cases, the social matters which are nowadays regulated through state intervention concern only particular interest-groups. In such cases moral discourse could only have the aim of

---

23. *Legitimation Crisis*, p. 117.

withdrawing legitimacy from the privileging of one side, which falsely claims to represent a general interest. When only particular interests are at stake, conflicts of action cannot be settled, even in ideal cases, through argumentation, but only through bargaining and compromise. Of course, the *procedures* of reaching compromise must for their part be judged from a normative standpoint. A fair compromise is not to be expected when—for instance—the parties involved do not have at their disposal the same positions of power or capacity to make threats. To give an example: when the complicated question arises of the effects of constitutional rights on third parties, one is entitled to expect that the ruling of the court will be supported by arguments; when it is a matter of the straightforward, but politically delicate, question of the location of a nuclear power station, the most that can be expected is that a fair compromise will be arrived at. Compromises are not only widespread as a matter of fact, but also, from the normative standpoint, occupy a position which is not in any way to be despised. This is why I do not have any difficulties with the pluralism of interests. After all, we anticipate that the pluralism of life-forms and the individualism of life-styles would increase at an exponential rate in a society which deserves the name socialist.

One of the novelties of your work as a whole, viewed against the background of classical forms of Marxism, is a shift from 'production' to 'communication', both as an analytic focus and as a source of value. At the same time, you have always emphasized that you regard yourself as a materialist. Could you specify the terms of the materialism you defend?

Right from my earliest publications I understood 'materialism' in the Marxist sense, as a theoretical approach which does not simply affirm the dependence of the superstructure on the base, the life-world on the imperatives of the accumulation process, as an ontological constant, so to speak, but which simultaneously explains and *denounces* this dependence as the latent function of a particular, historically transitory social formation. The transition from a production to a communication paradigm, which I advocate, does of course mean that the critical theory of society must no longer rely on the normative contents of the expressivist model of alienation and reappropriation of essential powers. The young Marx borrowed this model from the production aesthetics of Kant, Schiller and Hegel. The paradigm-shift from purposive activity to communicative action does not mean, however, that I am willing or bound to abandon the material reproduction of the life-world as the privileged point of reference for analysis. I continue to explain the selective model of capitalist modernization, and the corresponding pathologies of a one-sidedly rationalized life-world, in terms of a capitalist accumulation process which is largely disconnected from orientations towards use-value.

How far does the emergence of ecology, as a theory and a movement, qualify your earlier view that there is 'only one theoretically fruitful attitude towards nature'—that informed by an interest in technical control?

The awareness of ecological cycles, of biotopes, of human-environment systems has certainly brought forward new themes, new questions, perhaps even new disciplines. As far as I can tell, however, from the methodological point of view these ecologically inspired investigations move entirely within the inherited framework. So far nothing seems to suggest that alternative natural sciences can be developed in a non-objectifying attitude, for example in the performative attitude of a partner in communication—theories in the tradition of the romantic or alchemistic philosophies of nature.

II

What is the balance of your judgement on the political evolution you have witnessed, and lived through, from the fifties to the eighties, in the West? The conclusion of Strukturwandel, *your first major book, contains a kind of ambiguity. The overall direction of your account of the 'structural change' in the public domain in the advanced capitalist countries was a deeply pessimistic one—etching an unforgettable portrait of a degraded public life, in which the substance of liberal democracy is voided in a combination of plebiscitary manipulation and privatized apathy, as any collectivity of citizenry disintegrates. Yet you also evoked the possibility (more briefly) of a 'restoration' of the public domain, by the demo-cratization of parties, voluntary associations and media within it—but without giving much grounds for hope that this would occur. Looking back over a quarter of a century, do you feel things since have got worse or better, or have remained more or less the same?*

It is a perilous undertaking to recast the intuitive life-experiences of a political contemporary in the form of calculations of loss and gain. On the other hand I must admit that a proper theory of society, and a diagnosis of the present based upon it, can have no other point than to sharpen our perceptions for the ambivalent potential of contemporary developments. Let me try to give a very tentative and sketchy account from the perspective of the Federal Republic. On the one hand I have the impression that the tendencies to disintegration of a public sphere of the liberal type—a formation of opinion in discursive style mediated by reading, reasoning, information—have intensified since the late fifties. The mode of functioning of electronic media testifies to this, above all the centralization of organizations which privilege vertical and one-way flows of second- and third-hand information, privately consumed. We are witnessing an increasing substitution of images for words, and also that intermingling of categories such as advertising, politics, entertainment, information, which was already criticized by Adorno. Adorno's critique of mass culture should be both extended and rewritten. The display aspect of the centres of our large cities has indeed absorbed elements of surrealism in an ironic way, and promoted the neon-lit re-enchantment of a de-realized reality. The banal coalesces with the unreal, hellenistically de-differentiated customs blend with high-tech style, and the ruins of popular cultures with the highly personalized, consumeristically polished bizarre. The refuse dumps of civilization are camouflaged with plastic. The substance of the universal is dissolved into a narcissism which has forfeited everything individual, and become a stereotype. As I have suggested, Derrida and a capering deconstructivism give the only appropriate answer to this really existing surrealism. This is matched, somewhat more seriously, by another tendency which is also well advanced: a manipulation of mass loyalty which is both perfected and passed off as respectable, administered by political parties which have migrated from the life-world into the political system. At an earlier stage it was still said that the parties and their exponents procured the *acclamation* of the voting public. That is a touchingly old-fashioned expression for the staged performances, barred against all spontaneity, which run according to scenario and bring literally everything under control. At all events, *that* was the new quality which the last American presidential election attained—with an actor playing a president whose office is increasingly restricted to presenting this office to the outside world as a fictive reality. Reality is overtaking the systems-theoretic description which Luhmann gives of it: the political system *extracts* from the public sphere the legitimation it needs. That is the one side.

On the other side, the reactions to this evacuation of the public-political sphere are getting stronger. After all, our observations of how the provision of legitimacy is running into difficulties, and the mirror-image laments of the neo-conservatives about 'ungovernability', are not totally mistaken. I wrote *Strukturwandel* before the protest movement of the sixties—what is more, without having in any way foreseen it. In the Federal Republic at the present time there are increasing indications of locally fragmented, subcultural resistances, of defensive movements at the 'base', as well as of spectacular mass demonstrations which abruptly flare up, and then die down again. The peace demonstrations in the autumn of 1983, immediately prior to the stationing of the missiles, reached dimensions previously unimaginable in the history of the Federal Republic; they also had a previously unknown quality of, shall we say, disciplined aggressiveness. The sensitivity to threats to the protection of personal information, which was manifested in successful resistance against the planned census, against the introduction of a 'forgery-proof' identity-card and so on, is a further, admittedly less dramatic, symptom. Psephological monitorings of the erosion of traditional party ties, and of the increasing number of floating voters, also belong to this context. It is not only the successes of the Greens which are a sign of what we call over here 'party peevishness'. It seems to be generally the case that the ground is getting slippery. More or less unpredictable potentials for reaction are building up, which are mobilized by chance events.

These two contrary tendencies, of which I have given a few illustrations, testify to a polarization of the public sphere into official, desiccated sectors directed from above, and into local subcultures, which are difficult to define in socio-structural terms, in part connected with the old middle-class, in part 'post-materialistically' aligned, but in any event resistant, which have become the core of autonomous counter-public spheres—the old and the young, feminists and homosexuals, the handicapped and active unemployed, radical professionals, suburban housewives and so forth.

In work subsequent to Strukturwandel, *there emerges what might be called a counter-theme—that of a creeping 'legitimation crisis' of the prevailing order, with a decline, not of the public domain, but of the 'substitute programme' for it, or civil privatism and the 'ideology of achievement'. This more optimistic reading of the time was developed in* Towards a Rational Society *and* Legitimation Crisis. *How do you view this diagnosis today, from the vantage-point of the long recession and the neo-conservative wave that has accompanied it?*

Let's say that at that time I was already reacting to experiences with the student protest movement.

In the central essay of Towards a Rational Society, *you maintained that the dominant ideology in the West draws its lexicon from 'technology and science'—the socio-political order being fundamentally legitimated in the name of technocratic efficiency and necessity.*[24] *Couldn't one argue that it is rather 'democracy' that is the basic legitimating code of Western capitalism? If one analysed the speeches of Reagan, Thatcher, Kohl or Mitterrand, wouldn't one find that while the discourse of 'efficiency and prosperity' is a very important one, it is structurally subordinate to that of 'liberty and democracy'? How else, for example, are the stationing of missiles, the rollback of welfare programmes, the curbing of trade unions, justified?*

One could nevertheless defend the thesis that Reagan won his last election as the orchestrator of a mood of 'efficiency and prosperity'. On the other hand, it is certainly true that today a continuing technocratic practice, under the banner of neo-conservative attitudes and slogans, is no longer justified with technocratic ideologies. Technology and science, as an ideological programme, have lost much of their public effectiveness. My analysis of 1968 cannot be simply extended today; I already began to supplement it in 1973, in *Legitimation Crisis*. And in *The Theory of Communicative Action* I explore the 'crisis of the welfare state' which has developed in the meantime. The project of the welfare state has also become problematic in public consciousness, insofar as the bureaucratic means with which the interventionist state aimed to bring about the 'social restraint of capitalism' have lost their innocence. It is no longer merely the monetarization of labour power, but also the bureaucratization of the life-world which is experienced by broad strata of the population as a danger. Political-administrative power has lost the appearance of neutrality for the clients of welfare-state bureaucracies. These new attitudes are exploited by neo-conservatism, in order to sell the well-known policy of shifting the burden of problems back from the state onto the market—a policy which, Lord knows, has nothing to do with democratization, which rather effects a further uncoupling of state activity from the pressure for legitimation emanating from the public sphere, and understands by 'freedom' not the autonomy of the life-world, but a free hand for private investors.

How would you compare the 'new social movements' of the eighties with the student movement of the sixties, in terms of the direction and durability and likely effect of their protests against the established order?

Once again, I can only attempt to answer that with reference to the Federal Republic. Under the conditions of the boom, with a false

---

24. 'Technology and Science as "Ideology"', in *Towards a Rational Society*, London 1971, pp. 81–122.

understanding of the situation largely borrowed from orthodox Marxism, and in the narrow catchment area of the universities, our student movement already expressed, and in part made effective in the form of cultural revolution, a change of outlook which has continued to be manifest in the New Social Movements since the middle of the seventies. These movements, in conditions of persistent recession and increasing unemployment, have a more defensive posture, are less articulate than the students were in their day; perhaps they are more realistic in their understanding of the situation; above all, they recruit from broader social catchment areas. For example, the differences between the younger workers, apprentices, students and unemployed have been eroded within the framework of a youth culture whose unity is not simply a matter of image and appearances. Admittedly, this broader social basis does not yet indicate a power of veto strongly anchored in social structures. At the moment this 'anti-productivist' alliance is proving to have a certain socio-psychological contagiousness, but occupies no vital functional domains of industrial society. However, neo-conservative policies are the best way to secure a further influx to this alliance. Even if there are unforeseeable ups and downs in the manifestation of this capacity for resistance, I consider to be false the prognosis that people's anger will just as soon evaporate. The anger is structurally generated.

Do you continue to think that it was a mistake for the Greens to form a political party in West Germany, and to participate in electoral competition? How would you assess their prospects now?

Perhaps my warning at the time was fainthearted, but it was not unjustified. The predictable struggle between fundamentalist and re-formist wings may still destroy the party of the Greens. The experiment has a prospect of success only so long as this dialectical tension is not discharged onesidedly. Above all internally, in relations with themselves, the Greens must improve their ability to compromise. For this is precisely the problem which would have to be solved: how can the relative capacity for action, indeed the very existence of a political party, be secured, which must resolve within itself the contradiction between social movement and political system? Allow me to make a short detour in order to clarify this contradiction.

Recently the Federal Republic has been afflicted with the financial scandal of the Flick company. The scandal does not consist in the corruption of members of parliament, party leaders and ministers, who pocket illegal contributions for their party in return for favouring the interests of big capital. The privileged influence of the owners of capital on the state apparatus is secured in such a way, through functional connections and structures, that these risky and antiquated methods of corrupting individuals are not at all necessary. The Flick method is out of date and untypical. However, the procedure reveals something else, and indeed something quite trivial: the political parties are no longer able to finance themselves from members' contributions, and yet are only allowed to supply half their needs from taxation, since otherwise they would be obliged to admit publicly the extent to which they are already divorced from their base, and have become autonomous as organs of the state. Thus, measured by our normative self-understanding, the real scandal, if it is still experienced as a scandal at all, consists in the following: the parties engage with good conscience in the legitimation process almost exclusively from above—that is, from the perspective of an integral part of the state apparatus. In any event, they act so little from the perspective of a mere mediator in the process of forming public opinion that they overrun the public-political sphere with their interventions, instead of reproducing themselves out of it.

According to their own declarations, the Greens wish neither to be nor to become such a party. On the other hand, neither should they become submerged in the wake of the many subcultural and local counter-public spheres. As a party they must force the self-assured particularism of dissidents unconcerned with norms of civic equality through the filter of generalization, of equal consideration of interests. Perhaps this experiment should have been initiated after the capacity for self-organization had developed more strongly in different autonomous public spheres. Perhaps the experiment will succeed anyway—salutary effects are already stemming from it, for example on the internal life of the SPD, without which, if we are realistic about it, nothing can be moved.

How do you view the German national question, and the relationship between the two Germanies? Can the issue of 'reunification', or alternatively 'confederation', be raised from the Left today?

Willy Brandt has just made an impressive speech on this subject in Munich. Its tenor was: the German question is no longer open. I consider talk about a new German nationalism to be nonsense—it feeds more on inventions in the *New York Times* than on feelings here in Germany. The longing of many intellectuals for a lost German identity is as kitsch as the reunification rhetoric of CSU orators is mendacious. Long ago Kurt Schumacher, on his return from the concentration camps, was obsessed by the idea that he had committed an error at the end of the Weimar Republic—for this reason he wished, as Adenauer's opponent, to incorporate preventively right-wing feelings which in fact no longer existed. The West German Left should not repeat Schumacher's mistake today.

In Strukturwandel, *you point out Kant's failure to provide any theory of how the political power that could institutionalize the moral unity of a free civil society might itself be won—in other words, for ignoring (as you put it elsewhere in the book) the 'hard struggle against the ancient power' of Absolutism which was the price of the victory of a sovereign legislature.*[25] *Mutatis mutandis, could something similar be said, at any rate so far, of your own theory of 'domination-free communication'? How is the power that issued from the bourgeois revolutions Kant sidestepped to be transformed in its turn—through what kind of material struggles?*

'Freedom from domination' is presupposed by those who engage in *argumentation.* It would be a concretistic fallacy to assume that an emancipated society could consist in nothing but 'communication free from domination'. People who impute this to me make it a bit too easy for themselves. The release of a potential for reason embedded in communicative action is a world-historical process; in the modern period it leads to a rationalization of life-worlds, to the differentiation of their symbolic structures, which is expressed above all in the increasing reflexivity of cultural traditions, in processes of individuation, in the generalization of values, in the increasing prevalence of more abstract and more universal norms, and so on. These are trends which do not imply something good in themselves, but which nevertheless indicate that the prejudiced background consensus of the life-world is crumbling, that the number of cases is increasing in which interaction must be co-ordinated through a consensus reached by the participants themselves. Otherwise they must be transposed to media such as money or power, or controlled by a pseudo-consensus. This, in turn, is becoming less and less obtainable through ideologies, and is rather secured through the fragmentation of consciousness, and through barriers to communication which distort everyday practice in inconspicuous ways.

I recall these sociological considerations, which are developed in the second volume of *Communicative Action,* in order to make clear that I am no transcendental philosopher. I would not speak of 'communicative rationalization' if, in the last two hundred years of European and American history, in the last forty years of the national liberation

---

25. See *The Structural Transformation of the Public Sphere,* pp. 102–117, 79–88.

movements, and despite all the catastrophes, a piece of 'existing reason', as Hegel would have put it, were not nevertheless also recognizable—in the bourgeois emancipation movements, no less than in the workers' movement, today in feminism, in cultural revolts, in ecological and pacifist forms of resistance, and so forth. One must also bear in mind the rather more subcutaneous transformations in patterns of socialization, in value-orientations—for example, in the diffusion of expressive needs and moral sensitivities, or in the revolutionizing of sexual roles, in an altered subjective significance of waged work, and so on. Such long-term displacements in the motivational and attitudinal economy of the population do not hang in mid-air. Structurally they are above all based on the fact that the second industrial revolution augments labour productivity at a breakneck tempo while drastically reducing socially necessary labour time; for this reason it will require more and more absurd efforts, as Gorz, Offe and Negt argue, extending an old notion of Marcuse's, to hold the growing mass of those excluded and pushed to the margins in reserve for the role of full-time worker, which is set up as a norm by the capitalist labour market, instead of uncoupling income and social security from occupation, and doing away with the fetishism of the labour market.

The introduction to Theory and Practice *contrasts 'communicative action' with 'strategic action'—the arts of persuasion as against those of manoeuvre or constraint. The political distinction is very close to Gramsci's couplet of 'direction' and 'domination'. Your own commitment to the fullest possible exercise of the first, as the guiding principle of political practice, has always been unequivocal. Do you think that there are any grounds for supposing there to be limits to the suasive force of communicative action in advanced capitalism—possible or probable boundaries of enlightenment, so to speak? Or do you lean to the view that in principle a transition to socialism could rally the democratic assent even of those whom it deprived of their capital?*

You must be trying to have me on!

You have generally resisted a shift from procedural to institutional theories of democracy—criticizing, for example, proponents of 'council democracy' for confusing the two. But isn't the move an essential—even urgent—one if socialism is to be a credible project in the West? After all, if you could describe the transformation of the bourgeois public domain within capitalism, from the greater to lesser substance and vitality, as a 'structural change', wouldn't it seem evident that the transformations involved in passing beyond capitalism must involve far greater 'struc-

tural' changes in democracy, which can only be specified institutionally?

I think that one must distinguish between the idea of a democratic justification of political power and the institutionalization of this level of justification, which changes according to circumstances. The idea of a process of will-formation in which all those concerned participate freely and equally is one thing, the organization of opinion- and will-forming discourses and deliberations, which would come closest to this idea under given circumstances, is another. For example, one can only appropriately criticize bourgeois parliamentarianism, in its different phases and national contexts, if one keeps these two things separate. But from this it does not follow, as you seem to suggest, that the transition to socialism, however one may imagine this today in societies such as ours, would change nothing about the existing political institutions—or should change nothing. I am convinced that the competition of parties which have become more and more independent of their bases, and which carry on the business of providing legitimation in an essentially manipulative way, must be changed. I suspect that *another* kind of separation of powers would have to be introduced. Of course I also think that such transformations of political institutions should only be carried out in the light of the constitutional principles recognized today—by drawing on the universalist content of these principles. The whole wretchedness of so-called actually existing socialism can basically be traced back to a reckless disdain for the principles of the constitutional state—as if these principles did not also primarily belong to those productive forces, to those results of the bourgeois emancipation movement, which make socialism possible in the first place.

In the second volume of The Theory of Communicative Action *you suggest that 'in bureaucratic socialism crisis tendencies result from the self-blocking mechanisms of administrative planning, just as they do, on the other hand, from endogenous interruptions of the accumulation process.'* [26] *Given these formal limitations of both the market and planning, how do you envisage the operation of the economy in a democratic socialist society?*

How can I answer that in a few sentences? After fifty to sixty years of Soviet Russian development, no one can now fail to see that Max Weber was right, in other words: that the abolition of private ownership of the means of production in no sense does away with class structures as such.

---

26. *The Theory of Communicative Action*, vol. 2, p. 385.

Personally, I no longer believe that a differentiated economic system can be transformed from within in accordance with the simple recipes of workers' self-management. The problem seems to be rather one of how capacities for self-organization can be sufficiently developed in autonomous public spheres for the goal-oriented decision-making processes of a use-value oriented life-world to hold the systemic imperatives of economic system and state apparatus in check, and to bring *both* media-controlled subsystems into dependence on life-world imperatives. I cannot imagine that this would be possible without a gradual abolition of the capitalist labour market, and without a radical-democratic implantation of political parties in their public spheres. The secondary, although in no sense trivial, question then arises of how, under such altered initial conditions, plan and market are coordinated with each other, how their relative weights in the interaction of state and economy can shift. This would be difficult for me to anticipate, even if I had a better knowledge of economics. For every intervention in complex social structures has such unforeseeable consequences that processes of reform can only be defended as scrupulous processes of trial and error, under the careful control of those who have to bear their consequences.

The Frankfurt School tradition as a whole has concentrated its analyses upon the most advanced capitalist societies, at the comparative expense of any consideration of capitalism as a global system. In your view, do conceptions of socialism developed in the course of anti-imperialist and anti-capitalist struggles in the Third World have any bearing on the tasks of a democratic socialism in the advanced capitalist world? Conversely, does your own analysis of advanced capitalism have any lessons for socialist forces in the Third World?

I am tempted to say 'no' in both cases. I am aware of the fact that this is a eurocentrically limited view. I would rather pass the question.

Is there any significance in the modulation from your initial programme of a 'theory with practical intent' to your current description of your work as a contribution to 'the self-understanding of modernity', or does this simply reflect the variable kinds of work that you've produced over the years? Whom do you conceive as the addressees of your successive books—presumably these have varied too? Do you feel closer or more distant from your readership today than in the sixties?

Everyone changes during the cycle of his or her life-history; however, I am, if anything, one of those stubborn types, to whom a rigid bourgeois identity is attributed. For this reason I do not believe that I have changed any more in my fundamental orientations than was necessary to hold true to them in altered historical circumstances. I work as a philosopher and sociologist, and therefore the people to whom my work is addressed primarily occupy positions in the scientific and educational system: now and again I dabble in political journalism and write in daily and weekly newspapers, or in so-called cultural periodicals. In both cases it tends to be the left intellectuals who are interested in what I write—and of course my old sparring-partners on the other side. I don't think of myself as avant-garde, nor do I dream of a revolutionary subject. At the moment I am more distant from the attitudes of the politically active young people, including many students, than I was at an earlier period. In my view, they have become less political, more conservative in their ways of feeling, less theoretical, and at the same time more open to the inheritance—so dubious in our country—of political romanticism, of young conservatism, and so on. But please rather consider these as the usual prejudices which make the general ageing-process of the New Left—they do not diminish my unrestrained delight in discussions with my students, and discussions in general.

Could the Left expect from you some more direct treatment of socialism, a notion that remains at once relatively marginal in your writing (in the sense that it is never explored in its own right), yet presumably central to its overall purpose? Aren't you in a way logically committed to some programmatic account of the social order your work is concerned to bring about, beyond your diagnostic analysis of the present order which you reject? Could you contemplate your producing one day an equivalent for us of Hegel's Constitution of the German Nation *or Kant's* Scheme for Perpetual Peace—*a cross between the two today would virtually give us a sketch for a democratic socialism in a disarmed Europe! Hasn't the highest philosophical vocation traditionally embraced this kind of concrete thought too?*

The examples are too grand, but I must take your admonitions to heart. I should not talk about socialism only in interviews—even though there is otherwise hardly anyone who still does so. In a speech which I am delivering to deputies of the Spanish parliament next week,[27] you will see that, besides the things for which I am paid, I also reflect about normative questions, about questions of political and practical principles.

27- See 'Die Krise des Wohlfahrtsstaates und die Erschöpfung utopischer Energien', in *Die Neue Unübersichtlichkeit*, Frankfurt 1985, pp. 141–163.

Could you conceive of reassuming a more active political role, as you did in the time of the Sozialistischer Bund *in the late fifties, under other circumstances?*

Were I to rule that out, I would be someone other than the person I would wish to be.

7

Life-Forms, Morality and the Task of the Philosopher

Could you tell us something of the earliest direction of your interests? In particular, what was the relationship between your initial philosophical and sociological concerns?

There was no sociology at Göttingen, Zurich or Bonn, the universities where I studied. I took two or three terms of economics but my main courses were in philosophy, history and psychology. By the time I finished my dissertation, however, I was fed up with intellectual work generally, and philosophy particularly. In reaction, I maintained myself for the next two years as a freelance journalist. There I mostly just picked out problems as they came up—traffic control, civil service test procedures, or what have you. But I also developed one more persistent focus, the sociology of labour and industrial relations. Georges Friedman's work was translated into German at that time, which I read. It so happened that in the mid fifties this field was re-established as an area of professional research in West Germany. Nearly all my later friends, in fact, got interested in it too. The result in my case was an essay I wrote on rationalization of industry and rationalization of human relationships, which was published in *Merkur* in 1954. The key ideas in this article contain the kernel of much of what I later came to write in *The Theory of Communicative Action.* By chance Adorno read this article. One day one of my employers told me that he knew Adorno and offered to introduce me to him. I had no permanent job at the time. So that was the way I came to Frankfurt. I was already interested in sociology. So when I got a chance of the combination of Frankfurt and sociology, I was enthusiastic. There I learned statistics and did some empirical research—producing several studies during the three years when I learned sociology on the job, only one of which was published: *Student und Politik*, in 1961.

How much of Adorno had you read before you met him? How far were you aware of the tradition of the Frankfurt School?

I had read *Dialectic of Enlightenment* and Adorno had the feeling that some of his (or their) ideas had gone into my article on rationalization. I must confess that I wasn't thinking of them when I wrote it. But probably there's some truth in this—I've never really checked it. The context in which I had assimilated *Dialectic of Enlightenment* had been a quite different one. I had come across it when studying the early Lukács. I found *History and Class Consciousness* a marvellous book. But it was like a historical document for me—I felt, what a pity one can't take it up systematically. Whereas reading *Dialectic of Enlightenment* was a revelation: I suddenly realized that there were people who had been using Marx's theorems for their own systematic purposes, in the present. Nobody did that in West Germany, where there was a bad Restoration climate at that time. It is difficult for you to imagine how totally closed a world the Federal Republic was then.

Have you ever felt any tension in your subsequent career between your different interests?

Not any more. I don't really like the distinctions between the disciplines. I have never understood how one can distinguish between, say, political science and political sociology, or between social theory or political theory and related work in philosophy. It really makes no sense. Popper makes the nice comment somewhere that disciplines are historical accidents. That's more or less true. We never had any political science as such in Germany before about 1947–48, for example. People like Carl Schmitt or Hermann Adler taught *Staatsrecht* or public law. Today, I am in a philosophy department, but the reasons are rather external and institutional.

Turning to your philosophical formation, you've said that you found in pragmatism a corrective for the deficiencies of democratic theory in Marxism. Could you expand on this?

It was always my feeling that there was no adequate theory of democracy in Marxism. The orthodox accounts of it were functionalist analyses—which struck me as incomplete, at the limit even tautological. I also read Austro-Marxist authors like Karl Renner (who was certainly an influence on me) and Otto Bauer, and then the English Labour version of the same sort of approach in Strachey. They confirmed my impression that the orthodox analysis was insufficient. But more important was the deep, everyday experience we lived through after 1945: things got better with the reintroduction of democracy, and even simply of the rule of law (although I detest those people in Germany who play down democracy in favour of the rule of law). In these conditions, where was I to look for alternative accounts? One very important influence for me in the late fifties was Wolfgang Abendroth. He had several sides to his personality, but he was among other things a *Staatsrechtler*, and this reformist side appealed to me—especially his interpretation of human rights and the welfare state.

It was only later, in the mid sixties, that I became familiar with Peirce. Then I discovered that there was a missing branch of Young Hegelianism, one that led to a more or less radical-democratic humanism. You find this already on a philosophical level in Peirce. What stemmed from it was—I don't know whether the phrase was coined by Peirce himself— 'logical socialism'. What this meant was that not only Peirce's theory of signs, but also what he calls his analysis of categories, or his crazy ontology, led him to the idea that communities, and what occurs within them, have an internal impact on scientific research and on social conditions generally. This idea then turns up in the pragmatist tradition in various versions and on various levels. Royce, whom I don't know very well, developed a religious or transcendentalist version of the role of community. In Mead it took the fundamental form of the idea of universal discourse. In Dewey, it became an immediately political conception of democracy.

You've remarked that you were particularly attracted to Marcuse because of the existentialist strand in his thought. But there doesn't seem to have been any element of existentialism in your own formation?

When I arrived in Frankfurt and listened to Adorno lecturing or giving seminars, I was immediately struck by the fact that contemporary philosophy—as I knew it, two years after my dissertation—was completely ignored. The most recent thinkers ever cited were Bergson and Husserl—and the Husserl of the *Logical Investigations* alone. If Adorno mentioned Heidegger—which didn't happen very often—I had the impression that he had scarcely read him. It was not until a few years ago that I read his Inaugural Lecture of 1931, published posthumously, and realized that he must have known *Being and Time* at that time. But afterwards you couldn't discern any deeper knowledge of Heidegger, let alone Jaspers. Against this background, you may understand better what it meant for me, as someone who had been a thoroughgoing Heideggerian for three or four years, to read Marcuse for the first time. It was while I was working on the concept of ideology that I came across

Marcuse's early articles. There you could see the exact breaking-point between an orthodox Heideggerian and a Marxist. I still can show you the lines where Herbert made *the* substantive, *the* strategic criticism of Heidegger—namely where he rejects not just the ontological difference but the difference between history and historicity. So I can recognize my own point of departure, so to speak, from Heidegger in these texts of Marcuse. Then came *Eros and Civilization.* That touched me because of its direct political resonance. I always felt much closer to the practical attitudes of Marcuse. Not only to the practical attitudes, but also to the idea that the life of theory is a project of practical reason, or conducted in its name.

But you have been very critical of existentialist theories of morality—as versions of decisionism.

I was critical of decisionism from the very beginning—from the minute when I read Schmitt, for instance. I must say, however, that I didn't put Sartre so much in the category of decisionism. That may be surprising for you. But Sartre I liked for different reasons. For me he did not represent an existentialist ethic. He was just this marvellous phenomenologist who introduced you to extreme situations. I had been brought up in a high school between '45 and '49, where Sartre's theatre was a tremendous excitement. He was a door-opener to the world for us. That was how we looked out from our dusty closet. Sartre was a great figure for my generation.

You're critical of what you call the ahistorical way in which Heidegger was taken up in the United States. How do you feel a knowledge of Heidegger's political involvement should influence one's understanding of his philosophy?

In my next book, I have a chapter on that and I can give you the idea in a nutshell—though this will now become a very rough and one-sided idea. My thesis is that the whole Heideggerian notion of a history of Being cannot be derived from the internal development of his philosophy prior to 1934 or 1935. There is no real problem in his thought up to that date which would have made him rethink his whole project. The transition to his later philosophy—a process which took exactly ten years, from 1935 to 1945, between *An Introduction to Metaphysics* and the *Letter on Humanism*—was thus largely determined by external events. Heidegger had treated the whole framework of *Being and Time* without any obvious change up to 1933. Then he suddenly gave it a collectivist turn: *Dasein* was no longer this poor Kierkegaardian-

Sartrean individual hanging in the air, in *Sorge*. But now *Dasein* was the *Dasein* of the people, of the *Volk*. I can show that line by line. All his election speeches—and he made lots of them; he wrote for a local paper; he made a speech in Leipzig where there was a rally of scientists for the Führer, on a platform bedecked with Nazi flags (we have pictures of it); he made speeches at the University (all of them for the November elections) and also, of course, his Inaugural Address as Rector at Freiburg, although that is the least revealing—all of these publications and utterances show that he gave to *Being and Time* a national-revolutionary reading. In fact, he reinterpreted one substantive point in his theory, without touching any single category of the whole frame-work. Now, after a year or two—and I suppose it was only two years after and not just three months or so—he started to become hesitant about the whole cause with which he had been identifying. You must understand that he had really been fighting at the front of it. He had the nutty idea that he, as a spiritual leader, could set himself at the head of the whole movement. You have to be brought up in a German *Gymnasium* to have such notions. But now he became disillusioned. What was he to do? What if the whole philosophical project of *Being and Time*—identified with the movement from which he now retreated—were to be affected and discredited by it? Given Heidegger's personality structure, one solution was to interpret what had happened as an objective, fatal mistake, one for which he was no longer responsible as a person—an error which revealed itself like fate in a Sophoclean tragedy. You can trace the lines where he took this way out. But he also, of course, changed his interpretation of the role of fascism itself. As late as 1935, he had still seen it as a movement which accomplished the destiny of the national revolution, including the use of technology as Ernst Jünger had extolled it in *Der Arbeiter*. Later he turned this interpretation upside down: and by the late thirties and early forties fascism had become the epiphenomenon of a fate which had turned out to be not the salvation from, but the last act of, nihilism. It is these external reasons that lie significantly behind the emergence of the later idea of the history of Being. Internally, this idea is only related to his work on Nietzsche. You can trace back this idea via Nietzsche to Hölderlin, but in Hölderlin and in Nietzsche as well it was of course not an idea that had been linked to metaphysics, but to an idiosyncratic perception of the myth of Dionysos. Heidegger now used that Nietz-schean-Dionysiac messianism for his own quite different purposes.

Why do you think Heidegger lost enthusiasm for Nazism after 1935— when the regime was actually stronger because of its success in over-coming economic crisis and mass unemployment?

I can only speculate. The immediate reason is that he didn't succeed institutionally. But of course that was not the only reason. It was quite usual for German intellectuals to lose their enthusiasm for the regime in the second half of the thirties. Carl Schmitt became disillusioned a little later than Heidegger. He still wanted to write a constitution for the Third Reich in 1938. Gottfried Benn, on the other hand, I think, became disillusioned rather earlier, perhaps soon after 1934. You can see this in his *Doppelleben*. You cannot imagine what this legacy did to bourgeois students after the war—there were no other students—who encountered an essential continuity in the universities: there was no break in terms of persons or courses. The two pre-eminent thinkers— who determined the direction of my philosophical interests—were Heidegger and Gehlen. The expressionist poet with whom everybody identified was Benn. Nobody told us about their past. We had to find out step by step for ourselves. It took me four years of studies, mostly just accidentally looking into books in libraries, to discover what they had been thinking only a decade or a decade and a half ago. Think what that meant. My own two teachers, under whom I wrote my dissertation—Ernst Rothacker and Oskar Becker—were cases in point. There I could have short discussions, because of personal relations and even, in the case of Oskar Becker, who was a nice man, because of personal attachments. But in the cases of Heidegger, Schmitt or Jünger—who was never a Nazi, but was an outright anti-semite in the Weimar Republic— there was never a single sentence of regret afterwards. There was no apology or remorse afterwards by any of these people. The moral and psychological implication was devastating.

Turning to your own work now, could you comment on the relation between your theory of cognitive interests and your theory of communicative action? Is the theory of cognitive interests in some sense still in force, simply waiting for a reformulation, or has the theory of communicative action replaced it?

The role of *Knowledge and Human Interests* has changed in my mind, since I came to the conclusion that it was of secondary significance to defend or establish critical social theory in epistemological terms. This is what I didn't see when I wrote the book. Nor, for that matter, did Adorno or even the earlier Horkheimer—they too were fascinated by methodological problems, and gave them great importance. I don't any more. But that doesn't mean I dismiss them. Today, I think one should go ahead from a different angle, substantively, and then if people ask you, one might also argue the case methodologically. The theory of cognitive interests I more or less shared with my friend Karl-Otto

Apel—he has written further on it—and I continue to think that it's basically sound. But I would be a bit more cautious now. We have all the new arguments on the table from the post-empiricists. If only for that reason, one would have to reformulate the account more carefully and leave room for historical change. Nevertheless, I hold by the fundamental idea that there are constitutive relationships between scientific enterprises and everyday orientations. These internal relationships are so strong that they can predetermine—via the formal pragmatics of research—the possible channels of application or implementation of different types of knowledge. The correlation between these knowledge-types and the various disciplines is the weakest part of the theory. There one has to admit to several sins. But I think this too could be remodelled. However, I'm no longer interested in that—at least not just now. The intellectual situation has changed so much since I wrote the book. At that time, all these secondary, victimized minds of the postwar generation in Germany, including myself, were looking to Oxford and the London School of Economics and Cambridge, and even more so to America: and what did they tell us? You remember the empiricist and positivist climate. People like us in Frankfurt were so marginal in that discussion that we had step-by-step to reconquer certain dimensions. The first dimension was the quasi-transcendental question of the constitution of knowledge. For that Peirce was helpful. Today, everyone takes it for granted that theories are paradigm-dependent and paradigms are in some sense socially constituted and historically changeable. Analytical philosophers have done a wonderful job here. But for myself, I don't want to follow them too far in a historicist direction ...

One feature of your original theory that perhaps aroused most conventional resistance at the time was your notion of an 'emancipatory interest', constituting the specifically 'reflexive sciences' like psychoanalysis. Do you hold to this today?

There is one difficulty in the general theory which McCarthy showed me. Namely, once you accept that there is a category of sciences which I now, for purposes of convenience, call reconstructive, where do you place them? They are, in a way, successors to good old transcendental philosophy, although in a pretty detranscendentalized and desublimated form. I can see that they endanger the architectonics of the three cognitive interests. But I stick to the distinction I have made between rational reconstruction and self-reflection. So far as the latter goes, I cannot imagine any seriously critical social theory without an internal link to something like an emancipatory interest. That is such a big name! But what I mean is an attitude which is formed in the experience of suffering from something man-made, which can be abolished and should be abolished. This is not just a contingent value-postulate: that people want to get rid of certain sufferings. No, it is something so profoundly ingrained in the structure of human societies—the calling into question, and deep-seated wish to throw off, relations which repress you without necessity—so intimately built into the reproduction of human life that I don't think it can be regarded as just a subjective attitude which may or may not guide this or that piece of scientific research. It is more. So I would—and I think could—defend that part of the basic structure of the theory of cognitive interests too. Its formulation was perhaps too immediately fundamentalist for the present taste. No doubt I would present it differently today.

You have often emphasized the move from a philosophy of consciousness to a philosophy of communication in your own transformation of the Frankfurt heritage. How important do you feel this transition is in the general history of philosophy? Would you regard it as comparable in significance to the rise of the philosophy of consciousness itself at the beginning of the modern period?

Looking at it from a certain distance, it is obvious that in the Frankfurt tradition my work has represented a shift towards communication theory. But in other traditions there are equivalent moves. The whole history of analytical philosophy from Frege onwards was a sequence of such movements: first from consciousness to sentence, and then with the later Wittgenstein from sentence to utterance; and that means to context, and hence to life-forms, and ultimately to life-world. You have parallels in the Heideggerian tradition. When I was recently looking again at *Sein und Zeit*, I was surprised to see how monological its whole construction was. It was written in the wake of Husserl's cartesian ego, as a reply to it, but also still depending on it. The subsequent move into the area of a history of Being employs an appeal to language—yet there is no single analysis of language in the later Heidegger. The invocation of language is not really a serious one. On the other hand, Gadamer, while starting out from Heidegger, made a genuine move to hermeneutics proper—that is, to linguistically constituted contexts and life-forms. Maybe even structuralism can be taken as another legitimate parallel. If you look at it that way, as a threshold which has been crossed from very different angles more or less simultaneously, then I would expect—let me put this mildly—that this move might turn out to be a paradigm shift in a very strict sense. For prior to that we had only one paradigm in modern philosophy: that was, as Foucault nicely explains in *The Order of Things*, a subjectivity which is centred in the self-relation of the knowing subject.

But couldn't one reply that an argument has been going on between the two ever since Vico's critique of Descartes—that in fact theories of consciousness and communication are two traditions within modern philosophy, rather than a transition within twentieth-century philosophy?

My friend Apel has written a whole book on the Renaissance precursors of Vico's hermeneutic thinking, from Dante onwards. It does appear that just such a tradition did exist, but much more visibly in the Renaissance than later. After Newton, we find only figures like Vico on the other side. This tradition was an undercurrent which never became sufficiently explicit, clarified, highbrow if you like, to compete with the mainstream philosophical discussion. So we had Vico versus Newton, we had Hamann versus Kant, and then maybe within the German historical school we had Ranke, Droysen and Dilthey—to mention only its methodologists. There was a philosophy implicit in the historical school, as I learnt from my teacher Rothacker. But it presented itself only as the dualistic self-understanding of the humanities as against real science: it was not brought to the level of philosophical shift in paradigm. You can check that this is true in, for instance, Dilthey. For thinkers like Dilthey, Simmel or Bergson—those from which *Lebensphilosophie* took off—were finally fixated on the categories of a subject which—as in the early Marx—externalized its own essential forces into cultural objectifications. Their whole cultural criticism sprang from that starting-point—attacking the estrangement of those objectifications from the living productivity of the subject. These people too, *philosophically* speaking, were captives of the dominant philosophical paradigm—even while they fought it on another level.

Why do you think Adorno resisted the move—which you were to make— from what you describe as the impasse of his own philosophy of consciousness to a theory of communication?

I never talked about that with him. In any case, the shift to communication wasn't so clear a move for me yet. When I knew him, Adorno was at the height of an intellectual career. He had reached his solutions if you like. What he did in Frankfurt—at least while I was there, after 1956—was to elaborate ever further his *Negative Dialectics* and his *Aesthetic Theory*. He wasn't reading much else. He was so much focused on his own work that it would never have occurred to me to ask: look, shouldn't you consider this? All our discussions were immanently on his own terrain.

You've argued, however, that 'Adorno cannot appeal to any structure heterogeneous to instrumental reason against which the force of totalized purposive rationality must collide', because he had no confidence in the 'rationality which is immanent in everyday communicative practice' as a bulwark against such totalized purposive rationality.[1] Your phrasing seems to claim that such confidence can always be given to everyday communication as a source of human resistance. But could someone who lived through the epoch of fascism, as Adorno did, possibly have the same faith in the saving rationality of everyday communication? Surely that must have been one fundamental reason why he would never come to the kind of conclusions which you reached?

What I wanted to say is only that there has existed, as long as we can remember, a mode of social reproduction which is linked to linguistic communication. This does not mean that there cannot ever be historical circumstances under which this whole infrastructure might be eroded— even finally crushed. For the rest, if I understand you correctly, you refer only—only!—to different life-experiences. Of course, what you say is true—what can I add?

Isn't there a suggestion in your respectful criticism of the original Frankfurt School that their work possessed a logic which then went adrift at a crucial point: as if they took a wrong turning?

Maybe I did express it like that once. But no, they didn't really have either biographical or philosophical access to the alternative which I came to prefer. The categorial framework of their theory in the thirties left no space between the alienating systems of capitalist economy and state on the one hand, and subjective nature on the other. There was no room for ideas of the life-world or of life-forms (Dilthey or Wittgenstein). So they were not prompted to look into the no-man's-land of everyday life, which for them was a mere epiphenomenon either of the totalizing force of the administrative world, or of suffering nature. Intersubjective relationships left no philosophical trace. I've argued that there are some passages in *Negative Dialectics* that show Adorno had intuitions which could be and should be saved within a very different, communicative framework. But he himself was deaf to that alternative. You should realize that biographically the last political experience to which Horkheimer and Adorno spontaneously reacted was McCarthyism. That shaped their outlook for the rest of their postwar German

---

1. 'A Philosophico-Political Profile', p. 153, above.

existence. I think that for them the reconstitution of a more or less liberal, even democratic state in West Germany acted only as a confirmation of the intuition that the normative model for all that had been lost, and all that was going to be lost, was the liberal era of early capitalism. In that sense, the actual historical experience of the Federal Republic, of post-war West Germany, was more or less impenetrable to them. This does not mean, of course, that they were not in daily life, apart from theory, aware of the redeeming features of a Western constitutional regime—particularly Horkheimer.

You have sometimes indicated a utopian dimension of communication, which could be seen as rendering more concrete certain of Adorno's intuitions. Wouldn't that require, however, putting more stress than you usually do upon the intertwining of identity and non-identity in communication? Do you think it would be valuable to balance your emphasis on explicit consensus with more attention to the oblique aspects of communication?

That is just. What happened is this. If you enter a certain universe of discourse, you are forced to deal in the first instance with ideal or standard cases. But that this in itself is not enough is clear. As far back as the early sixties—when I was at Heidelberg—I did not treat communication so much technically as paradigmatically. If you look, for example, at my review of Klaus Heinrich,[2] you will see that I stressed the broken nature of all intersubjective relationships. In other words, even if these are idealized, they must still be conceptualized in such a way that their tensions remain irreducible—otherwise that whole structure collapses: tensions, not just between subjects, but reflexively as well, between different perceptions and self-perceptions of what constitutes an individuality and which nevertheless is perpetually in flux, in change, never identical with certain presuppositions which are nevertheless necessary and unavoidable. Today, having gone through more standard cases, I would say that you have to analyse idealizations in such a way that you stress *both*: the idealizations and their failures. For instance, there are no identical meanings in the terms in which we are now trying to communicate, from the third person's point of view there are *none*: it is easy for psychologists and for Derrida too (if he would analyse anything!) to show that there is only non-identity over the whole space of communication. On the other hand, we have simultaneously to realize that any human communication would break down the moment you

---

2. 'Von der Schwierigkeit, Nein zu Sagen', in *Philosophisch-politische Profile*, 2nd enlarged edn, Frankfurt 1981, pp. 445–52.

could not presuppose that we exchange identical meanings. You have to
show both. Only if you do so do you have the core of the idea. Of course
this is easy enough to show for meaning-identity. It is less easy—but still
not too hard—to show for pragmatic presuppositions in discourse. But it
is much more difficult to show—and it's from there you started—when it
comes to identity-formations of persons which are also always symbolic
constructions. It was with that problem I actually set out in the early
sixties. But it still lies before me. Here Adorno's categories are much
more appealing, since they are closer to the phenomena.

*What do you mean when you say, 'Unlike Nietzsche and his disciples,
Adorno has no illusions about the genuinely modern origins of aesthetic
experience, in whose name modernity falls victim to a levelling,
undialectical critique'?*[3]

That is one of the theses of my new book, *Der Philosophische Diskurs
der Moderne.* I think that from Nietzsche onwards—this is also true of
Bataille and Derrida—the experiential basis for the Other of Reason,
from whose standpoint they criticize reason as a narrowly objectifying,
instrumentalizing force, is a field which was only opened up with
modern avant-garde art, from Baudelaire to surrealism. In other words,
the self-referential criticism of reason is nourished—that is the key to it—
from an experience which is no older than avant-garde art. Yet this
experience is projected—by Nietzsche and his successors—backwards
into archaic origins, onto the Dionysian, the pre-Socratic, the exotic and
primitive. This kind of *nachgeahmte Substantialität* was completely alien
to Adorno and Benjamin. It never occurred to them to mystify
peculiarly modern experiences in this fashion. For that is what this
radical criticism of reason in effect amounts to, with its fabulation of
pre-civilizational states. We have had all that, in Germany, so immediately at hand that you can smell it ever afterwards: the artificial
mystification of something so close into something supposedly so
primordial.

*You've said that philosophical systems are no longer possible today and
that every philosophical work must tacitly forego systematic thinking.
Yet you certainly don't renounce in the same way systematic social
theory. In fact, you pursue it quite freely. What explains the contrast?*

It is in the strong notion of theory and of truth that the difference

---

3. 'A Philosophico-Political Profile', p. 155 above.

between metaphysics and post-metaphysical thought lies. The idea of theory since Plato was that of a thought capable of grasping the totality of entities, or the world as a whole; and the idea of truth implied a clearly non-fallibilistic element of fundamentalism. Yet these notions have been in a process of decomposition—as Marx said—since Hegel. In that sense, I think we are just contemporaries of the Young Hegelians still. Nothing has changed since then, basically. The decomposition has proceeded. But for some the farewell to philosophical systems was and is still so painful that they have to dramatize the whole question. This was true of Adorno and it remains true of Derrida. They made a drama of something which should be trivial by now: a fallibilist conception of truth and knowledge. Even I learnt this from Popper! But if systematic thinking in philosophy has this sense of strong theory- and truth-concepts, it does not in the field of science, where it is more or less innocent to speak of a systematic approach as opposed to, say, a historical one. History itself, of course, is also amenable to a systematic approach as opposed to, say, a hermeneutic one.

You make a very sharp distinction between the tasks that you will allow philosophy in the field of ethics, and substantive moral theories. But what difference does it actually make—other than one of a salutary pathos—to say that 'the philosopher ought to explain the moral point of view' and no more: 'anything further is a matter for moral discourse between participants', in which, if the philosopher happens to advocate any actual principles of justice, these can merely be an—unphilosophical—'proposal among citizens'?[4] Elsewhere, you go so far as to write: 'Everyday moral intuitions have no need of the clarification of the philosopher. In this area the therapeutic conception of philosophy, introduced by Wittgenstein, seems to me to hold without exception.'[5] In other words, philosophy leaves everyday morals as they are. Could you have written that in Germany in the late thirties?

Philosophers are not teachers of the nation. They can sometimes—if only rarely—be useful people. If they are, they may write books like that of Rawls, for instance. Rawls hasn't systematically cared when he speaks as a philosopher and when he speaks simply as a committed liberal in his society. This is what I think philosophers should also do: forget about their professional role and bring what they can do better than others into

---

4. See ibid., p. 158 above.
5. 'Discourse Ethics: Notes on a Program of Philosophical Justification' in *Moral Consciousness and Communicative Action*, p. 98 (trs. altered).

a common business. But the common business of political discourses among citizens nevertheless stays what it is. It is not a philosophical enterprise. It is the attempt of participants to answer the question 'what now?'—in these circumstances, for us particular people, what are or would be the best institutions?

Why is that not also true of what you say is the task of the philosopher: clarification of the general grounds or rules under which moral claims can be justified? You could say that's also our common business.

No, that's different. Because there you can develop arguments—within a fallibilistic framework, of course—which are *binding,* not just for us here and now, being members of a particular community, but which claim to be true, simply true. That is what I mean by 'explaining the moral point of view'. By the way, it is not an easy thing to do—at least not in our times.

Are you implying that by contrast it's an easy thing to arrive at a theory of justice?

What philosophy should seek to do is to maintain its competence in those areas where it can defend universal statements. Therefore in morality it is only the universal core of the moral point of view which is a matter for philosophers. Here they can do what they are equipped to. On the other hand, if they want to design just institutions for a certain type of society under given historical conditions, philosophers can only join those who are involved in the democratic process as active citizens or serve as assistants with a certain expertise. There they move within the horizon of a shared tradition from the start.

Would you say then that Rawls's Theory of Justice *is not a philosophical work?*

Yes. When he tries to explain the moral point of view through the construct of the veil of ignorance, he is doing what the philosopher can do as a philosopher. It is a reasonable proposal. But as soon as he moves to his two principles, he is speaking as a citizen of the United States with a certain background, and it is easy to make—as has been done—an ideological critique of the concrete institutions and principles which he wants to defend. There is nothing universal about his particular design for a just society. I think one could argue methodologically that *particular* moral principles always need agreement within particular communities. I can't think of any non-procedural, substantive principles which could be applied to everything at every time. It makes no sense. Justifying particular principles is a different task. Whether we call it philosophy of not, I'm the last to mind.

So ultimately you regard the question as an issue more of presentation than of substance?

No—it's definitely a question of substance for me: a very important one.

How far then could one compare your positions with those of the Oxford philosophers of the fifties, who also put a strenuous emphasis on the non-prescriptive role of the analytic philosopher, in keeping with the same Wittgensteinian recommendations? In their case, the restriction of philosophy to the elucidation of ordinary language uses—including the language of morals—had a notoriously conservative cast. Austin, whom you often cite, after all maintained that existing everyday speech and its stock of distinctions contained all the practical wisdom that preceding generations had found necessary, and so everything we should need or want to know. The suggestion was always that matters were being perfectly well handled out there in the non-philosophical world, and philosophers had no reason to interfere with them. How do you distinguish your view—letting citizens get on with things among themselves—from this? What if things and the way they are being debated are not very satisfactory? Mightn't the philosopher have some role here, between the teacher of the nation and the semantic amanuensis?

But there is a world of political difference between my position and theirs! The Oxford position was non-cognitivist: you restrict your business to linguistic and semantic analysis and leave normative questions to whomever. I defend a cognitivist position. In fact, I am defending an outrageously strong claim in the present context of philosophical discussion: namely, that there is a universal core of moral intuition in all times and in all societies. I don't say that this intuition is spelt out the same way in all societies at all times. What I do say is that these intuitions have the same origin. In the last analysis, they stem from the conditions of symmetry and reciprocal recognition which are unavoidable presuppositions of communicative action. Theoretically, the difference is clear. Practically, it is—or should be—clear too. For any attempt—not only mine—to defend a cognitivist-universalist ethical theory involves the public assertion that in your own society and in others all practical and political questions have a moral core which is susceptible to argument. The logic of this position thus directly affects the self-understanding of the existing political culture, which can no longer be immunized against rational demands for legitimation. That it has this political impact I know from my own experience over the past ten or fifteen years in West Germany. If there is one thing that makes our neo-conservatives wild, it is this. So I don't think that it is an apolitical stance.

Let me give two further motivations for my view. The first is that my restrictive view levels down the old philosophical claims to normative theory, be it in politics or in ethics. For it means that you put the responsibility for decisions on the shoulders of those who anyhow will suffer their consequences, and that at the same time you stimulate the participants who have to make up their minds in practical discourse to look around for information and ideas that can shed light on their situation—which can clarify their understanding of themselves. The problem, by contrast, with classical normative theories is that they give people the illusion that they simply need to find the theory and then act on it. Which is nonsense. You cannot just read Rawls and say, 'Look, these are the two principles—let's now reconstruct our institutions in keeping with them.' That is not our situation. The normative part of the theory should be only procedural, while everything else that matters for practical purposes should be learnt from science, from social theory and not from moral philosophy. What I have in mind is a certain division of labour where the limited role of moral philosophy leaves a larger space for social theory. I am sorry that social theory is basically not in any shape to perform the role I say it should.

There is also, however, on the moral side of the question, the Aristotelian argument, in the *Nicomachean Ethics*, that nobody can deal with ethical questions who has not been raised properly. I do not think that this is quite true. I feel inhibitions about saying that. But it is fair to ask: how could anyone focus on moral intuitions and reconstruct them, before having them—and how do we get them? Not from philosophy, and not by reading books. We acquire them just by growing up in a family. This is the experience of everyone, except perhaps the limit-cases of psychopaths with no moral sensibility whatsoever. There can't be anyone who ever grew up in any kind of family who did not acquire certain moral intuitions. The difference between these is then only in the degree of their universalization. The presuppositions concerned may not reach farther than your own kind, your own folk, your own nation. It is only modern developments which have brought a real push to universalize these intuitions. Thus, if I used the formulation that 'philosophy leaves everything as it is' here, that is partly true. For I don't believe that we can change moral intuitions except as educators—that is, not as theoreticians and not as writers.

Couldn't one make out a strong empirical case against this view? Think of Rousseau. It can be shown pretty clearly in cases like his that moral intuitions are not quite so naturwüchsig as you make them out to be—that they are more susceptible to illustration and advocacy of change.

That is important to add, for intuitions can become clarified, and that clarification may be very important. Just by entering the medium of words, something can change. Such transformations from 'know-how' to 'know-that' are sometimes only achieved through art or literature, or the work of artist-philosophers like Rousseau. I wouldn't deny that. But for me the problem is really a political one. What is the harm if I write something on civil disobedience as a political man, and not as a philosopher?

None at all. But one might reply—how many of your readers on civil disobedience forget that you are a philosopher? Your words have a different weight, because of your philosophy—as was true of Russell or Sartre.

Now you're talking about the sociology of reception ...

You've said that you defend the outrageously strong position that there is a universal core to all moral judgements. On the other hand, you argue that 'forms of life' can only be judged by cultural standards internal to them, which then permit 'clinical intuitions' as to their value—but you doubt whether these have any universal core, as moral intuitions do. Can these positions be reconciled? Take the example of the United States in the 1850s. Two opposed societies coexisted within the frontiers of the same state—North and South. Their differences were such that war eventually broke out between them. The principal defence of the slave-owners, in that conflict, was that Southern civilization was an integrated Lebensform—a way of life as a whole—which was threatened by Northern abolitionism, based on a quite other way of life. Given your postulates, how could you arbitrate the conflict between the two?

This is a very tricky question. I had to supervise a dissertation on the South, so I am a bit familiar with the arguments of its spokesmen, which I found at first sight rather persuasive. I think one needs to distinguish between two sets of questions. The first is the political and implicitly moral question whether the institution of slavery could be justified within the framework of a set of specific constitutional laws. The answer to that is not difficult. The Northern position was that slavery could and should be changed in accordance with the constitution, and also in accordance with moral intuitions, which were fortunately not just expressed in books, but were codified—as principles—in law. Few of the Southerners ever said that they would fight to the death on the ground of legal amendments, as such. But others could have objected on different grounds. They might have said, 'Look, in the end we will agree that slavery should be abolished. But in intentionally implementing this aim now, you will destroy a form of life in the South which has its own historical value, and whose treatment of its slaves is more or less preferable to the lot of your proletariat in the Northern cities.' Complicated questions are posed by this line of defence. To resolve them, it may be useful to look at another textbook example of these dilemmas. Would the English, on first entering India and encountering the ritual of burning widows, have been entitled to stop it? Hindus would have said that this institution—a burial rite—belonged to their whole form of life. In that case, I would argue that the English should have abstained, on the one condition t'at this life-form was really self-maintaining—that is, not yet in inevitab dissolution and assimilation to a different way of life. There could be no analogy to this example today, because there are no such traditional cultures left after three hundred years of capitalism. But the Indian case illuminates the American one, by contrast. For Southern society never represented a form of life which was freely chosen—if we can use this term as a naive-philosophical normative redescription of *naturwüchsig*. No unforced consensus could—counter-factually—have ever sustained it. For this was not a self-reproducing indigenous form of life, but an artificially produced one—an agrarian zone within a capitalist system of which the plantation South and the industrial North were equally part. If this common system could only flourish under a legal order that was more implemented in the North than in the South, then from a normative point of view there were no real grounds for maintaining the Southern form of life—even in the face of its own clinical intuitions.

Nevertheless, a problem still remains here. Southern society can be criticized once you just single out the dimension of justice. The question of freedom, of the violation of human dignity, is fairly straightforward. But this is not all there is to a form of life. If we say, for example, that a way of life is 'alienated', the judgement applies not to something which is generalizable, but to something concrete, to the totality of that life. All of us participate in different forms of life, and we have intuitions about more or less pathological cases—we sense whether people can grow upright in them or not. Now here I would make at least one general assumption: that there is no developmental logic to discover. For example, medieval societies, notwithstanding higher degrees of oppression than modern or primitive societies, could in certain circumstances be clinically healthier than either of them. It is possible that further research may refine our knowledge here, and eventually reveal certain universal conditions necessary for non-pathological ways of living together. I think that justice—historically conceived—may be one such condition. But if we do discover parameters for more, or less, repressed forms of life, they probably won't possess any directionality.

You've argued that 'even social theory would overstep its competence ... if it undertook to project desirable forms of life into the future, instead of criticizing existing forms of life'.[6] This position seems to raise two sets of problems—one concerning 'forms of life', and the other concerning 'projection into the future'. Taking the first, isn't there an inherent ambiguity—hence danger of confusion—in the notion itself? The term has a strongly cultural overtone, and in that register is acceptable enough. Your emphasis on the incommensurability of life-forms makes sense if we are comparing, say, national cultures in the West today. If someone says, 'I prefer living in Germany to living in France or England', the choice is not amenable to common value-judgement or argument: it is a question, if you like, of existential taste. But the term also has a holistic *connotation—it suggests a 'whole way of life' that then necessarily includes a* social structure. *That is the case, for example, in the contrast between North and South in the USA which we've just discussed. There political comparison and differential evaluation are surely inevitable, and indispensable. So the question arises, how do you theoretically demarcate a 'life-form'?*

I think I would do so by reintroducing the famous distinction between form and content. I'm not sure where this leads me. But I would retain Hegel's concept of totality for something de-Hegelianized: namely for a life-world which can be accounted for more or less only narratively and intuitively, in everyday language—not theoretically. Precisely because it has these holistic features, which are present to our daily self-understanding. We cannot but live in a total world. The world constitutes a totality—inevitably—in the background of our everyday activities. Now the problem is whether one can employ a theoretical language to analyse a concrete life-world, as a particular totality, or whether one refrains from that claim and restricts oneself to an analysis of the presumably universal infrastructure which all life-worlds share with each other. It is this infrastructure that I'm interested in. But social theory can, of course, also compare general features of a number of life-worlds—say plebeian

---

6. 'A Philosophico-Political Profile', p. 168 above.

subcultures in proto-industrial societies with those in pre-industrial or industrial societies, in terms of their optional structures in daily actions and transactions: how many options exist in different fields?—in order to pin down differences in the institutional core of these life-worlds. That you can do.

What about the second problem—your prohibition of projections into the future? Doesn't the way you put this rule out of court much too drastically any form of utopian thinking? Here too the ambiguities of the notion of a 'form of life' seem to be at work. For you say that Marxist theory cannot 'cash out the expression "socialism" in terms of a concrete form of life'.[7] This seems precisely to abstract the idea of a life-form from any 'institutional core'—as if it were essentially a culture, rather than a social structure. For Marxism certainly does specify institutional features of socialism, above all defining it as a classless society. But even setting that objection aside, is it the case that 'concrete forms of life' cannot be constructively projected in social thought? After all, you have yourself just spoken appreciatively of Marcuse's Eros and Civilization, *a utopian work which certainly attempts this. A more recent case would be Gorz's work, which also seeks to depict a future form of life, quite concretely. Do you really want to debar these kinds of projection from social theory?*

Look, I am convinced that we still live in the modern epoch—not in some post-modern sequel to it. The fact means, among other things, that everyday politics remains mediated by a *Zeitgeist* in which utopian and historical modes of thinking constantly intermingle. Utopian thought has been integrated into historical and everyday political thinking to such an extent that in the present period we manifestly suffer from an apparent retreat of utopian energies, from a closure of horizons. This is a typical indicator of the fact that utopian perspectives are constitutive of modern political thought. I think that social theories too live from their connection with these utopian contents—in spite of all denials from Fourier and Saint-Simon onwards. Nobody wanted to be utopian—it was not just Marx. However, the implicit connection of the theory of Marx with the utopia of self-activity—emancipation from heteronomous labour—suffered, I believe, from two mistakes. The first was the productivist bias which was built into this particular vision—as it was into all utopias from Thomas More onwards: namely, the idea that scientific control over external nature, and labour to transform it, is in itself liberating. The second error was more important, perhaps. It was

---

7. Ibid., p. 168 above.

not to realize that the only utopian perspectives in social theory which we can straightforwardly maintain are of a procedural nature. For the utopian lineaments of any future emancipated society can be no more than necessary general conditions of it. They cannot be in the nature of a design for a form of life. If Marcuse advocated a certain mode of socialization and concomitant changes in general structures in *Eros and Civilization*, or Gorz advocates a disconnection between employment and income, then I think these ideas can be formulated in a way that avoids the misunderstanding that social theory can project concrete or particular new forms of life. Gorz's scheme is essentially a demand for the abolition of the labour market and the reconstruction of the economy in such a way that certain imperatives of the occupational system can no longer invade everyday existence. But it is not a recommendation of one particular mode of life. It simply poses conditions under which people could then lead their lives—not individually, probably, so much as in their cultures. Similarly, I think that Marcuse's ideas could be reformulated as a principle that socialization processes should meet certain conditions such that the conflicts are not resolved by external discharge of aggression. The important thing—in the face of false, neo-conservative attributions—is to lay a clean conceptual cut between utopian perspectives in general and the projection of particular forms of life. The one refers to necessary conditions—and is what socialism is about. I don't say that socialists should abstain all the time from projecting concrete forms of life. But Marx was pretty hesitant about doing so. What he meant by socialism politically was just—we can say now after fifty years of Soviet history—*just* the abolition of the private ownership of the means of production. As the simple specification of a necessary condition, that was very cautious, I must say. But, we see today, not cautious enough.

You've often argued that the important shift to make in thinking about contemporary society is from a production to a communication paradigm. Critical social theory should no longer rest, you maintain, on the expressivist model of alienated labour and the re-appropriation of its essential forces. But is it really necessary for one model or paradigm completely to supersede the other? It is not clear from your reasoning why they couldn't complement each other. You started out by remarking that Marxist theory has traditionally been weak in the whole area of democracy. But it doesn't seem to follow from that negative deficiency that the positive concern of the theory with production has to fall by the same token.

We need to be clear about in which theoretical context, or at what level, the respective merits of the two paradigms are to be debated. At the very basic, quasi-anthropological level, I have proposed a conception of communicative rationality which does include the cognitive-instrumental elements of teleological action. In other words, the communication model is inclusive. When I introduce the idea of communicative action, I emphasize that all types of action display the same teleological infra-structure. So at that level I would maintain the inclusive character of one of the two paradigms, but not vice versa. On another level, we come to more specific assumptions about the evolutionary primacy of different sectors of our society. This is an empirical question. There, as you know, I have argued that the social-integrative core of the institutional framework of society undergoes developments which are at least as important as innovations in the forces of production and science. That is a second level. There is a third level, however, which is where I more usually compare the two paradigms: that posed by the question—where do social theories get their non-arbitrary, normative potentials from? Here, I have good reasons to maintain that the expressivist model is dependent on philosophical-anthropological assumptions, about how human beings are constituted, which acquire a methodologically dubious status. My procedure, by contrast, is to have recourse to a reconstruction of the intuitive knowledge we must inevitably possess, if we want to do something. That is a very different approach. Finally, and this is a fourth level, I think that the expressivist model inherited by Marx, which derived from the transference of certain aesthetic ideals into the sphere of industrial production, finds less and less empirical confirmation in the organization of contemporary labour processes. It becomes increasingly difficult to imagine how under current technical conditions, or even humanized versions of them with smaller-scale plant and equipment, work processes could ever be reintroduced that would bring with them the type of fulfilment originally derived from the exemplar of the artistic genius, who objectifies his most essential nature into his artefact and then contemplates and re-appropriates what he has externalized. I just don't think that our world affords a foothold for that any longer.

Isn't there some tension between these theoretical positions and the political judgements you yourself make about oppositional forces in West Germany today? For while you emphasize the positive potential of the Greens and the new social movements allied to them, as the basis for an 'anti-productivist alliance', you also say very positively that their weakness is that they 'occupy no vital functional domains of industrial society'.[8]

---

8. Ibid., p. 178 above.

Isn't that just because they are, indeed, marginal to production? You go on to remark that one of the most important effects the Greens might have would be to produce shifts inside the SPD—'without which, if we are realistic about it, nothing can be moved' in the country. Doesn't all this amount to conceding that, while an alliance—or capacity for joint action—between the new social movements and the labour movement is an important objective, its centre of gravity must lie in the majority of the population that is actually involved in classical forms of production?

In assessing the Greens, what is significant in the first instance is whether the potentials they represent are structurally generated or just contingently thrown up. My view is that there are systematic reasons why these potentials are still expanding. Now it is true they occupy no central functions, more or less by definition. That circumscribes the kind of power they exercise, in the second instance. This is not to say they have none. They lack the kind of power which the labour movement possesses, embodied in the strike. But they have a measure of the old reformist resource of the vote. That has a certain impact. You can see the effect from the fact that they behave more or less insanely in Parliament, yet increase their share of the vote in one election after another, till they can now get eight or nine per cent. That's not nothing. Thirdly, of course, these movements have a certain veto-power of disorganization too. For all these reasons, co-operation between the Greens and the Social Democratic Party, and even some of the unions, would not be ineffective in any case. But there are very strong opponents of it on both sides—the fundamentalist wing of the Greens (Petra Kelly is one of them), and the traditional right-wing of the Social Democrats.

What is your view of the SPD itself, then? The West German labour movement is in many ways one of the most strongly organized in Europe. The limitations of the social-democratic and trade-union tradition in the Federal Republic are obvious enough, but doesn't this also contain, or preserve, certain important cultural and political values? British writers of the Left have often seen working-class culture as a significant 'form of life' in its own right, embodying specific kinds of solidarity and struggle and self-education essential to the hope of any future socialism. Would you concede any pertinence of this emphasis to German working-class culture or the SPD—which has, of course, shifted somewhat to the left in recent years?

It is very difficult to put much hope in the West German labour movement today. The Bad Godesburg Conference of the SPD in the late fifties marked a fundamental turn in the history of the party. Abendroth saw this very clearly. The SPD opening to the middle class at that time was accompanied by a real political mutation. Thereafter it did nothing to counteract the steady erosion of the socio-cultural bases of the older social-democratic tradition. German working-class culture had been largely destroyed in the epoch of fascism and the Second World War—there was much less left after 1945 than in England. The self-organization of leisure-time, for example, in the clubs and colonies of the classical labour movement had disappeared. There are only a few traces of this heritage left in the Ruhr today. The party is now threatened even in its bastions by adverse sociological trends, as the unions are weakened by mass unemployment and technological change. The printers, traditionally the backbone of the politically educated labour movement, are an obvious case in point. The party now has great difficulties in recruiting younger people, as well—there is a breakdown of older motivations in the 18–32 age group. In many ways, the underlying situation of the SPD is worse today than it has ever been since the end of the War.

After a brief period of progressive initiatives under Chancellor Brandt, in a quite exceptional constellation which soon passed away, things got bad in the final years of Schmidt's rule. On the other hand, it is true that the party has become more politically active since the *Wende*—the installation of the Kohl government. For people like me, it is good luck that the SPD is now in opposition again—we are not so marginalized any longer. I vote for the SPD, and have always done so. Naturally, I would like to see an alliance between the SPD and the Greens, what is left of the labour movement and the new social movements. But this is not a *natural* alliance. How can unity be achieved among such heterogeneous groups—anti-productivist, old-productivist, new-middle-class? Above all, what kind of political vision can be developed beyond the impasse of the welfare state?

8

Critical Theory and
Frankfurt University

I

The intellectual climate of the period in which Critical Theory first emerged now strikes us as almost exotic, seen from the standpoint of the present. Neo-Kantianism, phenomenology and metaphysics collided with one another, the influence of Jung's and Klages' psychology was felt, all within the Humboldtian institutional framework of the university. Its students were drawn largely from a homogeneous social stratum, the educated bourgeoisie, and its white-bearded professors—such as Cornelius, the teacher of Horkheimer and Adorno—were of a type whose image was rather that of the homme de lettres. *Aside from their training in an academic Neo-Kantianism, Horkheimer, Adorno, Löwenthal, and to a certain extent also Benjamin, were inspired by psychoanalysis, which at that time was beyond the pale, by revolutionary radicalism, and by Jewish messianism; Bloch's* Spirit of Utopia *offered a theoretical synthesis, Lukács's* History and Class Consciousness *the epoch-making interpretation of Marx. Against this historical background, how much of the theory must be attributed to the (unique) authenticity of the people involved? How far is Critical Theory—as Dubiel has conjectured—'a personally embodied, and not always generalizable, form of life and thought'?*

At the Adorno conference which took place last autumn at the University of Frankfurt, Helmut Dubiel defended the contemporary relevance of the older Critical Theory in an ironical way. He criticized its claims unsparingly, and precisely in this way set the relevance and fruitfulness of the underlying questions in the correct light. A research tradition only remains alive when it can prove the validity of its old intention in the light of new experiences; and this cannot be done without abandoning outdated theoretical contents. But, of course, that is the normal attitude to theoretical traditions, and should especially be the attitude to a theory which is reflective about its own context of emergence. One of the ways in which Horkheimer distinguished 'critical' from 'traditional' theory was in terms of the fact that the former sees itself as a component of the very social process which it attempts, simultaneously, to explain. Adorno speaks for this reason of the 'temporal core of truth' [*Zeitkern der Wahrheit*]. In dealing with such a theory 'abandonment' or 'conservation' are not the appropriate alternatives. Instead, we should adopt an exploratory approach, and see how far we can now get with the attempt to continue critical social theory in an unreservedly self-correcting and self-critical mode.

On the other hand, you are right to point to the distinctive context of emergence in the 1920s, and to the specific outlook of the literary, Left–intellectual, Jewish–bourgeois milieu in cities such as Berlin and Frankfurt, in which motifs drawn from messianism and German Idealism combined with the contemporary cultural elements of expressionism, and of the new discipline of psychoanalysis, to form a unique structure which Merleau-Ponty was later to term 'Western Marxism'. The physiognomy of the spirit of that time is tied to an unrepeatable situation. At best, witness can be borne to such an intellectual formation, which has been historically superseded, through the presence of surviving, and commanding, personalities. At the Adorno conference which I just mentioned, the moving mode of address, the spontaneity, and the unaffected presence of Leo Löwenthal reminded us of that unique context, which is now irretrievably lost. Of course there are constellations in the past and present which have affinities with each other. Unfortunately, the double-sided combat of the old Frankfurt School against positivism on the one hand, and *Lebensphilosophie* and all kinds of metaphysical obscurantism on the other, has taken on fresh relevance. You have recalled C. G. Jung and Ludwig Klages—today the names would be Lacan and Guattari.

With regard to Critical Theory as—in Adorno's phrase—a 'message in a bottle', Löwenthal once remarked: 'Of course we were all amazed at the bang with which this bottle was opened in the sixties.' To what extent was it the specific historical background, and in the last analysis the confrontation of the theory with the totalitarianism of Hitler and Stalin, which gave rise to the explosive mixture of the 'old' Critical Theory? Is it so inconsistent to continue the idea of Critical Theory in the paradigm of the body formulated by post-structuralism? Is it not true for Foucault, as it was for Adorno, that sensitivity to suffering provides the measure of civilization?

The unpredictable shock waves set up by Critical Theory at the end of the sixties were undoubtedly connected with the fact that the theory was saturated with the biographical and historical experiences of exiled Jews and unorthodox Leftists. Because of this it was able to act as a catalyst in a situation where a part of the post-war student generation found themselves confronted with a past which had not been dealt with by their parents. But even the theoretical content somehow corresponded with the end of the Adenauer era. In contrast to the orthodox Marxists, of course, Horkheimer and his circle had applied all their energy to explaining the stability and capacity for social integration of developed capitalism—to the explaining not of crises, but rather the lack of crises with a revolutionary outcome. The *Bundesrepublik*, too, at that time— at any rate more so than today—conveyed the everyday experience of a well-ordered society [*formierte Gesellschaft*], as its champion Erhard called it.

In any event, it is in the nature of things that the historical effects of ideas cannot be predicted. Today the *Dialectic of Enlightenment* is read differently. Some read it with the eyes of the French post-structuralists. As Axel Honneth has shown, there are indeed similarities, for example between Adorno and Foucault. But Adorno would have defended himself against an *assimilationist* reading, perhaps with the formula which he often used: it is precisely the small differences which make 'all the difference'. Despite the radicality of his critique of reason, Adorno never gave up on what the great philosophers once intended with the notion of reason. Undoubtedly, the clinical condition of a civilization can be measured by the apparently peripheral victims, by the avoidable suffering which it demands of us. But when one surrenders to this critical impulse, is one then also entitled to deny the rationality of the criteria which are intuitively brought into play?

At the Adorno Conference in 1983, the vice-president of Frankfurt University spoke of a 'complicated relationship between Adorno and this University', hinting at the reservations concerning the critical philosopher which came to light in breaches of convention. Is this relationship any easier today? More generally: how hard is it for a scholar today when he openly describes himself as a Marxist? Would even such an internationally renowned philosopher as Jürgen Habermas have to sign a declaration of allegiance to the free-democratic constitution in Bavaria or Lower Saxony?

In my view the academic reservations about Adorno drew on similar dark sources to those which, two generations earlier, hindered the career of a Georg Simmel. Simmel was accused of having a relativistic attitude to Christianity. His unorthodox way of thinking and lecturing was experienced as provocative. His success with the students, and his effect on a broader public, aroused envy. Antisemitism blended with spiteful feelings against an intellectual who was also a literary success. These sources have tended to dry up in the meantime. What is more, it no longer exists, this last, incomparably productive generation of German–Jewish intellectuals who shaped the University of Frankfurt (above all in the twenties, and then once more through Adorno and Horkheimer after the war). Today similar reservations crystallize around other issues.

For my part, I experience the city and the University of Frankfurt today as a liberal milieu. Admittedly, that other university, which is located next to the seat of the government of Bavaria, could not bring itself—even after repeated attempts—to take the routine decision of granting the position of honorary professor to the director of the neighbouring Max Planck Institute, a position without any real power. That strikes me more as a curiosity than anything else. Less curious was the attempt on the part of the Albrecht regime to revive the oath of loyalty of the McCarthy era.[1] In this case it was not a matter of fidelity to the principles of our constitution, which forbid any interference with the freedom to teach. In 1977 it was a matter of declaring political submission to the concrete constitutional reality, the concrete order of a one-eyed regime. That was the background music to the German Autumn.[2]

There is something else which I find more worrying today—I am thinking of the defamatory campaigns of our neo-conservative colleagues. For example, yesterday I read an article with scholarly pretensions by Frau Noelle-Neumann in the *Frankfurter Allgemeine Zeitung*, which specializes in these things of course.[3] There it was stated that: 'The Habermasian overtones of the terms knowledge and interest, dating from the nineteen sixties, seem to have completely destroyed any claim for the self-critical, self-clarifying capacity of reason' (*FAZ*, 24 July 1984). It is not the glaring falsity of the assertion which disturbs me, but the deliberate propagation of such untruths. What is being increasingly destroyed in the *Bundesrepublik* is a culture of unselfconscious contact with those who have different political views, a culture which, in any case, is only weakly developed here, and which is difficult to restore—Rosa Luxemburg has become less a part of our landscape than Elisabeth Noelle-Neumann.

---

1. See note 10, p. 88 above. Ernst Albrecht (CDU) was the prime minister of Lower Saxony at this period.
2. See note 4, p. 87 above.
3. See note 3, p. 85 above.

The Zeitgeist *has turned away from Critical Theory in the course of the seventies. Slogans such as 'New Inwardness' [*Neue Innerlichkeit*], 'Thinking from the Belly' [*Denken aus dem bauch*], post-structuralism and* The Critique of Cynical Reason *have enjoyed a wild success. Sociology, which was already famed in Frankfurt in the 1920s, above all through the work of Oppenheimer and Mannheim, has acquired a reputation for bad abstraction, because of its critical stance. The end of the old* edition suhrkamp, *to use an institutional measure, can also be seen as the end of an inflationary excess of sociological analysis. Isn't there a touch of resignation about your introductory essay to volume 1,000 of the* edition suhrkamp, *which refers to 'preserving for posterity a document of the customs and outlook of our time'? To take this a step further, isn't sociological analysis a rather melancholy enterprise, when one recalls that its results are constantly changing and, what is more, play the role of fashionable slogans, of intellectual consumer products, which are sampled and then thrown away, so to speak?*

The document which I was speaking about in this context was not the *edition suhrkamp*, but a particularly repugnant example of that defamatory writing I was speaking about a moment ago. In any case, I do not feel at all resigned. The first three semesters I have spent teaching back here in Frankfurt have encouraged me, on the whole. Perhaps one should not apply psychological concepts to the tone of theories. People who wish to hold on to the utopian content of our best traditions, even in theoretical work, should not attempt to diffuse either pessimism or optimism. One should present one's concerns in such a way that a sensitivity to the ambivalence of the contemporary situation is heightened. An ability to bear frustration and a bit of ego strength are more useful for the patient drilling of thick planks than a happy-go-lucky nature. One should not judge the fate of sociology and social theory on the basis of unstable and short-lived fashions in intellectual reception. You are right to recall Oppenheimer and Mannheim; you could also have mentioned Heller, Sinzheimer, Grünberg, Tillich and many others—the University of Frankfurt has produced internationally famed social scientists in the seventy years of its existence, whose productivity no reasonable person can doubt. By contrast, the critique of sociology which appears today as 'anti-sociology' is a familiar ideological pattern, which can be traced back through the Nazi period far into the nineteenth century. This reflex belongs to the internal equipment of periods of reaction, so to speak. One should distinguish between the ongoing history of social theory, and the temporary effects of individual theories, which cannot help but disappoint the need for a *Weltanschauung*, if they truly deserve this name.

In a study of students in the early eighties, P. Glotz and W. Malanowski have highlighted a decisive danger for the university: the loss of confidence in its function of providing the younger generation with a practical orientation in life, a confidence which was once shaped by German Idealism. The university, as a modern service-sector enterprise, separates off the problem of personal identity from the specialized sciences, and hands it over to private initiative. You took a stance on this issue twenty years ago in your essay 'Vom sozialen Wandel akademischer Bildung'. Would you still stick to this position today, after the criticism of the 'opening to the community' and 'false democratization'? Is the task of academic education today still the 'retranslation of scientific results into the horizon of the life-world'?

I still hold what I said about academic education at that time to be correct. The university should not merely pass on knowledge: in one way or another it intervenes in the self-development of the young people whom it initiates into traditions of research. On the other hand, the task of fostering personal development cannot simply be split off from the serious business of teaching science, and handed over to philosophy, in accordance with a division of labour—for philosophy itself has now become one discipline amongst others.

You have often indicated that the role of philosophy as a fundamental or hyper-science, or as a type of thinking embodied in individual philosophers, is at an end. But can philosophy not be preserved at least as the placeholder for a claim to unity and universality? Can the cooperation of philosophy and the individual sciences which you encourage be practised?

I have just come from a conference where philosophers and psychologists spent a whole week discussing moral development. There are certain areas where cooperation works. On the other hand, even today philosophy does not merely have the task of defending the claim to unity and universality, as you rightly put it, in collaboration with other sciences.

Philosophy has always sustained a particularly intimate—admittedly also paradoxical—relation to everyday knowledge. It is simultaneously near to and remote from 'common sense' [English in the original]. Like the latter, philosophy moves within the horizon of the life-world, and stands in the same relation to the totality of the horizon of everyday knowledge, and yet it is radically opposed to common sense by virtue of its subversive power of reflection, its illuminating, critical and dissecting power of analysis.

Because of its affinity with common sense, with the knowledge which gives us our everyday orientation, philosophy is, rather more than the sciences, reliant on being represented by particularly convincing individuals. I mean something different by this than the traditional elitist self-conception of philosophy, which believed itself to be interwoven with an elevated way of life, as a religion might be with the distinctive path to salvation of the hermit or the wandering monk. It is important to practise philosophy with the same awareness of fallibility as any other science. The unity of work and person is a rather naive demand, against which Adorno always fought. But it is also clear that the academic teacher must stand for what he or she says, in a plausible way.

II

Between 1949 and 1954 you studied in Göttingen, Zurich and Bonn. Your most important philosophy teachers were Erich Rothacker and Oskar Becker. You were living in the atmosphere of Heidegger's philosophy. You made your escape from this atmosphere in 1953, when Heidegger's lectures, 'Introduction to Metaphysics', which were delivered during the Nazi period, were published without any commentary. At the same time you read Lukács's History and Class Consciousness, *and then* Dialectic of Enlightenment *'with fascination', as you put it in your interview with* Ästhetik und Kommunikation. *But the fascination was obviously not great enough to bring you to Frankfurt to hear the authors themselves. How did it come about that you became Adorno's assistant in 1956, and a staff member of the Institute for Social Research?*

As far as I remember, Frankfurt philosophy and Frankfurt itself as a place of study did not have a distinctive image in the early fifties which projected with any clarity beyond the immediate region—at least not from the perspective of a philosophy student in Bonn, from where one tended to look towards Freiburg and Heidelberg, or towards Göttingen. Adorno only became known to a wider public in the late fifties, mainly through his journalism. Frankfurt philosophy remained an enclave within the discipline for a long time. In any case, I had been working on my dissertation since 1952. So it was more a happy coincidence which brought me to Frankfurt, two years after having finished my doctorate, and then having worked as a freelance journalist. The editor of Musil's works, Adolf Frisé, to whose literary supplement in the *Handelsblatt* I contributed articles at that time, one day offered to introduce me to Adorno. The latter had read something by me in *Merkur*. In the course of this first conversation Adorno invited me to come to the Institute—

initially still on the basis of a research grant which Rothacker had obtained for me for a project on the concept of ideology. In the autumn of 1956 I was then taken on as Adorno's research assistant—I was, by the way, his first personal assistant.

In the interview just mentioned you spoke about the situation in Frankfurt, about Horkheimer's and Adorno's selectivity with regard to philosophical theories, the absence of the intellectual past of the Institute, and the 'electrifying role' of Adorno for a systematic reading of Marx and Freud. But up till now little has been said about the unhappy, indeed rather shameful circumstances of your departure from the Institute. I do not wish to appear indiscreet, but I could scarcely believe what Horkheimer had said against you when I read the relevant chapter of Wiggershaus's recent book on the history of the Frankfurt School.

As far as I am aware Wiggershaus's portrayal of Horkheimer's activities during the 1950s is correct. Horkheimer enjoyed a great reputation in Frankfurt; he was also careful to maintain good political contacts on all sides. We assistants in the Institute were not exactly enthusiastic about his political views, for example on the war in Algeria, or the question of German rearmament. Even his public behaviour and his policy for the Institute seemed to us to be the expression of an almost opportunistic accommodation, which was inconsistent with the critical tradition which Horkheimer, after all, embodied. However, I changed my opinion of Horkheimer when I read his diary entries for that period after his death. It is clear from them that, after his return from the USA, Horkheimer led an altogether split existence. He was a merciless observer and perceptive analyst of those false continuities which were so characteristic of the Adenauer period; but the fear in which he lived (and not only a need for recognition) made him keep up a facade, behind which he lived as if he were sitting on unopened suitcases.

Did the dividing line run between you and Adorno on the one side, and Horkheimer on the other?

It would not be true to say that, but Adorno never shared Horkheimer's prejudices against me, and he also kept me at the Institute despite Horkheimer's pressure.

Did you depart with a feeling of bitterness, when you left for Marburg in 1961 to take up a post as a Privatdozent?

Although based in Frankfurt, I prepared my *Habilitation* with Abendroth. My break with Horkheimer was a spontaneous move, which turned out not to be such a mistake, because I soon got the opportunity to finish writing *Structural Change in the Public Sphere* with the aid of a grant from the DFG [German Research Association]. I never taught as a *Privatdozent*, because Gadamer and Löwith had already called me to a chair in Heidelberg. I was very happy to be able to go to Heidelberg. Bitterness is not the right word. My very different attitudes to Horkheimer and Adorno at first remained the same as they had been during my time as an assistant. After I returned to Frankfurt as Horkheimer's successor in 1964, and even before that, Adorno never-theless repeatedly tried to ease the tense relation between Horkheimer and myself—eventually with some success.

What were the conversations and discussions between you and Adorno like? Were controversial issues worked through, or at least addressed? If one looks up the passages in Adorno's writings where he makes reference to you, one is struck by his readiness to agree. On one occasion he declares himself to be 'very indebted' to your book Structural Change in the Public Sphere, *on another he takes over from you the reproach of 'pseudoreality' directed at the protesting students. His most obvious references to you are in the 'Introduction' to* The Positivist Dispute in German Sociology, *where he interprets you—at least, this is my impression—in a way directly contrary to what you intended. Only in his interview with* Der Spiegel *does one detect a sharper tone, when he replies to your criticism that his dialectic surrenders to the 'darkest places' and to 'the destructive undertow of the death drive': 'I would say rather that a rigid inclination towards the positive stems from the death drive.' On the other side, it is clear that your 1963 essay in honour of Adorno's sixtieth birthday is marked throughout by a friendly proximity to Adorno, and that it was only later, after his death, that the differences were expressed in a less qualified and more decisive manner. The impression is hard to avoid that, as theoreticians, you treated each other in an extremely protective way. This was perhaps intensified on your side by the fact that Adorno—or so I imagine—was the kind of personality (the word is unavoidable) who could cast a harmonizing spell over those around him.*

You must not forget that I was separated from Adorno by a generation. I always remained the assistant, and then the younger colleague, who admired his senior and was on friendly terms with him. Gretel Adorno and my wife were also included in this constellation. As far as the theoretical relationship is concerned, it was of course never a question of two positions of equal weight. I don't believe that Adorno ever read a book of mine. We worked together in certain respects during my time as an assistant. Adorno always read my manuscripts very carefully, and covered them with annotations. Later he maybe read the odd article by me. Also, right up to the middle of the sixties, he probably assumed that there were no significant differences between us in our basic philosophical impulses. Theoretical discussions, which we often engaged in together, were always with reference to his texts. When I was still in the Institute, he used to come up to the first floor, where I had a room opposite Gretel's, in order to tell me about an idea, an inspiration, which he had just got excited about. That is what he did, for example, when he thought he had got clear about the internal relation between identity-thinking and the commodity form for the first time. I immediately expressed reservations on this point, by the way, which we then discussed, although I do not think I made any impression on Adorno with them. As far as the more profound differences are concerned, they were certainly already implicit—although I only really became aware of them later on. Your phrase, 'harmonizing spell', captures the situation very well, I think. The differences which I formulated in *The Theory of Communicative Action* only became clear to me *very* much later, through reading an essay by Axel Honneth.

You often speak of Adorno's genius, or of his 'genius-like' abilities. This seems to me to be an ambiguous expression. As we know, Kant only allowed for geniuses in art, a thesis which can be attributed to his narrow conception of science. But don't you also respect the same distinctions? I could put the question another way: is genius reserved for Adorno, or would the term be justified with regard to Horkheimer or Marcuse, indeed to any creative philosopher?

Adorno *was* a genius, I say that without a hint of ambiguity. In the case of Horkheimer or Marcuse, with whom, by the way, I had a less complicated and, if you like, more intimate relationship, no one would have ever thought of saying such a thing. Adorno had an immediacy of awareness, a spontaneity of thought, and a power of formulation which I have never encountered before or since. One could not observe the process of development of Adorno's thoughts: they issued from him complete—he was a virtuoso in that respect. Also, he was simply not able to drop below his own level; he could not escape the strain of his own thinking for a moment. As long as one was with Adorno, one was caught up in the movement of thought. Adorno did not have the common touch, it was impossible for him, in an altogether painful way, to be commonplace. But at the same time, in his case the elevated demands and the avant-garde claims were without the purely stilted and auratic features which are familiar from the school of Stefan George. If there was a pathos, it was the pathos of negativism—and this need not stand in contradiction to fundamentally egalitarian convictions. Adorno remained anti-elitist despite all his striking refinement. Furthermore, he was also a genius in the sense that he had preserved certain childlike characteristics—both the precocity and the dependency of those who have not yet grown up; when faced with institutions and bureaucratic procedures he was peculiarly helpless.

I would like to make a small jump, and use the term 'pseudoreality' which has already been mentioned in order to address the issue of your respective attitudes to the student protest movement. Obviously, we cannot do justice to this question with a couple of sentences, but I would not like to pass it over entirely. Whereas Adorno neither identified unreservedly with the student protest, nor took a clear distance from it, you—as someone with a strong interest in day-to-day politics, who was already known for his writings on the connection between the university, politics and the public sphere—both identified with the protest less reservedly, and were more clearly distanced in your pinpointing of dangers and illusions. Was the rage of the students primarily directed against Adorno because of his ambivalent attitude?

I think that your description is quite correct, although I caught my fair share of that anger too.

It is striking that the younger representatives of Critical Theory left Frankfurt very soon after Adorno's death. Von Friedeburg became the Minister for Culture in Hessen in 1969, and Negt became a professor of sociology in Hannover. In 1971 you left to become director of the 'Max Planck Institute for Research into the Life-Conditions of the Scientific-Technical World' in Starnberg. Did something comprehensive fall apart with Adorno's death?

Adorno's death represented a break, and everyone in Frankfurt experienced it as such. No one at the time could imagine a continuation which might have bridged over the chasm. Whether things would in fact have taken a very different course if Adorno had still been alive and working during the 1970s, who can say? As the reactions became harder, the hostilities deeper, as a pogrom atmosphere finally broke out in the autumn of 1977, I often wondered how Adorno would have responded, how he would have survived this totally repugnant malice.

In the collaborative volume, Die Frankfurter Schule und die Folgen, *you explain the widespread influence of the 'Frankfurt School' or 'Critical*

Theory' in terms of its 'largely fictive unity'. 'Today', you continue, 'the impulses deriving from Critical Theory are effective in scholarly discussion in so many different, sometimes opposed, directions, that one can no longer speak of the identity of a school, even given that such an identity once existed.' But does not the question remain of how such a fiction of unity could come into being? Was this not possible because Critical Theory was identifiable, and perhaps remains so, as an inter-disciplinary social theory with critical intent, or—to put this in more contemporary terms—as an expanded theory of rationality intended to ground a critique of society?

The Frankfurt School has become part of history. A shift towards historicization began in the late 1970s, with outstanding works such as that of Helmut Dubiel.[4] Since then we have been able to perceive more clearly the historical relationship between the deeper impulses of Critical Theory and the totalitarian determinants of the 1930s. Today it is only possible to take up again the same theoretical motifs across a divide which cannot be closed by an act of will. Nevertheless, in their philosophical core, the theories of Adorno and Benjamin, even of Horkheimer and Marcuse, possess a radiance, exert a fascination, which is not only infectious, but contains something of the purifying force of the very best—something of the steadfastness of the exoteric Kant. Even in *Dialectic of Enlightenment* the impulse of the Enlightenment is not betrayed.

---

4. Helmut Dubiel, *Theory and Politics*, Boston Mass. and London, 1985.

9

On Morality, Law, Civil Disobedience and Modernity

Herr Habermas, for you the intellectual is the defender of generalizable interests. In his public appeals and interventions, he orients himself towards the principles of a universalistic morality. But should we not take very seriously Arnold Gehlen's objection that such a 'hypermorality', as he calls it, which is not satisfied with regulating and generating norms for the neighbouring domain, the immediate field of action, but creates a universal and unlimited competence and responsibility, necessarily places excessive demands on the individual, and is—in the last analysis— unliveable?

Autonomous morality, which is a product of the Enlightenment, deriving from Rousseau's and Kant's conception of human freedom as self-determination, is inevitably alien to the reality of everyday life. We are dealing here with something violent, if you like—with an abstraction. This is also increasingly the case, by the way, for the theoretical sciences. Both of these, science and morality, can only become real and effective in a mediated form. However, moral codes which are anchored in concrete, particular, quite determinate forms of life only remain acceptable today if they possess a universalistic core. For, if the worst comes to the worst, they must be able to prevent an event such as the 'Shoah' from ever happening again. Otherwise they are worthless and cannot be justified. But, on the other hand, we should not be too sceptical as far as the practical validity of universalistic moral principles is concerned. There is hardly a constitution nowadays which does not have a section, written or unwritten, setting out fundamental rights. And it is obvious that—when something crucial is at stake—these basic rights are precious and dear to us, whatever the individual may otherwise claim.

But of course the Americans appealed to 'universal' principles of law, whose validity—they claimed—must be established all over the world, in the course of their 'action' against Libya. Shouldn't that cause one to have second thoughts?

Absolutely not! We are not talking about universalistic rhetoric, but about concrete actions. It is these which must be capable of justification. The action against Libya—which I considered so catastrophic that, for the first time in years, I joined a demonstration—this action contravened the law of nations, a whole series of evident norms. It deliberately and irresponsibly risked the lives of innocent people, for example; that is something which cannot be justified under any circumstances.

Was there not also a conviction at work behind the American action which has deep roots in modern European philosophy, namely an equation of might and right, which can already be found in Hobbes and Spinoza?

I don't think so. Rather, what drives the Americans is a meliorist conception of history. And even with Reagan it is more a matter of a cowboy philosophy (with some Lockean elements mixed in), which one cannot attribute to a whole nation. Of course, one must take into account the fact—and this has something to do with Hobbes—that a state of nature continues to prevail between states. Within a single country the expectation that universal principles will be applied is related to the fact that there is an authority, namely the state, which guarantees that all others will be held to the same principles. The problem is: how can international relations be bound by recognized principles of a universalistic morality, where there is—and perhaps should not even be—such an authority? For a world state, which many people in the past have dreamed of, would be something rather to be feared, as things stand now. As far as these private actions of Reagan's are concerned, one does not even need to go to the trouble of deploying moral arguments. Even on the basis of the premisses of American policy, these activities can be seen to be profoundly unacceptable and counterproductive. What is being played out at the moment is a narrow-minded foreign policy, which relates only to the USA, and is tied to the domestic political mood.

Not long ago, you made an appeal for the possibility and necessity of civil disobedience in a 'mature' democracy. Your opponents, for example in the Frankfurter Allgemeine Zeitung, *argue that even a universalistically grounded contravening of rules must bring about social disruption and, in the final analysis, 'civil war', since random groups and individuals will*

*raise such truth-claims, and then a struggle, a violent confrontation, must
ensue, in order to settle the issue.*

There are three things to be said about that. First: civil disobedience
cannot be grounded in an arbitrary private *Weltanschauung*, but only in
principles, which are anchored in the constitution itself. Second: civil
disobedience is distinguished from revolutionary praxis, or from a revolt,
precisely by the fact that it explicitly renounces violence. The exclusively
symbolic breaking of rules—which furthermore is only a last resort,
when all other possibilities have been exhausted—is only a particularly
urgent appeal to the capacity and willingness for insight of the majority.
Third: a position such as that defended by Hobbes, Carl Schmitt, or
even the *Frankfurter Allgemeine Zeitung*, in which the upholding of the
law is made not only the highest, but the exclusive ground of legitimation of a legal system, seems to me to be extremely problematic. After
all, one would very much like to know under what conditions, and for
what purpose, the legal peace should be upheld. For example, a crisis
situation in foreign or domestic politics might occur, in which, according
to this argument, it could appear useful or even imperative to exclude a
minority, for the sake of the legal peace of the overwhelming majority.

*And a peaceful legal order could also obtain in an Orwellian state, in a
totalitarian dictatorship.*

Of course!

*Herr Habermas, perhaps we could speak a bit more about the 'project of
modernity', which you consider to be both unfinished and worth
continuing. Others, for example certain contemporary French philosophers who are fashionable at the moment, proclaim it to be a failure and
drag it to its grave, with a certain grim satisfaction.*

First one must clarify what is meant by this elusive concept of
'modernity'. Initially, in other words at the end of the eighteenth
century, there was the experience of living in a society and a time in
which all pregiven models and norms were disintegrating, and in which
one therefore had to discover one's own. Seen in this way, modernity is
primarily a challenge. In positive terms, this epoch is essentially
characterized by the notion of individual freedom, and this in three
respects: as scientific freedom, as freedom of self-determination—no
norm is to be recognized whose point one cannot see for oneself—and as
freedom of self-realization. I am not just an apologist for modernity. I
am fully aware of its ambivalences, its dark sides; above all, the peculiar

feature of modern societies—and this is a structural property—that they continually endanger themselves in the course of the development of their potentials. At the moment I see such dangers above all in the economic and the military-strategic domain. To get the capitalist machine going again, people accept the need for two and a half million, perhaps soon three million or more, unemployed. The attempt is made to produce a majority consensus which is based on lack of sympathy, capable of coming to terms with the marginalization of minorities. Rational politics scarcely seems possible any more in this domain. Wackersdorf, for example, is a symbol for our inability to cope with our own productive forces, which—considered in themselves—are extremely useful.[1] Otherwise, we would hesitate to create unpredictable dangers for future generations through risks taken today.

Is it possible to summarize the notion of modernity?

First: it is not something we have chosen, and therefore cannot be shaken off by a decision, by an act of will. Second: it still has normatively convincing contents. Third: I am fully aware that in the social and economic development of modern society there are structurally anchored, self-generated dangers, which are only perceived in a one-sided way by neo-conservatives and post-structuralists. What is required is to grasp and endure the ambivalence and complexity of the whole process. By contrast, the neo-conservatives want a modernity which has been shrunken down to a restricted technical and economic sector, and which is then cushioned with pillows of cynically revived tradition. At the same time, the potentials of universalistic morality and autonomous art are devalued.

But is it not the case that essential positions of modernity are bound, in their possibility and validity, to presuppositions which have become obsolete today? For example, to God and the immortality of the soul, which at the very least play the role of postulates of practice in Kant, or to a teleological conception of history, in the Hegelian–Marxist tradition?

The problematic features of modernity become increasingly visible as its anchorings in pre-modern convictions are increasingly torn away. But the situation can be viewed in another light: certain potentials, those of

---

1. Wackersdorf, in Bavaria, was the site of a planned nuclear reprocessing plant for the West German electricity industry. Construction was begun in the mid-1980s but, against a background of violent protests and wildly escalating costs, the project was eventually abandoned in 1989.

Kant's philosophy of religion for example, were self-misunderstandings of modernity, even if helpful ones, which are perhaps no longer tenable today. Nevertheless, the normative substance of modernity, above all self-determination and self-realization, can be defended in a different, strictly post-metaphysical, form. The ideas of the Enlightenment are not simply pure abstractions: they are inserted into everyday communicative practice, and thereby into the life-world, as unavoidable, often counter-factual, presuppositions; in part they are also realized in the institutions of the political system, in however fragmentary a way.

But is not communicative rationality also a fiction, comparable to Kant's notion of God, or to the teleology of history?

That has yet to be shown convincingly. This is certainly the way the hard, empiricist naturalism of the neo-conservatives or an anarchic-cynical poststructuralism would see things. Even for me it is not simply a dogma. I cannot foresee how the world will look in a hundred years' time. In the meantime, I have gathered together a lot of arguments, which seek to show that this concept of communicative rationality is best suited to explaining why modern societies cannot be held together exclusively or even primarily through money and power.

At the moment it is possible to observe, even if at first only amongst a narrow social stratum, a tendency towards the aestheticizing, subjectivizing, and 'derealizing' of reality. The French thinkers are playing an important role here ...

An aesthetically inspired subjectivistic cynicism, which promises a kind of playful-amiable disengagement, is unquestionably a part of modernity; but I perceive in it the reflection of a skewed development. One could say things about this aestheticizing, one-sided lifestyle which would resemble those reservations concerning 'eroticized countercultures' which Max Weber formulated half a century ago. In the last analysis, what is at issue here are the attitudes generated by a bohemian lifestyle which has now become more widespread. Bohemia found its significant and necessary role, in the middle of the last century, as the form of life of those who nailed their existence, factually and literally, to the cross of aesthetic productivity. Separated from the selfless, self-consuming work of the avant-garde, a socially generalized lifestyle of this kind runs the risk of becoming merely the inverted image of an alienated everyday practice which is marked by a one-sided emphasis on the cognitive–instrumental. I say this, even though—heaven knows!—I sympathize with the subversive, playful and libertarian traits of the new subcultures.

The Role of the Student Movement in Germany

You have said that you think one of the essential functions of the student movement was to facilitate the cultural and political breakthrough of critical potentials which, during the Adenauer years, were limited to small circles of critical intellectuals on the edge of the dominant political culture. Could you explain this thesis in more detail?

When I look back over the history of mentalities in the *Bundesrepublik*, as a participating contemporary who still has no real historical distance, I find myself compelled by the image of a wavelike movement. Until the currency reform,[1] the symbolically and economically significant beginning of the restoration of capitalist relations, the great majority of the population, including the refugees and returnees, were crippled by the total defeat, which occurred against the background of the total victory proclaimed by Goebbels; they were stunned by what was perceived as a 'collapse'. The voices of those who had been opponents of Hitler, an anti-fascist coalition which soon began to fragment anyway, still had the lid kept on them, so to speak, by the suspicious allies; nevertheless they had a greater influence than at any time later. This was the period of the construction of parties from below, of de-Nazification, of political-cultural periodicals which seemed to spring up out of the ground (and of which only *Merkur* still remains), the time of an enormous cultural hunger in the universities, in the institutions of higher education, in the museums and theatres. Horkheimer's letters and diaries from that time portray extremely well the climate in Frankfurt University—the unreserved readiness to learn of the students, who were in fact not so young. Then came the Adenauer period, which was driven

---

1. On 20 June 1948 a currency reform was introduced in the three Western occupation zones of Germany, paving the way for the establishment of the 'social market economy'.

by a tremendous desire for stability and restoration, by a privately oriented, aggressive will to reconstruct. This period lasted until the beginning of the sixties—economically vital, culturally rigid and provincial (if one excludes painting), and yet already characterized by a kind of division of labour between politics and culture. In that period it gradually became apparent that the spirit of the times was leaning leftwards. The literary intelligentsia, which had acquired a certain influence, was in opposition. People like Sieburg were rather the exception.[2]

Then came the phase which you have in mind—Adenauer's last years, Erhard's interim period, and the great coalition leading up to the election of Heinemann. That is perhaps the most interesting phase for our present concerns. With the cracking of the rigid conservative veneer in the sphere of government, the outsider position of intellectuals, who tended to be Left-liberal, came to an end—along with the 47 Group,[3] which took on a political role, professors like Adorno and Mitscherlich began to acquire influence, while Jaspers and Kogon, who were already influential, became more radical. But above all the sounding board for the critical intelligentsia in schools and universities began to develop— the citizenship course in schools was reformed, and the *edition suhrkamp* acquired its distinctive image. Shortly before, the state prosecutor in Hesse had set up the first big Auschwitz trial, and the first debate in the Bundestag about time-limits on prosecution [*Verjährungsdebatte*] was successful.[4] These years between 1960 and 1967 were the incubation period, in which the cultural sphere, intellectual impulses, and non-institutionalized public opinion began to acquire political weight. The student movement was the subsequent explosion which no one foresaw, and which lasted for one or two years—and after which there followed the counter-revolution, fed by a hostility and resentment which has effectively lasted up to the present day: Marcuse's counterposing of revolt and counter-revolution fits the situation in the *Bundesrepublik* pretty well. It is as though the Right, discredited in the shadow

---

2. Friedrich Sieburg (1893–1964) was a journalist and travel writer who edited the literary section of the *Frankfurter Allgemeine Zeitung* from 1956 to 1964. He was a leading representative of conservatively oriented *Kulturkritik* in the early years of the Federal Republic.

3. The *Gruppe 47* was a loose association of writers and critics founded in 1947, with a platform which emphasized the social responsibility of the author. The annual meetings of the group were attended by figures such as Bachmann, Böll, Enzensberger, Grass and Johnson, and became a crystallization point for post-war German literature. The last conference occurred in 1967.

4. In 1964 the Federal parliament debated the possibility and necessity of lifting the twenty-year limitation on prosecutions for murder, with a view to the prosecution of Nazi war criminals. The limitation was lifted on 18 May 1965.

of National Socialism, had only been waiting for a pretext to rise up again against the 'Ideas of 1789'; only this ghostly projection can explain the intensity of the emotions aroused.

What role does the 'repressed' National Socialist past play in all this? Can the student protest be interpreted as a rejection of the deceitful contract between generations, the 'communicative silencing' [Lübbe] of German responsibility for the holocaust?

When Inge Marcuse suggested to me, in 1969 in Korcula, that—with the student rebellion–a generation had appeared for the first time in post-war Germany which was prepared to confront the heritage of fascism critically, and without reservations, I was hurt, indeed outraged. I knew my Frankfurt students, just as I knew my contemporaries, for example Alexander Kluge, who was writing his *Lebensläufe* at the end of the 1950s. I experienced the suggestion as an injury. In one respect I was probably right, because for the most part the left-wing students had a rather clichéd notion of fascism. At that time it cost a real effort to assert in public that the organs of state also carried out functions which helped to secure freedom, or that, in spite of everything, the *Bundesrepublik* was one of the six or seven most liberal countries in the world. It was difficult for me to find an audience for such statements, which were intended to introduce a sense of historical proportion. In another respect, however, I was wrong to react to Inge Marcuse as I did: the '68 generation was probably the first in Germany which did not shy away from asking for face to face explanations—from parents, from older people in general, in front of the television set, and so on. Lübbe was right about that, in the lecture which he gave on the fiftieth anniversary of 30 January 1933 in the *Reichstag*, certainly in a descriptive sense—it was only his evaluation which was ominous. The student protest was the staging of a public—and sometimes rather self-righteous—reckoning, also reaching into the private domain, with collective avoidance of the German responsibility, of the historical liability, for National Socialism and its horrors. When I was a student, in 1953, I wrote a comparable article on Heidegger's 1935 lectures, because I was outraged by the inability of the protagonists (such as Heidegger, Carl Schmitt, Gehlen and so on) to utter even one word admitting a political error. But I avoided any confrontation with my father, who was certainly only considered to be a passive sympathizer. In short, the generational clocks were set in such a way that the '68ers were able to insist, without any embarrassment, on a *specific* confrontation with the past. This confrontation had perhaps had something abstract about it up until then.

Could it be said that the fact that the anti-authoritarian revolt first made the 'left-over' questions of the thirties (the authoritarian character National Socialism, the relation between capitalist socialization and totalitarian rule) objects of public dispute fulfilled not only positive, critical functions, but also had regressive consequences for the movement itself? For example, the search for a 'proletarian' point of reference for the critique of capitalism, during the phase of disintegration of the student movement, or the neglect of the critical potential of the democratic-constitutional state itself (what Dany Cohn-Bendit, at the SDS revival meeting, called the 'emancipatory utopia of democracy').

The connection to Marxism and Freudianism was one of the great achievements of the incubation period, from the end of the fifties onwards; the commission on Marxism of the student association of the Evangelical Church should be mentioned here, as well as the Frankfurt Institute, or Mitscherlich, who organized a big Freud conference with Horkheimer in 1956, and who founded the Sigmund Freud Institute with the help of the Hessian government. The students appropriated and actualized this potential which was standing ready, with ambiguous consequences. They propagated all these things (Freud became the subject of church conferences, and Marx was behind the Vietnam protests), but they took up these rediscovered traditions with a new earnestness. They overlooked the historical distance separating the twenties from the sixties. In my view that was something positive, in the light of the history of German mentalities; for the first time the taboos against the Enlightenment elements of the German tradition were broken down. But on the other hand, this commitment to—or rather this libidinal cathexis of—particular theorems and concepts also had dogmatic consequences (a hindrance for any theory). This dogmatiza-tion led to a false revolutionary evaluation of the situation in our country, and to an equally illusory identification with the liberation struggles in Vietnam, Cuba, China and elsewhere. The young activists saw themselves as the arm of Che Guevara extending into the metropo-lises—into places such as this, where, to understand anything, one must first have grasped the relative success of social-democratic reformism. Of course, it was much easier for we left-wing children of the Adenauer period to grasp this, whereas Marcuse's and Adorno's theory of late capitalism tended to encourage the totalizing standpoint of the '68ers. The slightly older generation of the SDS (Preuss, Offe and so on) had been influenced by my *Structural Change in the Public Sphere* (1962), in other words by a welfare-state interpretation of the *Grundgesetz*, influenced by the reformist outlook of Abendroth, whereas the next 'generation', with Dutschke and Krahl, thought in more actionistic terms. The students who became active in 1968 were already so removed from the Nazi period that they could no longer accept as obvious what was obvious for Marx—that there could be no socialist emancipation without the realization of the freedoms enshrined in bourgeois principles.

Nevertheless, can your critique of student activism as 'left fascism' be sustained today, sine ira et studio*?*

I have already taken back this reproach, which was expressed hypothetically in 1968, in a spontaneous and context-specific way—in *Der Spiegel*, in autumn 1977. On that occasion I sought to explain, in a biographical context, why Left intellectuals in the *Bundesrepublik* reacted in a more sensitive, scrupulous, irritated way to the first stirrings of a rhetoric of violence, and of the use of violence, than their friends in other countries. What is more—and this is something which gave me particular pleasure—Dutschke thanked me emphatically for this explanation, when we met in Starnberg after Marcuse's death.

I am happy to say it again: seen with twenty years' hindsight, the tiny kernel of truth which the later emergence of terrorism brought to light in the reproach of Left fascism does not justify the grave connotations which this expression attached to the tactics pursued by Dutschke at the time, given that—in the heat of battle—nobody took seriously the hypothetical status of my question.

In your work in social theory, and also in moral philosophy, of the last decade, the category of 'post-traditional identity' plays a central role: as a form and precondition of social and personal self-identification and reflection, in which the universalistic potential of modernity in the West finally strips away its 'birthmarks' (Marx) of nationalism and historicism.

You have put it well. The collective identities which have developed under the sign of nationalism are post-traditional, even if you understand the term literally. But the universalistic elements of the democratic national state which emerged from the French Revolution—popular sovereignty and human rights—were always in danger of being overwhelmed by the particularistic self-assertion of one's own nation against all other nations. Since the Second World War a change of form has begun to appear, particularly in countries such as Germany and Italy, where fascism robbed nationalism of its last traces of innocence, which I investigated more closely in the context of the 'Historian's

Dispute' [*Historikerstreit*][5]. A transformation is occurring because we are obliged to appropriate our own history critically, via a spectrum of several, usually conflicting, readings. As Germans, we are particularly aware today that we cannot view ourselves as the inheritors of a triumphal history. This has nothing to do with negative nationalism, as those who want a positive nationalism believe. You are quite correct: the seed of the universalistic emancipation movements, which first made individualism possible, seems to be absorbed into a decentred historical consciousness and a more markedly reflexive appropriation of traditions, and to take on the shape of a post-nationalistically expanded identity. These tendencies broke through in the *Bundesrepublik* with the cultural revolution of the students, and since then they have spread through a diffuse social milieu, and in a transformed, more pessimistically tinged climate, they have even got stronger. This is all part of a subcutaneous, but widely influential, shift in attitudes, which took place under cover of the thirteen-year social-liberal coalition—and which was perhaps all the more effective because the Brandt government treated the '68 movement with a relatively high degree of understanding. This has to admitted, despite the *Berufsverbot* which Brandt helped to introduce (and which he later regretted).

Can the anti-authoritarian movement be considered as having been the first anticipation of a post-traditional public sphere?

The student protest scene brought about the first advance of a fundamental liberalization (Karl Mannheim once spoke of 'fundamental democratization'). I am thinking of the new individualism of lifestyles, oriented to libertarian models, but also the new forms of autonomous public sphere, in which the borderlines between demonstration and civil disobedience, between discussion, festival, and expressive self-presentation tend to dissolve. Here I perceive a long-term effect of the forms of protest of that period, and of what Marcuse, at the time, called a 'new sensibility'. The loosening of party ties in the areas dominated by service-sector industries, which is giving electoral strategists cause for concern, is perhaps only a symptom of the fact that, recently, more and more people have begun to demand the use-value of the principles of

---

5. The *Historikerstreit*, which occurred in the later 1980s in West Germany, arose from the attempts of conservative historians to 'relativize' the crimes of the Nazi regime, including the extermination of the Jews, and thus establish a positive image of the national past. Habermas played a central role in the critical response to this 'revisionist' offensive, which corresponded with the political aims of the CDU regime. For Habermas's contributions to this debate see section 9 of Jürgen Habermas, *The New Conservatism: Cultural Criticism and the Historian's Dispute*, Oxford 1989.

legitimacy of a constitutional democracy. They want democracy 'in cash' [English in the original], in the coinage of an active use of rights to freedom, to political participation, and to individualized mass consumption. And this is all taking place in de-differentiated spheres, where everything connects up with everything else: the existential demands of adolescent church conference-goers with the self-satisfied hedonism of the Yuppies, the desire for a politics of the first person singular with the cool calculations of commodity aesthetics and the seriousness of the information and argumentation which flood in from all over the world, and generate a nervy awareness of overcomplexity.

Can the optimistic 'subjectivism' of Herbert Marcuse, who conceptualized the flowing together of the universal-political and the personal in a (psychoanalytically interpreted) concept of liberation, be seen as an appropriate sketch of the emancipatory role of the '68 Movement? And what role did Critical Theory play in general?

Marcuse's socio-psychological theses certainly exerted a great influence over the self-conception of the rebellious students, from Berkeley and New York to Berlin and Frankfurt. But I would remind you that *One Dimensional Man*, which appeared in 1964, is a profoundly pessimistic book—not only the expression of a pessimistic mood, but negativistic in its fundamental assumptions. Marcuse himself only revised his view of the situation after being impressed by the success of the civil rights movement, and then of the American student movement. The interpretation of the revolt in terms of transformed psychoanalytical concepts, derived from *Eros and Civilization*, fitted well with the dispositions of a youth movement which was fundamentally bourgeois, in terms of its socializing experiences. In this way Marcuse certainly shaped the self-understanding of the activists. But the particular mixture of the private and the political, which resulted from such a socio-psychological perspective, may not have been entirely favourable to the discriminating perception of a complicated reality. In Frankfurt a version of Adorno, radicalized against his own wishes, and mediated by Krahl, was more influential than Marcuse. And outside Berlin and Frankfurt, on the German periphery so to speak, *Knowledge and Human Interests* may also have served as a stimulus.

What do you consider today to have been the decisive limitations of the student protest?

Of course, wisdom always comes with hindsight. But even at the time I believed, and stated, that the ingenuous use of the concept of revolution, and the undervaluation of democratic-constitutional traditions, was a misfortune. In general, the movement had the typical weaknesses of a youth movement—although its dynamic and power of conviction were also drawn from the same sources. Who can give one cause to reflect, if not one's own children? Willy Brandt's policies at the time cannot be understood without this dimension—and he stands for countless other older people, who were at first puzzled, then enlightened. Unfortunately our university is also full of people who learned nothing and only reacted—'with beans in their ears' [English in the original].

Anyone who does not simply shut their eyes in hostility must admit that this revolt was a decisive step for the political culture of the *Bundesrepublik*, only exceeded in its positive effects by our liberation from the Nazi regime by the Allies. What 1945 signified in terms of a transformation of our constitutional status, 1968 signified for the loosening up of our political culture, for a liberalization in forms of living and in relationships which is only making its full effects felt today. If I might use an image from the curio is debate over the double zero-option, at that time a wall of fire was set up by the expectations of legitimacy of the West German population, which will hopefully remain in place. Without the pressure of attitudes which emerged during that period, we would today have no Greens, no alternative scenes in the big cities, no awareness of the fact that subcultural and ethnic plurality enriches our streamlined culture—we would not have the degree of urbanity which is gradually being established, and it is likely that there would be less sensitivity on the part of the rulers towards the mood of the populace, perhaps there would not even be the so-called liberal wing in the CDU.

The Limits of Neo-Historicism

It has recently become clear that the Historikerstreit *is no mere scholastic controversy, but rather a debate about the Federal Republic's understanding of its own identity.*[1] *In what way, in your opinion, has Auschwitz so altered the conditions for the historical continuity of forms of life, that it is quite impossible to accept the conception of history which neo-historicism wishes to revive?*

Perhaps we should briefly clarify the term 'neo-historicism'. Since the seventies a kind of reaction against the increasing use of social scientific methods and approaches in the humanities has developed in the Federal Republic. This reaction sees itself as a return to the important nineteenth-century German tradition of the *Geisteswissenschaften.* The central catchphrase is the 'rehabilitation of narrative', in other words the narrative presentation of events as opposed to the claims of theoretical explanation. The *Frankfurter Allgemeine Zeitung* has started up a new section under the heading '*Geisteswissenschaften*' in order to promote this shift in a more popular form.

During the *Historikerstreit* it was above all Saul Friedländer who pointed out the limits and dangers of neo-historicism with regard to the historical presentation of the catastrophe of Auschwitz. No participant in the controversy objected to a 'historicization'—that is, a scientifically distanced account—of the Nazi period. But a hermeneutically unreflective procedure is questionable. If one tries simply to project oneself into the situation of the participants, in order to understand the actors and their actions in terms of their own surroundings, then one risks losing sight of the disastrous context of the epoch as a whole. In the

---

1. See note 5, p. 234 above.

kaleidoscope of trivial, colourful, or grey normalities, the only perspective which could enable one to recognize the radical ambiguity of that *apparent* normality tends to disintegrate. One should not pay close attention to the details merely for the sake of empathetic understanding—something which Martin Broszat, for example, who engaged in an interesting debate with Friedländer, does not do either. Dolf Sternberger has repeatedly insisted that 'the venerable doctrine of understanding [*Verstehen*] runs up against a brick wall ... The insane atrocity which is known by the name of Auschwitz cannot, in truth, be understood at all.'

Could you expand on this thought?

Neo-historicism relies on an assumption which is also defended by the neo-Aristotelians in contemporary practical philosophy. A practice is said to be comprehensible, and susceptible to judgement, only from the standpoint in the life-context and traditions in which it is embedded. That is plausible as long as we can be confident that practices can prove their worth simply in being passed on from one generation to the next and thereby continuing to exist, simply in terms of the strength of tradition. This conviction testifies to a kind of primal anthropological trust.

Historicism is nourished by this trust. And this is not so hard to understand. Somehow or other we rely on a deep-seated stratum of solidarity in our face-to-face dealings with other people, despite all the unpredictable, quasi-natural bestialities of world history. The unquestioned continuity of our traditions also depended on this confidence. 'Tradition' means, after all, that we unproblematically continue what others began and have taught us. We usually imagine that, were we to meet these forebears face to face, they would not completely deceive us, would not play the role of a *deus malignus*. In my view, it is precisely this basis of trust which was destroyed before the gas chambers. The complex preparation and extensive organization of a coldly calculated mass murder, in which hundreds of thousands—indirectly a whole people—were involved, took place, after all, with the appearance of normality preserved, and was even dependent on the normality of highly civilized social intercourse. The monstrous occurred, without interrupting the steady respiration of everyday life. Ever since, a *self-conscious* life has no longer been possible without suspicion of those continuities which are sustained unquestioningly, and which seek to draw their validity from their unquestionability.

I would like to turn to the question of the way in which the citizens of the

Federal Republic, and perhaps the Germans in general, could today constitute a collective identity. On the political level of national identity and sovereignty, 'Germany' looks, to say the least, like a problematic entity, to which no state organization corresponds. The form of national identity refers to historical consciousness, as the medium in which the self-consciousness of a nation is constituted. By contrast, you refer to a so-called 'patriotism of the constitution' [Verfassungspatriotismus], which is limited to the postulates of a generalization of democracy and human rights.

Could you please explain this universalist option? Do you simply renounce every kind of national-historical identity formation in favour of a purely formal-practical one, which no longer requires a fundamental reference to one's own tradition?

No, the identity of a person, of a group, of a nation or of a region, is always something concrete, something particular (which should also, of course, satisfy moral standards). We always speak of our identity, when we say who we are, and what we wish to be. Descriptive and evaluative elements are interwoven in this process. The figure which we have become through our life history, the history of our milieu, our nation, cannot be detached, in a description of identity, from the image which we present to ourselves and to others, and by which we would like to be judged, respected and recognized by others.

Now let us turn to the collective identity of the Germans since the Second World War. It is nothing new for us, after all, that the unity of our cultural, linguistic and historical form of life does not coincide with the organizational form of a state. We were never one of the classic nation states. Against the background of a thousand-year history, the seventy-five years of the Bismarck Reich are a short span; and even then the German Reich existed *alongside* Austria until 1938, to say nothing of the Swiss Germans, or the German minorities in other states. In this situation, I believe that for us citizens of the Federal Republic, a constitutional patriotism is the only possible form of patriotism. But this does not in any sense imply the renunciation of an identity, which can never consist merely in general moral orientations and characteristics, which are shared by all alike.

For us in the Federal Republic constitutional patriotism means, amongst other things, pride in the fact that we have succeeded in permanently overcoming fascism, establishing an order based on the rule of law, and anchoring it in a reasonably liberal political culture. Our patriotism cannot suppress the fact that democracy has only been able to strike roots in the hearts and motivations of the citizens, at least of the younger generation, after Auschwitz, and in a certain sense only because of the shock of this moral catastrophe. For this anchoring of universal principles one always requires a *specific* identity.

I have the impression that this post-conventional and post-national identity formation, which you defend, is proposed as a fundamentally valid form of life for the countries of Western Europe in general, as capable of replacing the form of national identity in a more or less distant future. And this in spite of the fact that nationalism is a specifically modern manifestation of collective identity. Am I right about this?

We need to keep two things distinct. In Germany nationalism took on an excessive, social-darwinistic form and culminated in racial delusions which served as a justification for the mass annihilation of the Jews. Consequently nationalism as the basis for a collective identity became drastically devalued in our case. And for this reason the overcoming of fascism constitutes the specific historical perspective in terms of which an identity based on the universalistic principles of the constitutional state and democracy is understood. But since the Second World War all European countries, and not only the Federal Republic, have developed in such a way that integration at the level of the nation state has lost significance and relevance.

These countries, too, are on the way to becoming post-national societies. I need only recall European integration, the supranational military alliances, the relations of dependence within the world economy, the economically motivated patterns of migration, the growing ethnic diversity of the population, but also the increasing density of the communication networks, which have heightened the *worldwide* sensitivity to violations of human rights, to exploitation, hunger, misery, and the demands of national liberation movements. On the one hand, this leads to reactions of anxiety and defensiveness. But at the same time there is also a spreading awareness that there is no longer any alternative to universalistic value orientations.

What does universalism mean, after all? That one relativizes one's own way of life with regard to the legitimate claims of other forms of life, that one grants the strangers and the others, with all their idiosyncrasies and incomprehensibilities, the same rights as oneself, that one does not insist on universalizing one's own identity, that one does not simply exclude that which deviates from it, that the areas of tolerance must become infinitely broader than they are today—moral universalism means all these things.

Initially, the idea of the nation state which emerged from the French Revolution had a thoroughly cosmopolitan meaning. One need only think of the enthusiasm which the Greek struggle for liberation aroused throughout Europe in the early nineteenth century. This cosmopolitan element must be revived and further developed today, in the direction of multiculturalism.

This transformation of the form of collective identity suggests a flexible structural transformation of modern ways of life, which is possible in the classic nation states. Yet I cannot imagine how, under such conditions of a radically decentred life-situation, the actual need for self-assertion and self-confirmation can be met. What is at issue is the identificatory and motivational force of purely formal, universalistic validity claims in general: how can the radically universalistic option or inspiration of a 'constitutional patriotism' provide an identity-shaping force which has not only moral legitimacy, but also historical plausibility?

Well, a commitment to the principles of the constitutional state and democracy, as I have said, can only become a reality in the different states (which are on the way towards becoming post-national societies), when these principles strike roots in the various political cultures in different ways. In the land of the French Revolution such a constitutional patriotism would have to take a different form than in a country which has never established a democracy through its own efforts. The same universalistic content must in each case be appropriated from out of one's own specific historical life-situation, and become anchored in one's own cultural form of life. Every collective identity, even a post-national one, is much more concrete than the ensemble of moral, legal and political principles around which it crystallizes.

When you appeal to a public use of tradition, enabling a decision to be taken as to 'which of our traditions we wish to continue and which not', an image emerges of that radical-critical relationship to culture which characterized the rationalist attitude of the Enlightenment. At this point I would like briefly to raise two criticisms of the Enlightenment. In the line of thought deriving from Gadamer, for example, there appears the objection that, for essential reasons, we cannot transcend tradition, especially not with the (supposedly) illusory intention of selectively continuing, or even excluding, certain tendencies. With respect to Hegel's critique, I would like to recall an idea which I will summarize from the Philosophy of Right*: 'A human being counts because he is a human being, and not because he is a Jew, a Catholic, a Protestant, a German, an Italian, etc.' This awareness is, for Hegel, of immeasurable importance, and only becomes inadequate when, in the form of cosmopolitanism, for example, it becomes set on opposing itself to the concrete life of the state. What would be the attitude to this problem of the Kantian*

universalism, deepened and renewed within the framework of discourse
theory, which presumably underlies the formal-pragmatic framework of
'constitutional patriotism'?

Hegel attached a pejorative meaning to the term 'human being'
[*Mensch*], because he considered 'humanity' [*die Menschheit*] to be a
bad abstraction. In his work the spirits of peoples or great individuals,
but above all states, appear as the world-historical agents. By contrast,
the totality of all subjects capable of speech and action does not
constitute an entity which can act politically. That is why Hegel ranked
morality, which concerns the vulnerability of everything which bears a
human face, below politics. However, that is a perspective very much of
its time.

Today cosmopolitanism can no longer be opposed to the concrete life
of the state in the same way as in 1817, for the simple reason that the
sovereignty of individual states no longer consists in the right to decide
concerning war and peace. Not even the superpowers can freely dispose
in this sense any more. Today all states are confronted with the
imperative of abolishing war as a means of resolving conflicts, precisely
for the sake of their own survival. For Hegel '*dulce et decorum est pro*
patria mori' was still the highest moral duty on earth. Today the duty to
serve under arms has become morally suspect to some extent. The
international arms trade, too, as it is carried on today, including by
France, has long since lost its moral innocence. For the first time, the
abolition of the state of nature between nations stands on the agenda.
With this development the preconditions for the self-affirmation of
peoples have changed. The order of precedence between the political
duties of the citizen and the moral duties of the 'human being' do not
remain unaffected either. It is contemporary circumstances themselves
which are compelling a moralization of politics.

Something similar is true of the critical attitude towards one's own
traditions. Hegel had already incorporated into his philosophy the
transformation in the awareness of time which took place in Europe
around 1800—namely the experience of the peculiar acceleration of
one's own history, of the unifying perspective of world history, of the
weight and urgency of the changing present within the horizon of a
future which must be responsibly assumed. The catastrophes of our
century have once more altered this awareness of time.

Now our responsibility extends to the past as well. This cannot simply
be accepted as something fixed and over and done with. Walter
Benjamin has probably defined most precisely the claim which is made
by the dead on the anamnesic power of living generations. Certainly,
we cannot make good past suffering and injustice done; but we have the

weak power of an atoning remembrance. Only our sensitivity towards the innocently martyred, from whose inheritance we live, can generate a reflexive distance from our own traditions, a sensitivity to the profound ambivalences of the traditions which have formed our own identity. However, our identity is not only something pregiven, but also, and simultaneously, our own project. We cannot pick and choose our own traditions, but we can be aware that it is up to us *how* we continue them. In this respect Gadamer's thinking is too conservative. This is because every continuation of tradition is selective, and precisely this selectivity must pass today through the filter of critique, of a self-conscious appropriation of history, or—if you wish—through an awareness of sin.

Discourse Ethics, Law and *Sittlichkeit*

Our principal theme will be your views on moral theory and ethics, particularly in the form which they have taken on since The Theory of Communicative Action. *We will first concentrate on the concept of morality, and on the relation between justice, law and an ethics of care. Then we will turn, in the second place, to questions concerning the universal-pragmatic foundations of a discourse ethics. What will be at issue is the validity of norms, the status of the so-called ideal speech situation, and the definition of democratic procedure. Third, I would like to discuss morality and ethics in connection with the distinction between system and life-world.*

How are we to understand the development which has led you from the sociological critique of the pathologies of modernity (in The Theory of Communicative Action *) to your moral theory (in* Moral Consciousness and Communicative Action *and in subsequent articles and lectures)? Can one understand discourse ethics as an answer, given from the standpoint of the individual, to the question of how an appropriate, non-pathological relation between system and life-world in modernity should look? Why have you been more preoccupied with questions of philosophical ethics since 1981, rather than with these sociological questions, which were left open by* The Theory of Communicative Action *?*

I don't see things in that way. The introduction of the concept of communicative rationality, theorized in terms of a pragmatics of speech, was the most important thing for the philosophical foundations of *The Theory of Communicative Action.* I did explore the development of law and morality in connection with Weber and Durkheim; but the two theoretical approaches which I relied on, discourse ethics and Kohlberg's theory of stages of moral consciousness, remained in the background at the time. I worked through these issues, which had been left open, in the following years. The title essay of *Moral Consciousness and*

Communicative Action dates from my time at the Institute in Starnberg, and stems from the research context there. The essay on discourse ethics emerged from a seminar which I held directly after my return to Frankfurt, and which was therefore held in a philosophy department. You should recall that since 1983 I have been working in a different professional environment: this also has an effect on which research interests are emphasized.

Your supposition is also incorrect in the sense that this concern with questions of moral theory connects up with problems which I had already treated in 1973, in the last part of *Legitimation Crisis*. There I proposed a model of 'repressed generalizable interests', in order to show in what sense one can distinguish between 'general' and 'particular' interests. Later, in *The Theory of Communicative Action*, I didn't return to these questions but sought to grasp social pathologies, which you rightly mention, with the aid of a two-stage concept of society—as deformations which originate in disruptions of the reproduction of the life-world (vol. 2, p. 143). In particular, I was interested in pathologies which emerge when a crisis-inducing, systematic disequilibrium in the economy or the state apparatus is displaced on to the life-world, and interferes with its symbolic reproduction (vol. 2, p. 385). Had I wanted to analyse these phenomena, which reveal the reification of communicative relationships and which are generated by monetarization and bureaucratization—what Marx called 'alienation', in other words—then moral-theoretical considerations would not have been appropriate. For such issues one would have needed a more precise account of the concept of systematically distorted communication. I have sought to explain this concept, on the basis of empirical research into family pathologies, as the interpersonal counterpart of those intrapsychic disturbances which psychoanalysis traces back to unconscious defences against conflict, and which it explains in terms of the corresponding defence mechanisms.[1] At all events, I have not returned to this notion of pathologies of communication since 1974. But I still think my suggestions are relevant, and feel confirmed in this view by the interesting work produced by Jim Bohman and Martin Low-Beer.

You present discourse ethics as a continuation and completion of your earlier work in moral theory, as well as an answer to the political agenda established by the public discussions of the 1980s. Do you feel a certain

---

1. Jürgen Habermas, 'Überlegungen zur Kommunikationspathologie', in *Vorstudien und Ergänzungen zur Theorie des kommunikativen Handelns*, Frankfurt 1984, pp. 226–70.

tension between these two poles, in other words between your own theoretical development, which derives from questions of the sixties, and the political themes of the eighties? Have these themes contributed to the turn which has led you from a more social and Hegelian ethics, to a more individual, and more Kantian, moral conception?

In fact I have been following the *same* research programme since around 1970, since those arguments concerning formal pragmatics and the discourse theory of truth which I first presented in my Christian Gauss Lectures.[2] On the other hand, anyone who preserves a certain political sensitivity (and a sensitivity to the politics of theory) will react to altering contexts. In the sixties one had to confront the theories of technocracy, on the one hand, and in the seventies the theories of crisis, on the other. From the mid-seventies one could feel the pressure of the neo-conservatives, as well as the post-structuralist critique of reason—and I replied to this with the concept of communicative rationality. Initially, this constellation did not alter in the eighties; for this reason I pursued the theme of the critique of the philosophy of the subject, and tried to make it more precise with philosophical means. In *The Philosophical Discourse of Modernity* I wanted to show that 'representational thinking' [*vorstellendes Denken*] can be dissolved by something other than the defeatism of the deconstructivists, or the contextualism of the neo-Aristotelians.

In context of this intersubjective autocritique of reason, I then responded to the conjuncture in which philosophical ethics finds itself today, and which is not entirely innocent. I worked out things which had already interested me in connection with Mead's ethics of communication (*The Theory of Communicative Action*, vol. 2, pp. 92 *et seq.*). For this reason discourse ethics connects up with the intuitions of Kantian moral theory, as Mead had already done, without taking over Kant's individualistic premisses.

Discourse ethics relates to specifically modern conditions (just as do The Theory of Communicative Action *and* The Philosophical Discourse of Modernity *). You defend the Enlightenment and modernity against traditionalism, on the one hand, and post-modernity on the other. Thus for you the concept of virtue is incompatible with modern conditions, just as it is for one of your chief opponents, the neo-Aristotelian Alasdair MacIntyre. How has it come about that all traditional and substantial*

---

2. 'Vorlesungen zu einer sprachtheoretischen Grundlegung der Soziologie', in *ibid.*, pp. 11–126.

*moral codes have become outdated? And what constitutes your solution:
is it a non-substantial morality which is better justified than MacIntyre's
solution, better than the return to traditional virtues which he proposes?*

In my view *After Virtue* has two fundamental weaknesses. First,
MacIntyre makes it too easy for himself in his critique: by choosing A.
Gerwith, he selected an untypical and rather easy-to-criticize example of
a universalistic position, instead of confronting Rawls, or Dworkin, or
Apel. Second, he gets into problems with his recourse to the Aristotelian
concept of praxis as soon as he attempts to extract a universal core from
the unavoidable pluralism of equally legitimate forms of life which is
typical of modernity. Where does he derive his equivalent for what
Aristotle could still rely on—I mean the metaphysical pre-eminence of
the polis as the model form of life, where human beings, and indeed all
human beings who are not barbarians, can realize the telos of a good
life? Because, in modernity, the plurality of individual life-projects and
collective life-forms cannot be prejudged philosophically, because ways
of living are handed over to the responsibility of socialized individuals
themselves, and can only be assessed from the standpoint of a participant, the element which can convince *everyone* is narrowed down to the
procedure of rational will-formation itself.

*In two respects discourse ethics offers a thin or minimal understanding of
ethics. In its approach it is deontological, cognitivist, formalist and
universalist; and it limits itself to justice as its central concern. In this
way, it excludes the traditional orientation to the good or to happiness (or
a combination of the two). Why this limitation to justice? Do you
consider this limitation to be a necessary feature of all modern ethics?*

Under modern conditions of life, none of the competing traditions can
claim *prima facie* general validity any longer. Therefore, even in
practically relevant questions, we can no longer back up convincing
grounds with the authority of unquestioned traditions. If we want to stop
settling elementary normative questions of collective life through direct
or concealed violence, through coercion, through the exertion of
influence, or through the power of the stronger interest, and instead
convince others without violence through a rationally motivated understanding, then we must concentrate on the range of questions which are
accessible to impartial assessment. We should not expect a generally
valid answer when we ask what is good for me, or good for us, or good
for them; we must rather ask: what is *equally good for all*? This 'moral
point of view' constitutes a sharp but narrow spotlight, which selects
from the mass of evaluative questions those action-related conflicts

which can be resolved with reference to a generalizable interest; these are questions of justice.

I am not claiming here that questions of justice are the only relevant questions. Ethical-existential questions are usually far more urgent—questions which oblige the individual or the collective to get clear about who they are and would like to be. Such problems of self-understanding can oppress us far more than questions of justice. But only the latter are so structured that they can be resolved in the well-considered and equal interest of all. Moral judgements must be capable of being approved by all those who might possibly be affected—and not, like ethical judgements, only from the perspective of my particular or our particular understanding of the world. For this reason, moral theories which develop a cognitivist approach are essentially theories of justice.

Why is the dimension of 'justice' not further differentiated? Why should the diremptions of modernity come to halt at the limits of Kant's three Critiques, and the corresponding spheres of value, so that justice can only be considered under one aspect? One could regard Michael Walzer's book Spheres of Justice *as one long argument for a breaking up of the concept of justice according to different spheres (membership, welfare, the economy, education, and so on); Walzer attempts to defend pluralism and equality in this way: 'The principles of justice are themselves pluralistic in form ... different social goods ought to be distributed for different reasons, in accordance with different procedures, by different agents.' (p. 6).*

I can agree to this statement without reservation, but not to the consequences which Michael Walzer would like to draw from it.

The fact that a norm is just, or in the general interest, means nothing other than that this norm deserves recognition or is valid. Justice is nothing material, no determinate 'value', but a dimension of validity. Just as descriptive sentences can be true, in other words express what is the case, so normative sentences can be right and express what we are required to do. But individual principles or norms which have a specific content are on a different plane—independently of whether they are valid or not.

For example, there are different principles of distributive justice. These are material principles of justice such as 'to everyone according to his need', 'to everyone according to his abilities', or 'the same for everyone'. Principles of equal rights, such as the principle of equal respect for all, of equal treatment and equal status before the law, are related to a different kind of problem. In this case it is not a matter of the distribution of goods and services, but of the securing of freedoms and inviolabilities. All these principles of justice can be grounded from the standpoint of universalization, and claim *prima facie* validity. But only with reference to concrete individual cases will it become apparent *which* of the competing principles is the appropriate one for the *current* context.

That is the task of discourses of application [*Anwendungsdiskurse*]. Within the family, for example, conflicts of distribution will be decided according to a principle of need rather than a principle of performance, whereas in macrosocial conflicts over distribution the situation may be reversed. That depends on which principle best suits the situation, described as fully as possible with all relevant details. But I consider a general alignment of principles of justice and spheres of action to be highly problematic. In discourses of application, considerations of the kind which Walzer puts forward can find their place; but here they must prove their worth from case to case, according to the context.

The limitation of moral theory to questions of justice leads you to distinguish sharply between 'moral questions' (which can be decided in a fundamentally rational manner, from the standpoint of universalizability), and 'evaluative questions' (which pose issues of the good life, and are accessible to rational discussion only within the horizon of a historically concrete form of life, or of an individual life history). In the last analysis, do you exclude the possibility of convergence between justice and the good life? John Rawls, who specifically asserts a priority of justice over the good, assumes such a congruence, 'at least in the case of a well-ordered society'. According to his view, a moral theory should also specify the relation between the just and the good.

Indeed, in a society which had at its disposal all the resources of a modern society and which was also well-ordered, i.e. just and emancipated, the socialized individuals would enjoy not only autonomy and a high degree of participation, but would also have a relatively wide field of opportunities for self-realization, that is, for the conscious projection and pursuit of individual life-plans.

You separate justice from the good life, but you include aspects of care and responsibility in your concept of justice. How is it possible to make Carol Gilligan's 'care' and 'responsibility' components of your discourse-ethical conception of justice? The ethics of care relates to concrete others, not to the generalized other. It demands a contextualizing rather than a formal-abstract way of seeing. It keeps in mind social relations, not fixed roles, and it traces moral questions back to conflicting interests, not to opposing rights. How can all these differences be subsumed under formal justice?

Let me handle the first and the last two aspects in pairs.

The impression that a deontological ethics such as that of Kant requires us to neglect the concrete other, and his or her particular situation, arises only from a one-sided concentration on questions of grounding, which is avoidable. Kant restricted morality as a whole to Rousseau's perspective of the lawgiver, who considers how a certain material can be regulated in the common interest of all citizens, and thus from the standpoint of universalizability. In this way the problematic of application disappears from view. The unique constellation of a case demanding a decision, the concrete characteristics of the people involved, first come into play *after* the foundational problems have been solved. However, as soon as it has become clear which of the *prima facie* valid norms is most appropriate for the given situation and the conflicts to which it gives rise, the fullest possible description of all relevant features of the context must be given. Klaus Günther gave his excellent enquiry into discourses of application the title: *The Sense of Appropriateness* [*Der Sinn für Angemessenheit*, Frankfurt 1988]. Practical reason cannot bring itself into force merely through foundational discourses alone. In the process of grounding norms practical reason expresses itself in the principle of universalization, whereas in the application of norms it appears in the form of a principle of appropriateness. When one is clear about the complementarity of grounding and application, then one sees how discourse ethics can do justice to those reservations which you share with Carol Gilligan, and also with Seyla Behabib.[3]

Let's now consider the other reservation, that deontological ethics are only concerned with rights and not with needs, and also neglect the dimension of relations of belonging, as opposed to the dimension of fixed roles. If we look back historically at the individualism of the Kantian tradition, then this doubt is justified; but it does not apply to discourse ethics. For the latter takes up the intersubjectivist approach of pragmatism, and conceptualizes practical discourse as the *public* practice of a shared, reciprocal taking over of perspectives: everyone finds him- or herself required to take over the perspective of each other person, in order to test whether a ruling is also acceptable from the perspective of everyone else's understanding of the world and of themselves. Justice and solidarity are two sides of the same coin, because practical discourse is a procedure which, on the one hand, allows every individual to make his or her 'yes' and 'no' felt, and thereby satisfies an individualistic

3. Seyla Benhabib, 'The Generalized and the Concrete Other', in Seyla Benhabib and Drusilla Cornell (eds) *Feminism as Critique*, Minneapolis 1987, pp. 77–96.

understanding of equal rights. But, on the other hand, in moral discourse the social bond which requires all participants in argumentation to remain aware of their belonging to an unlimited community of communication [*unbegrenzte Kommunikationsgemeinschaft*] remains intact. Only with the securing of the existence of the communication community, which demands of everyone, in the ideal assumption of roles, an unselfish, empathetic activity, can those relations of reciprocal recognition be reproduced, without which even the identity of each individual would disintegrate.

How should we understand the separation of law and morality? According to Durkheim and Weber, these are two separate spheres, which emerge from the decay of traditional ethics; but somehow they remain bound to each other through a common centre. Ought one to understand law and morality in modernity as merely different forms of institutionalization of procedures which have the same purpose?

Positive law and post-conventional morality complement one another, and together are superimposed on traditional customary ethics [*Sittlichkeit*]. From a normative standpoint, it is not difficult to grasp the incompleteness of universalistically grounded moral norms. A norm which passes the test of universalizability only deserves general recognition on condition that it is also actually obeyed by everyone. But it is precisely this condition which a morality of reflection, which breaks with the unquestioned character of traditional *Sittlichkeit*, cannot guarantee. Thus the premisses of a demanding, post-conventional mode of grounding themselves generate a problem of expectations: the following of a valid norm can only be expected from someone who can be sure that all others are also obeying the norm. Kant already justified the transition from morality to state-sanctioned law in this way. And Kant already recognized the subsidiary problem, which arises from the use of the medium of state power. Political power is not a characterless medium; its use and organization must themselves be submitted to moral limitations. The idea of the constitutional state [*Rechtstaat*] is intended to answer this difficulty.

In Kant, and in early liberalism, there is a conception of the rule of law which suggests that the legal order itself is exclusively moral in character, or at least is a form of implementation of morality. This assimilation of law and morality is misleading. The political element of law brings completely different aspects into play. Not all material which requires, and is accessible to, legal regulation is of a moral nature. Even if lawgiving had reached a sufficient approximation to the conditions of a discursive formation of will and opinion, the decisions of the lawgivers could not be based only on moral grounds—and especially not those of the lawgiver within a welfare state. *Pragmatic* reasons for a (more or less fair) balancing of non-universalizable interests play a considerable role, as do *ethical* reasons for the accepted self-understanding and the preferred life-form of a collective, in which different identity-securing traditions encounter each other, and must be brought into harmony with each other. For this reason, the claim to legitimacy of positive law, even if it is supported by a rational formation of will, cannot be reduced to a claim for moral validity. Along with the pragmatic and ethical grounds, something else feeds into the legitimacy of law: *legitimacy* is sustained by a broader spectrum of validity-aspects than is the obligatory force [*Sollgeltung*] of moral norms of action.

Furthermore, the validity of law is constituted by two components; the rational component of the claim to legitimacy is combined with the empirical component of the enforcement of law. The validity of law must be able to ground two things together for the addressees. It must ground the cognitive expectation that general observance of the individual legal norm will be compelled if necessary (with the consequence that the legality of behaviour, mere conformity to norms, is *sufficient* for the law); but at the same time legal validity must ground the normative expectation that the legal system as a whole deserves recognition for good reasons (entailing that law must always *make possible* more than mere legality, namely an obedience stemming from insight into the legitimacy of the legal order).

Let us move on to the theme of the grounding of discourse ethics in a pragmatics of speech, in particular to your further development of Toulmin's analysis in The Uses of Argument, *of Wittgenstein's 'language-games', and of Chomsky's 'universal grammar', into a formal pragmatics. On this methodological level I would like to confront you with an argument which is a variation on the old objection against the Eurocentrism of your defence of the Enlightenment, and your concept of evolution.*

One might ask whether the whole concept of formal pragmatics is not based on a misleading generalization from examples of the Indo-European family of languages. Benjamin Lee Whorf compared 'Standard Average European' with non-European languages, and discovered that such central things as, first, the function of verbs, second, the temporal structure, and third, the grammatical relation of subject and predicate were fundamentally different from the characteristics which you take to be universal. I cannot go over the details here. But there seems to be a wealth of linguistic data which puts the approach of universal pragmatics in question, or even refutes it. Perhaps you may reply that non-European languages are less developed; but then you take over the burden of proof in showing how a development is possible in the deep structures of grammar.

The Sapir–Whorf hypothesis was discussed exhaustively in the 1950s, and on the whole with negative results. The superficial structures of individual languages can obviously show sharp divergences, without affecting the correspondence in the basic semantic structure of simple assertoric sentences, or in the basic pragmatic structure of the speech situation (e.g., personal pronouns, space and time deixis). What Whorf had intuited were, rather, differences between linguistic worldviews, which Humboldt had already been interested in, although without drawing consequences which would favour a linguistic relativism. In order to avoid this, there is no need to take refuge in notions of an evolution of language systems. Evolutionism is quite inappropriate with regard to natural languages. It is clear that the grammatical complexity of languages scarcely varies over time.

Today Whorf's intuitions have been applied on another level, namely in the rationality debate sparked off by anthropologists, and which has since split into various branches. I consider the decisive point of *this* controversy to be whether we must take account of an asymmetry which arises in the interpretive capacities of different cultures, when some have introduced so-called 'second-order concepts' [English in the original], and others not. These second-order concepts fulfil necessary cognitive functions in the process whereby a culture becomes reflexive, thus enabling its members to take a hypothetical stance towards their own traditions and to undertake on this basis a cultural self-relativization. Such a decentred understanding of the world characterizes modern societies. So the dispute concerns whether such cognitive structures signify a threshold which requires similar processes of learning and adaptation from *every* culture, once it has been crossed.

The contextualists maintain that the transition to post-metaphysical concepts of nature, and to post-traditional ideas of law and morality, only characterizes one tradition amongst others—and in no sense the process of tradition becoming reflexive in general. I don't see how this thesis can be seriously defended. I think that Max Weber was right, particularly if one adopts the cautiously universalistic interpretation which Schluchter has given to his thesis of the general cultural significance of Western rationalism.[4]

---

4. Wolfgang Schluchter, *Die Entwicklung des okzidentalen Rationalismus*, Tübingen 1979, pp. 15 *et seq.*

Your moral theory takes the form of an investigation of moral argu-
mentation. And you set up, as the single principle of morality, a principle
of universalization which is supposed to play the same role in moral
argumentation which the principle of induction plays in empirical-theor-
etical questions. According to this principle, a norm is only valid when it
could be accepted in actual argumentation by all those potentially
concerned; this means that it must satisfy the interests of all participants.
But must the participants be in agreement about the consequences of the
general following of a norm? Often they can only reach a shared realiza-
tion of their inability to agree. There would be a certain analogy here to
the process of political will-formation, which expresses a consensus
concerning the fact that certain controversies and themes must be handed
over to other forms of settlement.

Argumentation is not a decision procedure which results in resolutions,
but a procedure for resolving problems which leads to *convictions*.
Naturally, an argumentative dispute over the truth-claim of assertoric
sentences, or the claim to rightness of normative sentences, can
conclude in such a way that no agreement is reached; in this case, the
question will have to be left open for the time being, although with an
awareness that only one side can be right. In practical discourses it can
indeed turn out that the relevant conflict is not moral in character. It
may involve an ethical-existential question, which concerns the self-
conception of certain persons or of a certain collective; in this case even
the most rational answer will only be relative to the goal of my—or our—
good or non-spoiled life, and will not be able to claim universal validity.
Or perhaps what is involved is the pragmatic question of balancing out
opposed, non-generalizable interests; in this case those involved can
always aim for a fair or just compromise. Thus the failure of attempts at
argumentation in the domain of practice may also mean getting clear
about the fact that it is not moral discourses, but discourses of self-
understanding or negotiations which are required.

　　Even in parliamentary decision procedures there is a rational kernel;
for, depending on the case, political questions can be treated discursively
both from an empirical and pragmatic, and from a moral and ethical
standpoint. These legally institutionalized processes of opinion formation are, of course, structured to produce decisions in a limited time.
The order of business combines truth-oriented opinion formation with
majoritarian will-formation. From the standpoint of discourse theory,
which tests such a procedure for its normative content, the rule of
majority decisions should, of course, have an internal relation to the cooperative quest for truth. The basic idea is that a majority decision
should only be taken under discursive conditions which make it possible

to assume the rationality of the result. The content of a decision which has been taken according to correct procedure must be able to count as the rationally motivated, although fallible, result of a discussion which was prematurely ended under the pressure of the need for a decision. For this reason one should not confuse discourse, as a procedure for forming moral or ethical judgements, with the legally institutionalized procedure of political *will*-formation, even if this is mediated by discourses.

Your cognitive standpoint in the domain of moral theory is based on an analogy between truth-claims and normative validity-claims. But this analogy can only be sustained when the norms which lie behind the principle of universalizability are given something like an unconditional normative validity. But how can, and why must, moral theory ignore those other norms, which are in force de facto without being valid in the strict sense? And is this exclusion possible without severing the dialectical relation between abstract morality and social ethics?

Regarded from the performative standpoint of their addressees, norms appear to have a claim to validity analogous to that of truth. 'Analogous' means, of course, that the obligatory force of norms should not be assimilated to the validity-as-true of sentences. The differences appear not only at the level of rules of argumentation, and of the kinds of arguments which are permissible; they already begin with the fact that normative validity claims are embodied in norms, in structures which are of a higher level than moral actions and regulative speech acts, whereas truth-values can only be ascribed to individual assertoric sentences, and not to theories. In this latter case the higher level constructions, namely the theories, owe their validity to the body of true sentences which can be derived from them, whereas particular commandments or prohibitions, by contrast, derive their validity from the underlying norms.

A further interesting difference consists in the fact that holding sentences to be true does not affect the dimension essential to the truth of sentences, namely the existence of states of affairs. By contrast, holding norms to be right directly affects the dimension of action regulation which is essential to them. As soon as a norm of action is sufficiently recognized and adhered to within the circle of its addressees, it constitutes a corresponding practice—irrespective of whether the norm can be justified and *deserves* recognition, or whether it is only *factually* adhered to, for false reasons for example, or out of sheer habit. For this reason the distinction between the validity [*Gültigkeit*] and the social currency [*Geltung*]—that is, the general holding-to-be-valid [*gültig*]—of a norm is important. I agree with you to this extent.

But I then become unsure whether I grasp the meaning of your question. The *moral theorist* naturally chooses a normative standpoint; he shares the standpoint of the addressees of a norm, who take part in discourses of grounding and application. In this perspective, we must initially abstract from existing traditions, habitual practices, and current motives—in short, from the ethical customs established within a society. On the other hand, the sociologist is in the first instance interested in these ethical customs. But he takes up the attitude of a participant observer. We cannot simultaneously take up the second-person standpoint of the addressee of a norm and the third-person standpoint of a sociological observer. You are presumably thinking of the complicated case in which someone interprets in one attitude the knowledge which has been acquired in another attitude. This is the case with a sociologist, who measures a descriptive account of a belief in legitimacy against the grounds which could be adduced for the legitimacy of the actual social order which he observes, from the perspective of *possible* addressees. In a similar way, the participant in argumentation (or the moral theorist as his philosophical alter ego) changes his role as soon as he considers with the eyes of a legislator the empirical aspects of the material needing regulation, and incorporates the practicability or acceptability of regulations into his considerations. One must keep these different viewpoints, and their distinct objects, separate. However, such differentiation does not support the argument for a sociological short-circuiting of moral theory.

You then go on to speak of empirically valid norms without (normative) validity. Strictly speaking, this formulation is only appropriate for conventions such as table manners, which are habitual and generally accepted, without requiring or being capable of rational grounding.

From the ontogenetic standpoint, the conditions for a discourse ethic are only satisfied at Kohlberg's last, post-conventional stage. But only a minority of the adult population reaches this stage (if the relevant long-term investigations can be relied on). But in this case we are confronted with the paradox that we have post-conventional social institutions, while a majority of the population remains on a pre-conventional or conventional level of moral consciousness. How is this possible? And how can this be reconciled with your assertion that normative structures are the pacemakers of social evolution? If the answer lies in the fact that post-conventional morality is embedded in structures of law, then you must be able to offer a plausible explanation of how such a situation can become stabilized.

Social innovations are often spurred on by marginal groups, even if they later become generalized throughout society on the institutional level. This may provide an explanation for why positive law in modern societies can be conceptualized as an embodiment of post-conventional structures of moral consciousness, although many members of the society only display a conventional level of moral consciousness. The conventional understanding of a post-conventional system of law need not lead to instabilities; it often impedes radical interpretations, which could lead—for example—to civil disobedience.

In any case, findings concerning the moral consciousness of the populace are problematic: there is much dispute about whether Kohlberg's methods of data collection do not produce artificial results. For example, children master the moral judgements of a particular stage performatively long before they are in a position to make this intuitive knowledge explicit when providing answers to the well-known dilemmas.

The question of whether normative validity has a sense comparable to that of truth is only a variation of a question which was originally posed in your interview with New Left Review, *and which remained unanswered: 'How do you conceive the relation between philosophical and scientific truth-claims? Are philosophical truth-claims cognitive claims, and would a rational consensus ultimately guarantee the truth of the consensus theory of truth itself?'*[5]

In my view philosophy today plays two roles simultaneously—an interpretative role, in which it mediates between the life-world and the specialized cultures of experts, and a more specific role within the system of organized knowledge itself, where it co-operates with the various reconstructive sciences in particular. Here it produces statements which make a claim to truth. Even the discourse theory of truth contains assertions which must be defended against competing theories of truth within the corresponding universe of discourse.

But your question also expresses another doubt. You seem to suggest that the self-referring character of philosophical statements, in this case statements concerning the theory of truth, must lead the discourse theory of truth *ad absurdum.* I don't see things in that way. Naturally, the reconstruction which I have proposed of our intuitive understanding of truth, with the help of a theory of discourse, may prove to be false, or at least insufficient. But the everyday or scientific practice which

---

5. See p. 161 above.

depends on the correct use of this intuitive knowledge remains un-affected by these attempts at reconstruction and their revision. It is not practical knowledge itself which can be refuted, but only the false description of it.

A decisive concept for your conception of moral grounding is that of performative contradiction, which you have taken over from Karl-Otto Apel (without the overtones of transcendental philosophy which it has in his work). The argument behind your use of performative self-contradic-tions seems convincing in the narrow sense that no one involved in communicative action can systematically contrast its presuppositions without putting his or her own rationality and responsibility in question. But how is it possible to justify in this way the claim that one approach to moral theory is better than another?

The demonstration of performative self-contradiction plays a role in the refutation of sceptical counter-arguments which varies from case to case. It can also be developed into a method, and then serves—as it does in Strawson—in the identification of indispensable preconditions of a practice, for which there are no functional equivalents in our form of life. Apel and I use this method in order to bring to light general pragmatic presuppositions of the practice of argumentation, and to analyse these in terms of their normative content. In this way I have sought to ground a principle of universalization as a moral principle. The first aim here is only to show that moral-practical questions can indeed be decided by adducing grounds, in other words in a rational manner. These general presuppositions of argumentation have the same status in discourse ethics as the construction of the 'original position' in Rawls' theory of justice. Which is the better version of a Kantian ethic must then be demonstrated in the discussion between such theoretical approaches. This professional debate has many aspects, and can certainly not be decided by a direct recourse to performative self-contradictions.

What is the status of the 'ideal speech situation'? Is it partly counter-factual? Or is it part of a society imagined as a life-world? Or is it merely a hypostatization? How do these three themes fit together, if at all? You adopt the first thesis in Moral Consciousness and Communicative Action *(p. 92). The second thesis results if one understands discourse ethics as a further development of the third of those fictions, mentioned in* The Theory of Communicative Action, *which are necessary if one wishes to grasp society as a whole as a life-world—I am referring to the assumption of completely transparent understanding (vol. 2, p. 149). The third thesis is attributed to you by Wolfgang Schluchter. He maintains that the logic of your argument implies a transformation of the ideal speech situation from a necessary presupposition of communication into an ideal to be realized, and thus its hypostatization.*

We can leave the second position to one side, because in the passage in question a concept of the life-world is under discussion which I myself reject as idealistic. The first position states only that the community of communication, unlimited in social space and historical time, is an idea which we can approximate to in actual conditions of argumentation. We orient ourselves in terms of this idea on every occasion when we strive to ensure that (a) all relevant voices are heard, (b) the best of all available arguments, given the present state of our knowledge, are accepted, and (c) only the non-coercive coercion of the better argument determines the affirmations and negations of the participants. Unfortunately, I once dubbed the state in which these idealizing presuppositions would be fulfilled an 'ideal speech situation'; but this formula can give rise to misunderstanding, because it is too concretistic. It can induce the kind of hypostatization which Schluchter ascribes to me, although with reservations.[6] In doing so Schluchter relies on the formula 'prefiguration of a form of life' [*Vorschein eines Lebensforms*] which I had already taken back ten years ago.[7] But at no time have I 'hypostatized the unlimited community of communication, transforming it from a necessary presupposition into an ideal to be realized', as Schluchter, drawing on Wellmer, assumes.

In fact I would hesitate to describe this community of communication as a regulative idea in Kant's sense, because what I mean by an 'unavoidable idealizing presupposition of a pragmatic kind' does not fit the classical contrast between the 'regulative' and the 'constitutive'.

The idea of the truth of statements, which we assert—fallibilistically— here and now, is regulative from the standpoint of participants. On the one hand, all currently available grounds justify us in claiming truth for p; on the other hand, we can never be certain that p will survive all future objections—we can never know whether it would count among the valid statements which would be confirmed over and over again *ad infinitum* within the unlimited community of communication. However, the universal pragmatic presuppositions of argumentation in general are in no sense merely regulative, since these conditions must be fulfilled *hic et nunc*, in an adequate approximation, if we wish to engage in argumentation at all.

---

6. Wolfgang Schluchter, *Religion und Lebensführung*, Frankfurt 1988, vol. 1, pp. 322–33.

7. *Vorstudien und Ergänzungen zur Theorie des kommunikativen Handelns*, p. 126n.

Along with the validity-claims raised in communicative action, the tension of the ideal becomes part of the social facts, a tension which participating subjects become aware of in the form of a power which bursts contexts apart, and transcends all merely provincial criteria. To use a paradoxical expression: the regulative idea of the validity of utterances is constitutive for the social facts generated through communicative action. To this extent, as Schluchter remarks, I go beyond Kantian themes; but I do this without taking on board Hegel's way of thinking. Already in Peirce the idea of the unlimited community of communication serves to replace the eternal dimension, or the supratemporal character of the unconditionality of truth, with the notion of a process of interpretation and understanding which transcends the limitations of social space and historical time from the inside, *from the world outwards* as it were. Learning processes should build a bridge *within* time to the unlimited community of communication which reaches beyond all temporal distance; they should realize *within* the world the conditions which are presupposed by the unconditional demands of transcending validity-claims.

This conception, introduced in terms of theory of truth, also shapes the notion of society which is developed from the standpoint of communicative action; for communicative interactions can only run along the rails of intersubjectively recognized validity-claims. With these unconditional validity-claims transcendence enters the life-world and saturates its symbolic structures. For this reason, even the counterfactual assumptions of communicatively acting subjects can count on support from social reality: every actually raised validity-claim which transcends the context of our present life-world creates a new fact through the affirmations and negations of those to whom it is addressed. The results of the interplay of innerworldly learning processes and world-disclosing innovations become sedimented through the mediation of this cognitive-linguistic infrastructure of society. This is the Hegelian element which Schluchter senses, but which—from his Kantian standpoint (and falsely in my view)—he can only understand as the impermissible objectification of a regulative Idea.

You understand discourses as the way in which communicative action, which for its part is located in the life-world, becomes reflexive. By contrast, every normative element disappears on the level of the social subsystems which are steered by money and power. You have already explained, elsewhere, how your use of the expression 'norm-free sociality' has led to misunderstandings. Even after the decoupling of system and life-world which occurs in modernity, system integration remains bound to the life-world in an indirect way, namely through the legal institution-

alization of the steering media. Your claim is only that, in the last instance, the integration of the subsystems is not dependent on the social integration achieved through communicative action. You state: 'It is not binding illocutionary effects, but steering media, which hold the economic and administrative systems of action together.' This reply makes your conception more flexible, but you still maintain that the media of money and power require a strategic attitude on the part of actors. I have doubts about this.

Your image of the economic actor shares significant features with the models of neo-classical economics. Why do you neglect the arguments developed by institutionalist economics, which show that the model of purely strategic and utilitarian action died out, at the latest, with Adam Smith's 'invisible hand'? A. Etzioni's latest book contains abundant argument and evidence to show that 'the most important basis for decisions (even in market behaviour) lies in the affective and normative domain. This means that human beings make decisions on the basis of non-rational or pre-rational considerations chiefly because they draw on normative-affective sources, and merely in the second instance because they only possess limited intellectual capacities' (The Moral Dimension, 1988, p. 90).

I think this is a misunderstanding. I use the terms 'system' and 'life-world' as concepts for types of social order which are distinguished according to the mechanisms of social integration, in other words the way in which actions are intermeshed. In 'socially integrated' domains of action the enchainment or sequence-building occurs via the conscious-ness of the actors themselves, or via their intuitively present background knowledge of the life-world; in 'systemically integrated' domains of action order is produced objectively 'over the heads of the participants' as it were, and indeed by means of a functional interlocking and reciprocal stabilization of consequences of action, of which the actors need not be conscious. The concept of the life-world must be introduced in terms of a theory of action. Only if the concept of systems were introduced in this way could one produce the unambiguous one-to-one relation between systemically integrated domains of action and types of purposive-rational action which you attribute to me.

In fact I introduce the concept of systemically differentiated and self-steering, recursively closed domains of action with reference to the mechanisms of functional integration, and specifically to the steering media of money and power. These certainly have their correlates on the level of social action, namely media-steered interactions. But this does not in any way prejudge the rationality of the decision procedures used by participants in interaction. The medium determines the criteria according to which conflicts will be decided in the last instance. To this extent, the structural limitations of media-steered interaction provide an opportunity for more or less rational planning of action; but they neither make rational orientations of action necessary, nor can they oblige actors to adopt them. For this reason, the empirical evidence which you cite is compatible with a description of the economy and administration in terms of a theory of media.

You have taken over the concept of the state as a system, and the concept of power as a medium, from Talcott Parsons. Both ideas suggest a separation of politics and administration. Thomas McCarthy has criticized this approach, on the grounds that such a separation contradicts both the empirical evidence, and your own concept of democracy; if self-determination, political equality and the participation of citizens in decision processes are the marks of a true democracy, then such a democratic government could not be a political system in your sense. You emphasize yourself that the democratic state cannot be reduced to positive law. In the case of civil disobedience, legality must be handed over to those who bear the ultimate responsibility for the legitimacy of rule, namely the citizens. How can one interpret civil disobedience in this way, without abandoning the separation of politics and administration which underlies the system concept of the state and the steering-medium concept of power?

I do not count legitimation processes as such as part of the power-steered administrative system—they take place in the public sphere. Here two contrary tendencies collide and intersect with each other: the communicatively generated power (H. Arendt) which arises from democratic processes of opinion and will formation runs up against the generation of legitimacy by (and for) the administrative system. It is an empirical question how these two processes impact on each other, and which overpowers which—the more or less spontaneous formation of will and opinion in public communication circuits, on the one hand, and the organized production of mass loyalty, on the other. A similar interaction occurs in the institutionalized forms of political will formation, in parliamentary bodies for example. Only with their complete transformation into state apparatuses would the political parties become *entirely* absorbed into an administrative system, which would then be self-programming (within the limits of current law).

But to return to your question: the border between the communicatively steered formation of political will and opinion, on the one hand, and power-steered administration on the other, could be eliminated, under modern conditions of life, only at the cost of a de-differentiation of public administration. The creation of communicative power and the assertion and application of administrative power follow two different logics.

By contrast, civil disobedience—in the sense of a non-violent infringement of law serving as a symbolic appeal to a differently minded majority—is only an extreme case where one can study the interplay between non-institutionalized public communication and the constitutional formation of a democratic will. One can influence the other, because institutionalized will formation is guided by an idea which I mentioned a moment ago: in parliaments, a formation of opinion oriented towards truth should precede majority decisions as a kind of filter, so that these decisions are entitled to the presumption of rationality.

How can power, even when regarded as a steering medium, be compared to money? In The Theory of Communicative Action *you do indeed (again like Parsons) list the differences between these two media, with regard to measurement, circulation, and accumulation, but then go on to maintain that both make the co-ordination of action equally independent of the resources of the life-world. But the ways in which money and power are institutionalized in the life-world reveal considerable differences. For example, obedience is the appropriate attitude with regard to administration, whereas the market requires an orientation to enlightened self-interest. Accordingly, these two attitudes would have to be classified as belonging to different stages of moral consciousness. How can one explain such differences when both steering media occupy a more or less parallel position in the architectonics of your theory.*

The contradiction which you have set up can be resolved in the following way. The two media, money and power, operate symmetrically insofar as they secure the coherence of differentiated, self-steering systems of action independently of the intentional efforts, in other words the co-ordinating activities, of the actors. They are asymmetrical as regards the form of their dependence on the life-world, although both are legally institutionalized, and thus anchored in the life-world. Whereas the capitalist economy also subsumes the production process, including the activities of labour (as the substrate on which exchange-value depends), the democratic state apparatus remains dependent on sources of legitimation which it can never *entirely* bring under control through the use of administrative power. Here communicatively generated power constitutes a substrate which can never be as completely cut off from its roots in processes of discursive (and therefore administratively uncontrollable) opinion and will formation, as can production for the market from the life-world context of living labour.

But this asymmetry should not mislead one into dissolving the administrative system into the categories of the life-world. Of course the asymmetry constitutes a necessary condition for demands to be made on the administrative system in the name of life-world imperatives; and, unlike consumer decisions, these demands do not have to be formulated immediately in the language of the corresponding steering medium—either prices or regulations—in order to be 'comprehensible' to the system. This can be seen in the different ways in which politics and administration deal with law—either from a normative standpoint or instrumentally.[8] The administrative system deals with law, in the first instance, in an instrumental manner; from the perspective of the application of administrative power, what counts is not the practical rationality of the grounding or application of law, but the effectivity of the application of a programme which is partly pregiven, and which it partly shapes for itself. The normative grounds which are supposed to justify the posited norms in the language of politics are considered by the administration as restrictions and subsequent rationalizations of decisions which have been generated elsewhere. At the same time, normative grounds are the only currency in which communicative power can make itself effective. It can operate on the administrative system in such a way that it rations the stock of grounds from which administrative decisions, which stand under constitutional restrictions, are obliged to nourish themselves. Not everything which the administrative system could do is permissible, if the prior political communication and will-formation has discursively devalued the requisite grounds.

Behind the last three questions lay the argument that your analysis of the pathologies of modernity requires completion from the opposite point of view. You say that the systems colonize the life-world. But there are also contrary tendencies. Normative expectations and democratic processes of will formation can impinge on the two subsystems to such an extent that they can no longer be held together by systemic mechanisms alone. Thus your analysis of tendencies towards legal regulation could be complemented by an analysis of social movements which aim for a democratization of the economy, rights of consultation for consumers, and so on. Why do you neglect these issues? Would the results of such investigations explode the architectonics of your theory?

At the time, my principal concern was to develop a theoretical instru-

---

8. Jürgen Habermas, 'Volkssouveranität als Verfahren', Forum für Philosophie (ed.) *Die Ideen von 1789*, Frankfurt 1989, pp. 28 *et seq.*

ment which would allow me to identify phenomena of 'reification' (Lukács). But this attention to the systematically induced disruptions of communicatively rationalized life-worlds was one-sided in its direction. It did not exhaust the potentials which the theory of communicative action offers. The question of which imperatives set limitations on which side, and to what extent, must be treated empirically, and should not be prejudged on an analytical level in favour of the systems. In response to similar objections of Johannes Berger I have already emphasized, in the preface to the third edition of *The Theory of Communicative Action*, that the colonization of the life-world, and the democratic blocking of the dynamic of systems which remain insensitive to the 'externalities' which they generate, are equally valid analytical perspectives. A one-sided form of contemporary diagnosis is in no sense built into the theory as such.

In a series of articles (after Moral Consciousness and Communicative Action *) you have dealt with the Hegelian concept of* 'Sittlichkeit ', *or—let us say—of a 'pragmatic ethics', in order to mediate between discourse ethics and social reality. You assess the rationality of a form of life by the extent to which its participants are capable to—and are encouraged to— develop a moral consciousness based on principles, and to translate this consciousness into action. But can one equate rationality and morality? In this way* Sittlichkeit *or pragmatic ethics seems to be reduced to the existing normative context of a society. But then the question arises of whether the social norms are also valid—or at least of whether they foster such valid norms. You seem to want to keep validity or the pure 'ought'* [Sollen] *within the framework of Kant's individualistic morality, while Hegel's effort to bring 'is' and 'ought' together is abandoned.*

The concept of communicative rationality includes several validity aspects, not only the moral or obligatory validity of commandments and actions. For this reason, the rationality of a form of life cannot be measured purely in terms of the normative contexts, or the motivational potentials, which support the translation of post-conventional moral judgements into practices. At the same time, one essential measure of the liberality of a society seems to me to be how far the models of socialization and the institutions, the political culture, the identity-securing traditions and everyday practices in general, embody a non-compulsive, non-authoritarian form of *Sittlichkeit,* into which an autonomous morality can be incorporated, and can take on concrete form. Intuitively we very quickly sense—as if we were ethnologists living in an alien society—how emancipated, how sensitive, how egalitarian the environment really is; how minorities and marginal groups, the handicapped, children and old people are treated; what social meaning illness, loneliness and death possess; how much of the eccentric and deviant, the innovative and dangerous, people are accustomed to tolerate, and so on.

In your question two issues seemed to be mixed up. When I take up the distinction between morality and *Sittlichkeit* in the normative attitude of a moral theorist (or of a participant in argument), I am concerned with different things than when, in the role of a sociologist, I compare the moral ideas of the individuals observed, or the moral content of their legal principles, with the established practices of the society, the manifestations of concrete *Sittlichkeit*. Even from this sociological perspective, however, it could not be said that the whole normative substance is contained in the heads of those who make judgements (or in the legal textbooks)—and thus is exhausted by a universalistic morality. Naturally, habitual ethical practice, however much it may deviate from the accepted morality, is also part of this normative substance.

In your 1988 'Howison Lecture' in Berkeley you made a further attempt to mediate discourse ethics and society. In the lecture you state that the application of norms requires an additional discourse in its own right. The impartiality of a moral judgement cannot again be secured through a principle of universalization, when it comes to application. But how can a new relativism be avoided, when a so-called 'principle of application' serves as a substitute in all cases of context-sensitive application of norms?

The logic of discourses of application can be investigated from the normative standpoint of the philosopher or the legal theorist. Ronald Dworkin gives examples of this, and also proposes a theory; Klaus Günther has given this approach a convincing formulation in terms of discourse theory.[9] He shows that the principle of appropriateness, no less than the principle of universalization, brings into play the impartiality of judgement in practical questions, and thereby makes possible a rationally grounded agreement. Even in discourses of application we must rely on grounds which are valid not only for you or me, but in principle for everyone. It is important to avoid over hasty conclusions: an analytical procedure which demands sensitivity to context need not itself be context-dependent and lead to context-dependent results.

---

9. Klaus Günther, 'Ein normativer Begriff der Kohärenz', in *Rechtstheorie*, vol. 20 (1989) pp. 163–90.

In the Howison Lecture you make clear that ethical questions, in contrast to moral ones, do not require a clean break with an egocentric perspective, because they remain related to the telos of my particular—or our particular—form of the good life. You also introduce maxims of action as a kind of bridge between morality and ethics, since these can be assessed both from a moral and from an ethical standpoint. How are these maxims related to normative validity-claims? Do not such maxims somehow claim simultaneously both empirical and normative validity?

It is indeed true that ethical questions, questions of self-understanding, are oriented towards the goal of my particular—or our particular—good life: 'not gone awry' [*nicht verfehlt*] might be a better expression. We look back at our life-history, or at our traditions, and ask ourselves, with that ambiguity which is characteristic of strong preferences, who we are and would like to be. The answers must therefore relate to the context of a particular life-perspective which is assumed to be binding for certain persons or for a certain collective. Such answers cannot claim to determine an exemplary form of life which is binding on all—in the way that Aristotle understood the polis. But, relative to the given context, ethical questions can be answered in a rational manner—that is, in a way which everyone finds convincing, and not just those directly concerned, from whose perspective the question is posed.

You also touch on another point: what are maxims? By this term I understand, as Kant did, rules of action or habitudes which constitute practices, or even the manner in which a life is lived as a whole, by relieving actors of the daily burden of making decisions. Kant had in mind above all the maxims of early bourgeois society, still stratified into professional groups. In my lecture I stated that maxims can be assessed both from an *ethical* and from a *moral* point of view. What is good for me, according to the way I see myself and would like to be seen, need not be equally good for all. But the fact that maxims can be judged from a double perspective does not give them a double character.

Once again, it is important to distinguish between a normative discussion, of the kind we are having now, and a sociological discussion. From the standpoint of the sociological observer, maxims may seem to be a good class of phenomena by means of which to study the concrete *Sittlichkeit* of a group. Maxims enjoy social currency; therefore they are also normatively binding on actors, as long as what is involved is not pure convention. For this reason we can change perspectives and shift from observation to judgement, in other words, consider whether the reasons for which *they* have chosen their maxims would also count as good reasons for *us*.

You defend ethical cognitivism against the sceptics, but you leave moral feelings on one side. However these come into play—at the very latest—in the application of norms. What function do moral feelings have? Don't feelings and 'inclinations of the heart' have an intrinsic value? Or do they only play the role of a catalyst for the development of moral conscious- ness, so that they become superfluous, once a certain level of moral competence has been developed?

Moral feelings are a grand theme, and offer a wide field for investiga- tion. I will limit myself to a few remarks.

First, moral feelings play an important role in the *constitution* of moral phenomena. We would not even perceive certain action-related conflicts as morally relevant if we did not *feel* that the integrity of a person were being threatened or harmed. Feelings provide the basis for our *perception* of something as a moral issue. Whoever is blind towards moral phenomena has a blindness of feeling. He or she lacks the sensorium, as we say, for the suffering of a vulnerable creature who is entitled to the preservation of his or her integrity, both personal and corporeal. This sensorium is obviously connected with capacities for sympathy and empathy.

Second, and above all, moral feelings—as you rightly say—give us an orientation for the *judgement of morally relevant individual cases.* Feelings build the experiential basis for our first intuitive judgements: shame and guilt are the basis for self-reproaches, pain and the sense of injury for our reproaches against another person who has harmed us, indignation and rage for the condemnation of a third person who has injured someone else. Moral feelings are reactions to disruptions of patterns of intersubjective recognition, of interpersonal relations, in which the actors participate from a first-, second-, or third-person standpoint. For this reason moral feelings are so structured that the system of personal pronouns is reflected in them.

Third, of course, moral feelings play a role not merely in the appli- cation of moral norms, but also in their grounding. Empathy, at the very least—in other words the capacity to transport oneself by means of feeling across cultural distance into alien and *prima facie* incomprehens- ible life conditions, patterns of reaction, and interpretive perspectives— is an emotional precondition for the ideal taking over of roles, which requires each person to adopt the standpoint of all the others. To see something from a moral point of view means that we do not elevate our own understanding of the world and our self-understanding to the status of criteria for the universalization of a mode of action, but also test their universalizability from the perspective of all the others. This demanding cognitive achievement would scarcely be possible without that generalized sympathy which becomes sublimated into a capacity for fellow feeling, and points beyond our emotional ties to those closest to us, opens our eyes to 'difference'—in other words to the individuality and autonomous significance of the other who remains in his or her otherness.

Of course moral feelings, despite the cognitive function which they fulfil, cannot monopolize the truth. In the last analysis it is moral judgements which span a gap that cannot be filled in with emotions. In the end we must rely on moral *insight*, if everyone who has a human face is to have a claim to moral protection. That all human beings are brothers—and sisters—is a counterfactual notion which is hard enough to hold on to in itself; the broad horizon of humanity would prove to be even more fragile were it to be spanned only by spontaneous feelings. For this reason your question is not so easy to answer. Certainly, feelings make us sensitive to moral phenomena; in questions of the grounding and application of norms they have, in addition, an invaluable heuristic function. But they cannot be the *ultimate* authority for the judgement of the phenomena which they reveal.

You have often emphasized that a narrow conception of morality demands a modest self-evaluation on the part of moral theory. According to your conception, the philosopher should explain the 'moral point of view' and, as far as possible, define its claim to universality. Everything else should be left to those who are themselves involved in moral argumentation. It seems to me, however, that in your most recent writings, this modesty and separation of roles is replaced by a new three-way distinction, in which a neo-Kantian morality (discourse ethics) is mediated, by means of an expanded conception of practical reason, or perhaps even Kierkegaard's 'radical choice', with a restricted form of Hegelian Sittlichkeit (or pragmatic ethics). How do you understand these connections?

I take the task of philosophy to be the clarification of the conditions under which both moral and ethical questions can be rationally answered by those concerned. There corresponds to the moral standpoint, which allows us to perceive the generalizable interests which we have in common, an ethical decision in favour of a self-conscious conduct of life, which first gives a person or a group the attitude which is required in order for them to appropriate critically their own life-history and identity-securing traditions, in the light of an authentic life-project. But philosophy cannot take over from those concerned with the answering of substantive questions of justice, or of an authentic, non-failed life. Philosophy can help to avoid confusions; it can insist, for example, that ethical and moral questions not be confused with each other, and thus answered from an inappropriate perspective. But when philosophy makes a material contribution to a theory of justice—as does Rawls in parts of his book—or when it seeks to develop a normative outline of an emancipated society—as do Ernst Bloch or Agnes Heller—then the philosophical author steps back into the role of an expert, who puts forward his or her proposals from the perspective of a participating citizen.

Whoever goes beyond the procedural questions of a discourse theory of morality and ethics, and sets out *directly*, in a normative attitude, to develop a theory of the well-ordered or emancipated society, will soon find him- or herself running up against the limits of his or her own historical standpoint, and its unreflected context of emergence. For this reason I argue for an ascetic understanding of moral theory and even of ethics, indeed of philosophy in general, in order to make space for a critical theory of society. The latter can assist in the scientific mediation and objectification of processes of self-understanding in a quite different way; it should neither fall prey to hermeneutic idealism, nor fall between the stools of philosophical normativism and sociological empiricism. This is approximately, and from a negative viewpoint (the point of view of avoidance), the architectonics which I envisage.

Index

H. = Habermas